# God's Gift ◆ Our Choice

**Grades 9 and 10**

Produced under the auspices of the
North American Division of Seventh-day Adventists
Office of Education

Published by
**Pacific Press® Publishing Association**
Nampa, Idaho

# TABLE OF CONTENTS

# WELCOME TO YOUR RELIGION CLASS

This section is intended to provide you with some general information about this textbook and about your religion class.

## • THE CROSSROADS SERIES OF RELIGION TEXTBOOKS •

The **CROSSROADS SERIES** is the title of the series of religion textbooks for Seventh-day Adventist secondary schools, grades 9 through 12. This textbook is a part of the series.

The logo for the **CROSSROADS SERIES** symbolizes the theme of the series—that the cross of Jesus Christ is at the very center of Christian faith. God's revelation of Himself in the cross reveals the only sacrifice for sin and the ultimate significance of life to each person and to every nation. Thus the cross stands as the decisive moment of truth for all humankind through all ages. The logo, in symbolic form, portrays the centrality of the cross with all paths (roads) of human experience and personal decisions leading to and from it.

May you meet Jesus at the crossroads of your life and in each decision you make. This is the prayer of those who have prepared these textbooks, and we join our prayer with those of your teacher.

## • GOAL OF THE CROSSROADS SERIES •

The goal of the **CROSSROADS SERIES** is that through your study of Scripture in this class you will come to know the loving and redeeming God of Scripture. His self-revelation has its focus and fulfillment in the life, death, resurrection, and intercession of Jesus Christ. His substitutionary death on the cross is the sole basis of Christian assurance. With Christ as Saviour and Lord, each believer is enabled, through the Holy Spirit, to experience a life of worship, growth, and service. Each person is then eager to proclaim and be ready for His return.

## • VERSIONS OF THE HOLY BIBLE •

The NEW INTERNATIONAL VERSION, referred to as NIV, is used as the primary version of Scripture for the **Memory Focus**, scriptural references quoted in the narrative section of the lesson, and for answers to **Into the Bible** activities and **Projects**. Other versions of Scripture have also been used when the particular version enriches the meaning of a given reference. Lesson 6 of book 1 will assist you in understanding the difference between a version of the Holy Bible and a translation or a paraphrase.

## • REFERENCE BOOKS FOR THE RELIGION CLASS •

Reference books are essential to the religion class. It is important that the following general reference books and books by Ellen G. White be available in your classroom.

1. General reference books

   a. *The Seventh-day Adventist Bible Commentary*, Vols. 1–8
   b. *The Seventh-day Adventist Bible Dictionary*
   c. *The Seventh-day Adventist Encyclopedia*
   d. A Bible concordance

e. A Bible dictionary
f. A Bible atlas
g. *The Seventh-day Adventist Hymnal*
h. A current set of encyclopedias
i. A high-school or collegiate dictionary
j. A thesaurus

2. Books by Ellen G. White
a. Conflict of the Ages series
      *Patriarchs and Prophets*
      *Prophets and Kings*
      *The Desire of Ages*
      *The Acts of the Apostles*
      *The Great Controversy*
b. *Selected Messages*
c. *Steps to Christ*
d. *Testimonies for the Church*

## • MEMORIZATION OF SCRIPTURE •

Each lesson contains a verse labeled **Memory Focus**. Your teacher will assign certain of these verses to be memorized. The references should first be understood, both as to their meaning and to their application to your life. The memorized texts should be reviewed at the end of the lesson and throughout the school year.

## • GRADES FOR THE RELIGION CLASS •

Whatever the school policy is regarding grades for the religion class, it is important that you understand your grade is not an evaluation of your spiritual growth or experience. Rather, the grade is an evaluation of the work you do in your religion class and how well you have mastered the content.

Your grade can be based on the following:

1. Class discussion and participation.
2. Your answers to the Into the Bible activities.
3. Completion of and/or answers to Projects.
4. The results on quizzes and tests.
5. Mastery of the assigned Memory Focus.
6. Other criteria identified by your teacher.

# unit

# Jesus and His World

# Jesus' Life–Birth to Ascension

Unit one is an introduction to the gospel story and covers the early years of Jesus' life. The content is drawn from the four Gospels. The unit emphasizes Christ's redeeming work and explores the roles of faith, grace, and obedience in our personal salvation.

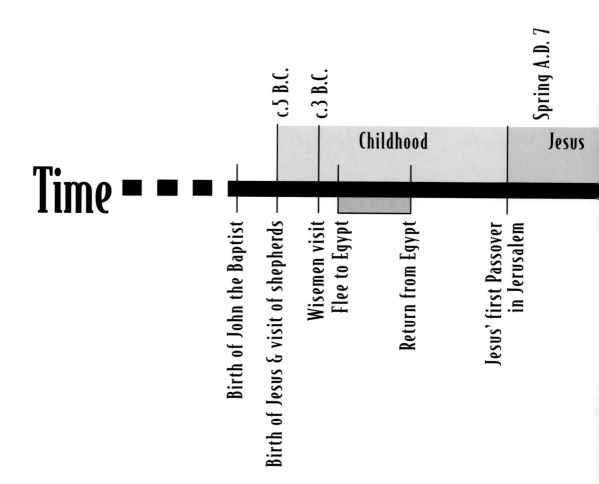

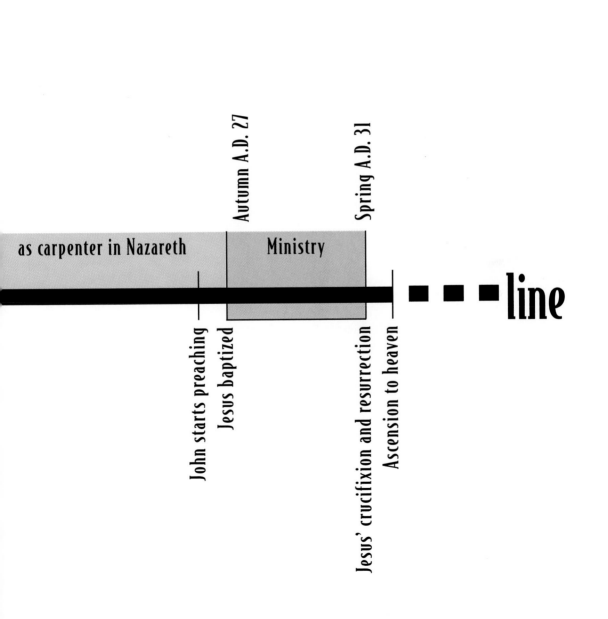

as carpenter in Nazareth

Ministry

line

Autumn A.D. 27

Spring A.D. 31

John starts preaching

Jesus baptized

Jesus' crucifixion and resurrection

Ascension to heaven

# CLARITY

I can see and understand only a little about God now, all I know is hazy and blurred, but someday I will see everything clearly, just as clearly as God sees into my heart right now (Paraphrase, 1 Corinthians 13:12).

# Ever Wonder Why?

**Lesson Scripture: 1 Peter 3:15, 16, TEV**

Not long ago, a group of adults was asked: If you could ask God just one question, what would it be? Their responses reflected deep concerns about salvation, the nature of evil, and the future. Adults would ask God things like, Why do good people suffer? How can I know that I'll be saved? Is there one true religion? Will the world eventually destroy itself? Why does a good God allow evil to exist?

Then the same question was put to a group of children. What one question would they ask God? Their responses were no less meaningful than the adults', but they were really very different—more down-to-earth. For instance, children would ask God, When You got elected, did You get all the votes? Instead of letting people die and having to make new ones, why don't You just keep the ones You've got now? How come You only have ten rules, but our school has a million? I know You are really powerful, so could You beat up the kid down the street?

If you could ask God one question, what would it be?

**CHANGE IS NEVER EASY**

As we go through life, we reach times or situations in which we have to make adjustments in the way we think. The examples above illustrate one of those life experiences that force us to change—simply, growing up!

As we all know, or can remember, children think

about things differently than adults do. For them, life is less complicated. So what they value, what they think about God, and how they solve problems all share a certain simplicity.

When children turn into teenagers, some unsettling changes begin. Life doesn't seem so simple anymore, and neither does the way we think about things. The questions get a lot more complex, and the simple black-and-white answers that used to satisfy us now just lead into murky areas of gray. We start questioning everything we once believed in or trusted.

When you add all this mental turmoil to the physical changes going on during teen years, you've got a recipe for real anguish. It's helpful to remember that readjusting our mental maps is a natural part of growth.

It's the normal outcome of social and spiritual development. Sooner or later it happens to everyone, and most of us come out the other side of this process with our basic values intact.

The apostle Paul surely must have known that growing means continually examining and evaluating our ideas and habits. As we mature, old beliefs need to be reinforced or replaced with better ones. That's what he means in 1 Corinthians 13:11, 12, TLB:

"When I was a child I spoke and thought and reasoned as a child does. But when I became a man my thoughts grew far beyond those of my childhood, and now I have put away the childish things. In the same way, we can see and understand only a little about God now, as if we were peering at his reflection in a poor mirror; but someday we are going to see him in his completeness, face to face. Now all that I know is hazy and blurred, but then I will see everything clearly, just as clearly as God sees into my heart right now."

## ANOTHER WAY WE CHANGE

At any age, confronting new information or having new experiences can call for some mental adjustments. This can be very exciting, but it's also kind of scary. We get a lot of security from holding on to what we've always believed. When these basic beliefs are challenged, it can threaten our peace of mind.

Jesus created a lot of turmoil and unrest among the Jews of His day, precisely

because He tried to get them to look at things in a new way. They had some long-held, cherished ideas about what God was like and who the Messiah would be. Jesus told them that He Himself was the most accurate reflection of God that they could hope for, but most of them refused to give up their old ideas. "The world didn't recognize him [Jesus] when he came. Even in his own land and among his own people, the Jews, he was not accepted" (John 1:10, 11, TLB). Blinded by fear and pride, the Jews clung to their old beliefs and rejected the Messiah.

Because they could see Him and touch Him and argue with Him in person, the Jews' biggest problem was seeing Jesus as divine. Christians today often have the opposite problem. For us, Jesus has become remote, a figure from the past, removed from everyday life. Even though His story doesn't begin "Once upon a time . . . ," we may think of Him more as a legend than as a living person.

Perhaps Peter anticipated this problem when he argued, "We did not follow cleverly invented stories when we told you about the power and coming of our Lord Jesus Christ,

but we were eyewitnesses of his majesty" (2 Peter 1:16, NIV).

How can we change our minds on this subject? How can we take Jesus out of the realm of make-believe and make Him a part of the real world we live

in every day? How can we be friends with Jesus?

A good place to start is with a modern translation of the Bible. Read a paragraph or a chapter every day on the life of Jesus. Then spend some time thinking about what you've just read. Talk to others about what you're learning. This will go a long way toward making Jesus real in your mind.

Another effective way to make Jesus come alive is through your imagination. Practice some simple meditation for a few minutes each day. Take an event in Jesus' life, and relive it in your mind. Change the time and setting to our world today, and put yourself in the picture as an observer or participant. What would you have heard if you were a wedding guest at Cana? How would you have felt if you were one of the five thousand fed with loaves and fishes? What would you have seen if you were hiding behind a pillar in Pilate's courtroom?

We can change our minds. We can look at spiritual things in a new way.

It takes creativity and discipline, but if it renews our faith and commitment to Jesus, the effort is worth it.

## Memory Focus

"Be ready at all times to answer anyone who asks you to explain the hope you have in you, but do it with gentleness and respect" (1 Peter 3:15, 16, TEV).

### OR

"Let the words of my mouth and the meditation of my heart be acceptable in Your sight, O Lord, my strength and my redeemer" (Psalm 19:14, NKJV).

## Into the Bible

1. Why does Jesus, whom the Bible describes as the "exact likeness of God's own being" (Hebrews 1:3, TEV), seem to act so differently from the God of the Old Testament?

   A. Read the following texts, and describe the contrast between God's declaration in the Old Testament and Christ's response to a similar situation in the New Testament:

| GOD'S DECLARATION | CHRIST'S RESPONSE |
|---|---|
| Leviticus 20: 9, 10 | John 8:1-11 |
| Deuteronomy 20:17, 18 | Matthew 5:44, 45 |

    B. How do Exodus 34:4-7 and Romans 5:9 help resolve the problem?

**2.** Though maturing involves changes in the way we view things, we must be careful that on important issues we do not change our minds too quickly or for the wrong reasons. Use the worksheet provided by your teacher to identify guidelines for making changes in our spiritual and moral convictions.

 # Projects

**1.** On one page, write a description of the kind of person you think Jesus would be if He were a teenager today, living in your neighborhood and going to your school. Your teacher will give you a list of suggested questions. Be prepared to share your ideas in a class report.

**2.** Team up with a friend, and conduct a survey of three or four people, asking the following questions. Summarize each person's answers on a single page.
    A. What are your personal beliefs about Jesus?
    B. Is the biblical story of Jesus true? Partially true? A legend? Explain your answer.
    C. Do you believe Jesus is coming back to earth? Explain your belief.
    D. If Jesus were on earth today, what social or moral issues do you think He would be actively involved with?

 # Focus Questions

**1.** Do you have some beliefs that you can't imagine changing or giving up? Which ones? Explain why.
**2.** Have you recently changed your mind about an important issue? How and why did that happen?
**3.** The Jews based their religious beliefs on what we now call the Old Testament. So why were their ideas about God wrong in the end?
**4.** How would the world be different if we were still waiting for the first coming of Jesus?

# THE GOSPEL

The strongest argument in favor of the gospel is a loving and lovable Christian
(*The Ministry of Healing*, 470).

# Why Four Gospels?

**Lesson Scripture: John 20:31, 32**

ho is the Messiah? A king— yet willing to stoop low in service and sacrifice. God—yet He became a man. He is like a diamond that when held up to the sun reflects all the colors of the rainbow.

Why are there four Gospels? There are four because each one reflects a different dimension of who Jesus was. Each one was written to a particular audience. Each Gospel paints a particular portrait that emphasizes an important aspect of Jesus' mission and character.

1. Matthew's Gospel is the kingly Gospel. Matthew was a Jew, writing to the Jews with the desire to show Jesus as the true King of Israel, the fulfillment of Old Testament prophecy. The key word in Matthew's Gospel is *kingdom.* It appears eighty times.

2. Mark's Gospel is really Peter's Gospel. Mark was the apostle Peter's penman in Rome, writing Peter's portrait of Christ for the Romans, who cared little for Jewish prophecy or about a man's ancestry. The Romans ruled the world by strength. In Mark's Gospel, Jesus is shown as God's anointed servant, filled with power, but who uses His power to serve and save others (see Mark 10:45).

3. Luke's Gospel is written to

the educated Greek world. Luke himself was a Greek, the only non-Jewish writer in the Bible, so he is particularly suited to his task. The Greeks were concerned with human perfection in all areas: physically (they originated the Olympic games) as well as mentally (they were the great philosophers). And they wanted to understand how to attain eternity. In Luke's Gospel, Jesus is presented as the ideal man and the Saviour of all humanity.

4. John wrote his Gospel for the church at the end of the first century. At this time, false ideas were spreading about who Christ really was. John set out to show that the man Christ Jesus was truly God. He presented Christ as the Son of God (Jesus' main title in this Gospel), the eternal Word, who was "with God, and was God . . . [and] became flesh and made His dwelling among us."

Now let's dig deeper into each individual Gospel. We will begin, as the New Testament does, with Matthew.

## THE GOSPEL ACCORDING TO MATTHEW: JESUS AS THE KING

Matthew is the first and most complete Gospel. Matthew is the Jewish Gospel, setting the story of Jesus the Messiah against its Old Testament background. Matthew's account is the bridge between Old Testament prophecies about Jesus and New Testament fulfillment in Jesus. A key phrase, which recurs over and over throughout Matthew's Gospel, is "All this took place to fulfill what the Lord had said through the prophet" (Matthew 1:22, NIV).

At the beginning, Matthew shows Jesus is a descendant of two great Jewish heroes (1:1). He calls Jesus the "Son of David," the great King of Israel, thus showing Jesus to be David's promised heir, and the "Son of Abraham," the father of the Jewish nation.

By appealing to Jewish history and prophecy, Matthew's Gospel links the New Testament with the Old. Christianity is not completely new. It is the fulfillment of Judaism. It completes what had been promised.

Matthew's Gospel is the only one that speaks of the church,

which is Christ's community of believers gathered together as His new kingdom on earth (see Matthew 16:17, 18). Remember that the key word in Matthew's Gospel, appearing eighty times, is *kingdom*. Over His church— and through His church in the world—Jesus rules as King and exercises His authority.

The final third of Matthew's Gospel especially focuses on Christ's kingly victory. From the time of His triumphal entry into Jerusalem until His ascension into the heavens, Jesus is pictured as the King who rules and conquers all His enemies through His willingness to die for our sins and rise victorious from the tomb. In Christ's great victory on the cross, Matthew is telling us that all the hopes of all the prophets have been fulfilled.

## THE GOSPEL ACCORDING TO MARK: JESUS AS THE CONQUERING SERVANT

Next, we turn to Mark's Gospel, the shortest and most action-packed of the four. The earliest traditions unanimously connect this Gospel with a certain person and a certain place. The person is the apostle *Peter*, and the place is *Rome*. One

early church leader actually called Mark's Gospel "the memoirs of Peter." In 1 Peter 5:13, Peter calls Mark his "son."

Mark's Gospel was written around the time of Peter's martyrdom in Rome in A.D. 65, during the first great persecution of Christians by Emperor Nero. At that time, the great apostle's voice was silenced, but his testimony to Christ lives on.

Once this link to Peter is recognized, Mark's Gospel comes alive with images and actions that remind us of Peter's personality. It begins where Peter's contact with Jesus began and ends with a special and personal reference about Peter from Jesus (16:7).

Peter! Always the man of action (often too much so). Peter was always ready to jump into the middle of things. Whatever he did, he did with vigor. Remember: Who wanted to hop out of the boat and come to Jesus on the water? Who cut off the servant's ear in the garden? Who was the first to rush into Jesus' empty tomb?

So, in this Gospel, we have Mark's organization of Peter's testimony about Jesus' mighty deeds. It is a Gospel full of vivid, action-oriented, eyewitness events. And because of this, it is perfectly suited to reach the Roman world with the story of Jesus. For the Romans also were people of action. They gloried in power and conquest; they were more

interested in deeds than in words. And that's the kind of a Jesus they meet here.

The key word in Mark's Gospel is *immediately*. It occurs forty-one times in sixteen chapters, eleven times in the first chapter! Everything seems to

happen with a sense of urgency and speed. And wherever Jesus is, big things are happening—fast. After the first thirteen verses of Mark's Gospel, we are at the same point in the story of Jesus that it takes both Matthew and Luke four long chapters to reach.

The focus in this Gospel is clearly on actions more than words. Mark includes only four of Jesus' parables but eighteen miracles—more than any other Gospel. Power goes forth from Jesus as He conquers demons, disease, and even death. But His power is not like the raw military might of Rome. Mark sets forth the compassionate Christ, who conquers by the *power of love* rather than the *love of power*. Mark shows us a Jesus who demonstrates that self-sacrificial love is ultimately the mightiest force on earth.

This brings us to the key theme in Mark's Gospel: Jesus' sacrificial death on the cross. The final six chapters (over 40 percent) of Mark's Gospel focus on the events surrounding the crucifixion. The key verse is Mark 10:45. It has two parts, which summarize the two main divisions of the book:

"For even the Son of Man

did not come to be served, but *to serve* [the main theme of Mark 1–8:30], and *to give his life as a ransom* for many [the main theme of Mark 8:31]" (Mark 10:45, NIV, emphasis added).

Mark's Gospel records only one of the seven statements of Jesus from the cross, the terrible cry of separation from God: "My God, my God, why have you forsaken me?" (Mark 15:34, NIV). Why, indeed! There can be only one reason, given Peter's powerful picture of Jesus. It is His sin-bearing love. The Lord laid on Him the iniquity of us all. And because of this sin-bearing love, a new and living way to God has been opened for sinful humanity.

Mark's story of the crucifixion makes one more important point in light of his intended audience. That point is found in Mark 15:39, where the Roman centurion who witnessed the final scenes of Jesus' trial and death exclaims, "Surely this man was the Son of God!" (NIV). This pagan soldier is meant to show us that the way to God has been opened not only for Jews, but for the Gentile world, as well.

And that theme leads us into the third great Gospel, a Gospel written by a Gentile-Greek to offer a universal Saviour to the Gentile-Greek world.

## THE GOSPEL ACCORDING TO LUKE: JESUS AS SAVIOUR OF ALL

Luke is the only non-Jewish writer in the Bible. He was a Greek physician and close friend and traveling companion of Paul, the "apostle to the Gentiles" (see Colossians 4:11-14 and 2 Timothy 4:11). Between the two of them, they wrote more than 70 percent of the New Testament.

Luke was highly educated. The introduction to his Gospel is written in the classical and formal Greek, used only in royal documents and official correspondence. In it he dedicates his Gospel to Theophilus, a name that means "lover of God." Was there a dignitary named Theophilus? We don't know, but surely Luke intended this dedication for all who honestly seek to know and love God.

The Greeks longed for two things: human perfection and a way to immortality. In Jesus, Luke declares, God has

answered both longings. Here is the ideal human as God intended—perfect in character because He is perfect in self-sacrificing love. And here is God's universal Saviour, the way of salvation for any and all who will accept Him.

Just the fact that Jesus was God's ideal for humanity is not the gospel. His life only makes more obvious how poorly our lives reflect the love and purity of God. But Luke makes clear that from His birth, Jesus came with one primary mission: to be the Saviour of all humanity—Jew and Gentile, black and white, male and female, rich and poor. As if it were brand new to you, listen to that oh-so-familiar proclamation of the gospel by the angel at Jesus' birth:

"Do not be afraid. I bring you good news of great joy that will be for all the people. Today in the town of David a Savior has been born to you; he is Christ [Messiah] the Lord" (Luke 2:10, 11, NIV).

There are two themes of special interest in this Gospel:

1. Luke's account is called the Gospel of womanhood because of his special emphasis on the part women play in Jesus' ministry and the new status, dignity, and freedom Jesus offers them.

2. Another dominant theme in Luke's Gospel concerns Jesus' teachings about money. One out of every seven verses in this Gospel has to do with the constant, subtle danger of allowing money and the lust for possessions to become our "god" (e.g., Luke 12:15-34; 16:11-15).

But above all else, Luke presents Christianity as a rescue religion for those who know they are lost. Luke is the Gospel of God's free grace, of His unlimited love reaching down to the lowest and the least. Jesus is seen as the "friend of tax collectors and 'sinners'" (Luke 7:34, NIV). If we were looking for one key verse that sums up the entire Gospel, we would find it in Jesus' own words: *"For the Son of Man came to seek and to save what was lost"* (Luke 19:10, NIV, emphasis added).

With this offer, Luke gives a strong warning. He makes it plain that his good news of salvation is only for sinners—only for those who recognize their need. There is no place in Christ's kingdom for the self-righteous, the self-sufficient, and the self-satisfied. "He has scattered those who are proud in their inmost thoughts . . . but has lifted up the humble. He has filled the hungry with good things but has sent the rich away empty" (Luke 1:51-53, NIV).

These two spiritual classes of people (the proud and the needy) are found throughout this Gospel. A good example is Luke 15:1, 2:

"Now the tax-collectors and 'sinners' were all gathering around to hear him. But the Pharisees and the teachers of the law muttered, 'This man welcomes sinners and eats with them' " (NIV).

Luke develops this contrast in such famous parables as the prodigal son and his older brother and the Pharisee and the publican, which Luke introduces with these words: "To some who were confident of their own righteousness and looked down on everybody else, Jesus told this parable" (Luke 18:9, NIV).

Out of this contrast, Luke repeatedly teaches two primary and interrelated lessons:

1. We are all equally lost in ourselves and UNWORTHY of salvation. Not worthless, but unworthy.
2. We are WORTH EVERY-THING to God.

We are of such value that Jesus would give Himself up to die before He would give us up. And by dying in our place, for our sins, He can rescue anyone who knows their need. Even a dying thief (see Luke 23:39-43) whose life was a total loss until he found Jesus—and Jesus found him—at Calvary.

## THE GOSPEL ACCORDING TO JOHN: JESUS AS GOD

The first three Gospels are known as the Synoptic (same view) Gospels because of their many shared stories and common teachings of Jesus. The fourth Gospel is very different from the other three. It has a distinctive and deeper purpose.

John wrote long after Matthew, Mark, and Luke and assumes their portraits of Jesus are well-known. He is the last living apostle, and he sets out to write the most deeply spiritual Gospel. His message can be summed up in three crucial phrases: *eternal life* through *believing in* the *Son of God.*

"Jesus did many other miraculous signs in the presence of his disciples, which are not recorded in this book. But these are written that you may *believe* that Jesus is the Christ, the *Son of God,* and that by believing you may have [eternal] *life* in his name" (John 20:30, 31, NIV, emphasis added).

The key word in John's Gospel is *belief,* or *faith.* One or the other translation of that same Greek word appears ninety-six times in this Gospel. Every story ends with either someone believing or refusing to believe. For John, the belief or faith that saves has only one object—the divine *Son of God* (in this Gospel Jesus is called the *Son* in relation to the Father over 138 times).

The divine Son of God is John's special portrait of Jesus. The apostle wants us to understand that Jesus was as fully and truly God as He was fully and truly a man. He wants Thomas's great confession of Christ, found at the end of this Gospel, to be ours: "My Lord and my God!" (John 20:28, NIV).

The divinity of Jesus is made central, right from the first verses where John introduces Him as "the Word was God . . . made flesh":

"In the beginning was the Word, and the Word was with God, and *the Word was God.* He was with God in the beginning. Through him all things were made; without him nothing was made that has been made. In him was life, and that life was the light of men. . . . *The Word became flesh* and lived for a while among us. We have seen his glory" (John 1:1-4, 14, NIV, emphasis added).

Why is the divinity of Jesus so crucial? Because if Jesus is God, then all that He does has infinite and eternal value. There is no problem too large for Him to conquer (not even death), no sin too deep for Him to forgive, no situation in which He lacks sufficiency. If He is God, then He is capable of imparting *eternal life* to all who believe in Him.

No verse better sums up John's goal and sets forth his three crucial phrases than the most famous Bible verse of all, John 3:16:

"For God so loved the world that he gave his one and only Son, that whoever *believes*

**26**

in him shall not perish but have *eternal life*" (NIV).

Like Matthew, Mark, and Luke, John does not offer the salvation of Jesus apart from His sin-bearing death on the cross. Even John 3:16 must be read in that context, as the verses that come just before it prove. Jesus told Nicodemus that to see or enter the kingdom of God, he must be born again (John 3:3-8). Nicodemus asks how this can happen (John 3:9), and Jesus responds by pointing to His own sin-bearing sacrifice on the cross: "Just as Moses lifted up the snake in the desert, *so the Son of Man must be lifted up, that everyone who believes in him may have eternal life*" (John 3:14, 15, NIV, emphasis added).

It is not enough to see Jesus as a great teacher or moral example. John's Gospel makes it abundantly clear we must see Him as the divine Son of God who chose to become *the Lamb of God who takes away the sins of the world.*

### CONCLUSION
One gospel—the good news of an all-powerful Saviour and King, of the God who became a man to redeem His people from their sins through His death on a cross. It is a gospel too big for one perspective. Too grand to be limited to one people or group. Too deep for just one approach.

And so Scripture presents the story as a four-sided diamond. Four accounts through the eyes of four evangelists. And just as a diamond, when held up to the sun and turned slowly, gives off the entire rainbow of colors, these four portraits of Jesus, taken together, give us a complete picture of His work for our salvation.

 **Memory Focus**

"Jesus did many other miraculous signs in the presence of his disciples, which are not recorded in this book. But these are written that you may believe that Jesus is the Christ, the Son of God, and that by believing you may have life in his name" (John 20:30, 31, NIV).

 # Into the Bible

1. Matthew, Luke, and John put a genealogy (list of ancestors) near the beginning of their Gospels. The oldest name in each of these genealogies helps indicate the particular group of people each Gospel is written to—and its distinctive theme. Where the genealogy starts or ends gives a strong indication of the target audience and main theme of that Gospel. Complete the worksheet provided by the teacher.

2. Read Matthew 1–3. List the six verses in these chapters where Matthew indicates that the coming of Jesus fulfilled something the prophets had said would happen. Use the worksheet provided by your teacher.

3. At many significant points in the ministry of Jesus, Luke specifically records that Jesus took time for prayer, showing how vital and necessary prayer was to our Lord. There are seven instances where Luke mentions Jesus praying (Luke 3:21; 6:12; 9:18, 29; 11:1; 23:34, and 23:46).
   Choose four of these instances, and do the following:
   A. Identify the instance.
   B. Write out your opinion as to how Jesus felt about prayer during His ministry.

4. In the first half of his Gospel, John relates seven miracles that demonstrate the complete power of Jesus to conquer every problem, no matter how serious or great, through seven great miracles. They are found in John 2:1-11; 4:46-53; 5:1-15; 6:1-15; 6:16-21; 9:1-41; and 11:1-44. Read each story, and then, on a sheet of paper, summarize in one sentence what Jesus did in each miracle.

 # Projects

1. Luke records events that showed Jesus' compassion and respect for the women He encountered in His ministry. The following verses contain four examples of events involving

women: Luke 7:11-17; 8:1-3; 13:11-13; 23:27, 28. Divide into groups. Read each of these instances, and then discuss the aspects of the story that show the respect and compassion Jesus had for women in a time when many treated them as second-class citizens or simply as property. Use the worksheet provided for this project, and share the results with the class.

2. The story of the prodigal son in Luke 15:12–32 is Jesus' direct response to the charge made against Him by the Pharisees in Luke 15:1–2. Read through the parable of the prodigal son. Be prepared to discuss the following:

   A. The steps the son took in his return to his father.
   B. Who the older brother represents (what religious attitude).
   C. Why Jesus ends the story with the unresolved discussion between the older brother and the father.

3. The special covenant name for God in the Old Testament was Yahweh, which literally meant "I Am." Six times in the Gospel of John, Jesus takes the title "I Am" and completes the sentence to show how He supplies all that we lack (for example, John 8:12: "I am the light of the world"). The six "I am" statements of Jesus are found in John 6:47-51; 8:12; 10:9; 11:25; 14:6; and 15:1-7. Read the statements in their context, and complete the worksheet provided by your teacher.

4. To review this lesson, draw a picture that will illustrate a unique aspect of each Gospel. Use the directions provided by your teacher.

························································

## ☉ Focus Questions

1. Did Jesus do the things prophets predicted He would do simply to fulfill the prophecy? Explain.
2. Why were four books in the New Testament written regarding the life of Christ?
3. Compare John 20:30 and 21:25, and describe what this might mean regarding Jesus' stay here on earth.
4. Which Gospel do you prefer, and why?
5. How does Jesus' attitude toward women compare to that of Paul?

# HUMANITY

God likes people.  He sent His Son to be one *(Quips and Quotes)*.

# The Chosen Land

**Lesson Scriptures: Genesis 12:1-3;
Deuteronomy 11:8-21;
John 17:15-18**

Think how radically different your life would be if you lived in Afghanistan or Kuwait instead of in the United States.

What you eat, how you dress, the kind of house you live in, even how you spend your time would be different if you lived in another country. It would even be somewhat different if you lived in another part of the United States, Canada, or Bermuda. Our lives are affected and our thinking influenced by where we live.

Can you really understand someone if you don't know much about where or how they live? What about people who not only lived in another place but also lived in another time?

To be more specific, as we begin our study of Jesus, what do we need to know about the time and place where Jesus lived to best understand what He said and what He did?

Jesus lived about two thousand years ago in the narrow strip of land Israelis and Palestinians now struggle for. This is an important bit of land today and was even more important during Christ's life on earth. The land was called Canaan when God first asked Abraham to leave his hometown of Ur in Babylonia to journey there. Canaan was a crossroads, a sort of bridge between the continents that are now known as Asia, Africa, and Europe. It was a connecting link between two major civilizations of the ancient world—

Egypt to the South and Babylon/Persia to the east. Trade caravans traveled through Canaan carrying goods and news. It was this little land, so strategically located, that God chose as a home for Abraham and his descendants.

## SIZE OF BIBLICAL PALESTINE

Biblical Israel was small, about the size of the states of Vermont or Maryland. It measured about 150 miles from north to south and varied from between 25 to 75 miles from east to west. The distance from the Sea of Galilee to Jericho was about 65 miles. Since the method of transportation used by the common people was walking, this smallness made travel possible from one part of the country to another.

Although cities at the time of Christ were small compared to modern cities, they had grown considerably from the time we first read about them in the Bible. Have you ever wondered how the people of Israel were able to walk around the city of Jericho seven times in one day? At the time Solomon was king of Israel, Jericho occupied only five acres. No doubt, at the time the Israelites took the city, it was even smaller than five acres. By contrast, a modern freeway cloverleaf covers about 40 acres.

When Solomon was king, Jerusalem occupied about 45 acres, not including the 35 acres on which the temple stood. By the time Jesus was on earth, Jerusalem had grown to 140 acres, still not very large if measured against the size of cities today. The streets were narrow, no more than four or five feet wide, and the city was densely populated. The crowds were noisy as they pushed along the streets with their goods piled on their backs and sometimes driving their animals before them.

Jesus did not spend all, or even much, of His time in Jerusalem. With His disciples, He walked among the cities and towns of Judea and Galilee, sometimes passing through Samaria.

## DAILY LIFE IN BIBLICAL PALESTINE

The daily life of the people was different from the life we live today. Most people lived in houses built of packed earth that were frequently destroyed

by heavy rains and floodwaters. When Jesus told the parable of the foolish man who built his house on sand, He was talking to people whose houses had been washed away if they had been unfortunate enough to build on low-lying, sandy land. The little one- or two-room houses usually had flat roofs made of baked mud bricks. The bricks were placed over tree limbs that formed a crude framework. When you visualize the construction of the roofs, you can better understand how the paralytic's friends could easily remove part of the roof and lower him down through the opening to the place where Jesus was standing.

Usually the windows were built on only one side of the house, away from the sun. Palestine is a warm land, and the walls without windows helped to keep the house cool. Of course, with no electric lighting and the sun blocked out of the house, it was usually dark inside, even in the daytime. You will remember that the woman in the parable who lost one of her ten coins lighted a lamp before sweeping the house to search for the coin. Jesus also reminded the people

that it was useless to light a candle and put it under a bushel. Candles had to be put on candlesticks if they were to provide light in the house.

## UNDERSTANDING BIBLE STORIES

To understand how strange it seemed to Jesus' disciples when they found Him talking with the Samaritan woman, you

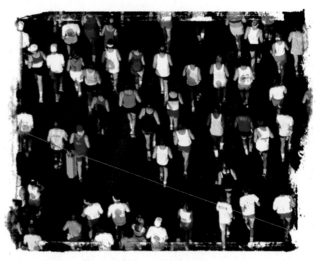

need to understand how much Jews hated Samaritans. Even to begin understanding how upsetting it was for Jewish leaders to hear the parable of the good Samaritan, you need to know something of the history of hatred that went back hundreds of years. It was based on the

belief that Samaritans were unclean and unfaithful to God. You will learn the reasons for this hatred in the following lesson.

At one time, Jesus told His disciples it was harder for a rich man to enter the kingdom of heaven than for a camel to pass through the eye of a needle. Most of us try to think of a camel getting through the eye of a sewing needle. It may be that Jesus was talking about a small opening in the gate of a city. Usually, city gates were closed at sundown. Anyone wanting to enter after that was admitted through a small door in the gate. The passage was too small for a camel to pass through unless its load was taken off its back and it could be coaxed through the opening on its knees.

### PARABLES

Many of Jesus' parables and sayings were based on the ways people earned their living in Palestine two thousand years ago. There were, of course, some who were rich, but there were also many poor people who were slaves or day laborers. Most of the people were peasants, small landowners, fishermen, farmers, shepherds, or craftsmen. You can find parables or references in Jesus' teaching about all these groups. These were the common people who the Bible says heard Jesus gladly.

The common people were not highly regarded by the religious leaders. Most had little education and were not so strict in keeping the legalistic traditions that the religious leaders tried to impose on them. Still, life centered around the Synagogue, and the Sabbath day found the people there. We know they were concerned about pleasing God because of the way they came to hear John the Baptist preach and later crowded around Jesus.

Jesus used parables, a popular way of teaching at that time. Without the many types of entertainment that we have today, the people loved to hear stories and, no doubt, repeated them over and over. In this way, many lessons Jesus wanted people to understand were locked in their memories.

Imagine how Jesus would live if He had been born on earth in the twentieth or twenty-first century instead of two thousand years ago. How would He dress? How would He travel? In what part of the world would He live? Would He be on radio? On television? And how would His parables and illustrations be different? We know that the things He said and did were designed to reach the people in the time and place in which He lived. We must understand that time and place if we want to understand what Jesus is saying to us.

# Memory Focus

"Jesus went throughout Galilee, teaching in their synagogues, preaching the good news of the kingdom, and healing every disease and sickness among the people. . . . Large crowds from Galilee, the Decapolis, Jerusalem, Judea and the region across the Jordan followed him" (Matthew 4:23-25, NIV).

# Into the Bible

1. What do these Old Testament references tell us about Palestine?
   A. Exodus 3:8
   B. Numbers 13:17-20, 23-27
   C. Joshua 24:13, 14
   D. Nehemiah 9:25
2. The lesson narrative tells about the unique assortment of people and varying landscapes that no doubt affected the life, teachings, and ministry of Jesus. Use the worksheet provided by your teacher to discover what objects of nature Jesus used to illustrate spiritual truths, and explain what lesson you think Jesus was trying to teach.

3. Read about the Promised Land in Deuteronomy 11:8-21, and answer the following questions:
   A. How do verses 8 and 9 relate to the fifth commandment in Exodus 20:12? What does obedience to God have to do with living a long life?
   B. In what ways was Palestine different from Egypt? What spiritual lessons was Israel to learn from this?
   C. What important truth was God teaching His people by linking rainfall to obedience? Also, see Deuteronomy 28:12-14.

 # Projects

1. Obtain a map of Palestine as it was at the time of Christ. Locate the names of the towns and cities, bodies of water, and major provinces (as specified by your teacher).
2. Study the map and graphs of Palestine as it was when Christ lived there. These will be provided by your teacher. Determine the following:
   A. The distance from Bethlehem to Jerusalem.
   B. The distance from Capernaum to Jerusalem.
   C. The difference in altitude between Jerusalem and Jericho.
3. Make a scale drawing of your state, province, or island with Palestine superimposed on the drawing.
4. Identify some reasons why God chose Canaan as the homeland for His people.

 **Focus Questions**

1. What are some similarities and differences between your home state, province, or island and Palestine?
2. What are some similarities between your hometown and one of the towns/cities in Palestine?
3. What principles should be considered when making a choice of a place to live?
4. If Christ were coming to earth today rather than when He did, where would He come to live? Why?
5. Give some examples of parables Jesus told that were influenced and shaped by the type of land and lifestyles around Him.

# HUMILITY

Lord, when we are wrong, make us willing to change;
when we are right, make us easy to live with *(The Daily Walk).*

# The Chosen People

**Lesson Scriptures: Deuteronomy 4:5-9; 7:6-9; Galatians 3:7-9**

It's hard to beat the excitement of being chosen for something special. It's fun to receive an award, be hired for a great job, or be elected as a student association, class, or club officer. To be chosen makes us feel good and builds our confidence.

Being chosen may mean that we have the talents and abilities for the job, that people see us as capable and responsible. Or it may mean that we are liked and that others want to see us succeed. Whatever the reason, being chosen usually gives us a boost. We all need to be chosen sometimes.

The great news is that each of us has been chosen by God. How do we know this? The promise is in 1 Thessalonians 1:4, TEV. "We know that God loves you and has chosen you to be his own." Paul also makes it clear how much God values us, "in that while we were yet sinners, Christ died for us" (Romans 5:8, NKJV).

When Jesus came to this world, He was born into a chosen people. Through God's call to Abraham, the Jewish people inherited a sacred and unique mission. They were to be God's representatives in this world. God called them to demonstrate the blessings that would come to a nation that worships Jehovah. But these blessings were not only for the Jewish people and nation. God expected them to share the blessings He gave them with others.

Moses explained to the children of Israel why they were

chosen. "The Lord your God has chosen you out of all the peoples on the face of the earth to be his people, his treasured possession. The Lord did not set his affection on you and

choose you because you were more numerous than other peoples, for you were the fewest of all peoples. But it was because the Lord loved you and kept the oath he swore to your forefathers that he brought you out with a mighty hand and redeemed you from the land of slavery, from the power of Pharaoh king of Egypt. Know therefore that the Lord your God is God; he is the faithful God, keeping his covenant of love to a thousand generations of those who love him and keep his commands" (Deuteronomy 7:6-9, NIV).

The Jewish nation knew that God loved them and was with them. For years in the wilderness, He did miracle after miracle that showed His love. When the people finally crossed the Jordan River into Canaan, the miracles continued.

Without God's help, they could not have conquered the land. Yet Israel often disobeyed God and even worshiped idols. Why? The Israelites made all sorts of excuses for their disobedience. We know that through the years they were strongly influenced to worship idols by the surrounding nations. But in the end, the reason was simple. God chose Israel to be His people, but Israel didn't always choose God's plan.

The history of the Jewish nation as told in the Old Testament shows a pattern of neglect, defiance, and rejection of God. They were not committed to accepting God's plan and did not seem to understand Him. Therefore, Israel was not an effective witness to God's love, nor could they tell of God's plan to redeem them. They did not even understand the role of the Messiah, so when the Saviour was born, they did not recognize Him and were not ready to receive Him.

Why is it important for us to understand the failure of Israel? So that we will not make the same mistakes. The Bible states that "all these things happened to them [Israel] as examples to warn us against doing the same things" (1 Corinthians 10:11, TLB). Let's take a look at just where Israel went wrong.

In the beginning, the Israelites recognized that they existed as a unique nation because of God's greatness, not theirs. They had been slaves when God called them out of Egypt. He cared for them in the wilderness and educated them for forty years because they were slow learners—slow in learning to trust and obey God. When the twelve tribes of Israel first entered the land of Canaan, they were united under God's rulership. It wasn't long, however, until they began to worship heathen gods, as did the nations around them. The history of this period is one of prosperity, rejection of God, invasion by an enemy nation, repentance, prosperity, then apostasy, in a never-ending cycle.

The Israelites wanted a king so they could be like the nations around them. God granted their request, but instead of leading the people in the worship of Jehovah, many of the kings permitted, and even encouraged, wickedness. At the death of Solomon in 931 B.C. nearly five hundred years after Israel entered the Promised Land, national unity came to an end. The nation split into two separate kingdoms—Israel to the north and Judah to the south.

After rejecting the appeals of God's prophets to repent of their corrupt and immoral ways, Israel fell to the Assyrian army in 722 B.C. When the Israelites were carried off as captives, people from nearby regions repopulated the land, bringing their idols with them. As time passed, marriages occurred between the idolaters and the few Israelites who were left behind. Gradually, the heathen religion became mixed with the worship of God. A temple was built on Mount Gerizim where sacrifices were offered to idols.

North of Judea was Samaria, home of those Jews who had not been taken into captivity and who intermarried with the people of Canaan. This mixed race, called Samaritans, was considered by the Jews in Judah to be defiled and impure. The Jews despised and shunned the Samaritans because of both their religious and cultural differences. This hatred between the Jews and the Samaritans still existed when Jesus lived on earth more than six hundred years later.

After the fall of Israel, the people of Judah followed in their footsteps. They, too, "mocked God's messengers, despised his words and scoffed at his prophets" (2 Chronicles 36:16, NIV). They, too, were taken captive to Babylon. The southern kingdom fell in 605 B.C., and its people lived in captivity for seventy years.

At the end of this time, a few dedicated Jews returned to rebuild Jerusalem, restore the temple, and occupy the land. Never again did the Jewish people worship idols. They had learned their lesson, but in an effort to safeguard their religion, they avoided close contact with people of other nations. They developed a lifestyle full of rules and regulations in order to gain God's favor.

Still, many people who came in contact with the Jews learned about their God. Some, such as the wise men who followed the Bethlehem star, even heard about a Messiah who was to come and began to look for Him. Israel did not, however, share their knowledge of God's love or give a true picture of the Messiah. They did not fulfill the mission God had given them to do.

With Jerusalem serving as the spiritual and political center of the nation, most of the Jews lived in the southern region of the area now known as Palestine. In Christ's time, this area was known as Judea, a Greek/Roman translation of *Judah* meaning "a Jewish nation."

Galilee, the most northern of the three provinces of Palestine, was also inhabited by a mixed race of Jews and Canaanites. In time, these people became Jewish and were known as Galileans. They retained a distinctive accent

and dialect. The pure-blooded Jews of Judea despised the liberal, open-minded Galileans for some of the same reasons they hated the Samaritans. These strong ethnic feelings of hostility were still in evidence during the lifetime of Jesus. Eleven of Christ's disciples were from Galilee and were recognized as Galileans because of their speech.

When we look back at the history of the Jews, we can't help but wonder what went wrong. How could a people chosen by God to bring salvation to other people not experience salvation themselves? When they had so many evidences of God's love and forgiveness, how could they have so much hostility in their hearts? Perhaps the most important question we can ask is, What can we learn about ourselves as we study the history of the chosen people?

 ## Memory Focus

"'You are my witnesses,' declares the Lord, 'and my servant whom I have chosen, so that you may know and believe me and understand that I am he. Before me no god was formed, nor will there be one after me. I, even I, am the Lord, and apart from me there is no savior'" (Isaiah 43:10, 11, NIV).

 ## Into the Bible

1. Read the following texts and identify the mission of the chosen people.
   A. Deuteronomy 4:5-9
   B. Isaiah 43:10-12
   C. Isaiah 49:6
2. Read the following texts and describe the reasons for the failure of the Jewish nation to carry out their divine mission.

A. Deuteronomy 28:47, 48
B. 1 Samuel 8:4-7, 19-21
C. 2 Kings 17:9-18
D. 2 Chronicles 36:14

 **Projects**

1. **STUDY GUIDE:** The following questions are based on chapter 2, "The Chosen People," in *The Desire of Ages.*
   A. What three specific tasks was Israel to accomplish for God?
   B. Why did Israel fail to carry out these divine purposes?
   C. Having been cured of the worship of graven images, what did they do in order to escape the temptation of idolatry?
   D. What began to happen as the Jews continued with their ceremonies?
   E. What kind of Messiah did the Jews expect?
   F. How did the Jews interpret the prophecies that foretold of Christ's first coming?

2. To illustrate God's desire to save each sinner, Jesus told two parables about people who hunted for things they had lost: a shepherd who lost one sheep and a housewife who lost one coin (Luke 15:1-12). This man and woman were familiar types to Jesus' audience. If Jesus were alive and preaching in North America today, what kinds of people might He use to illustrate the same idea? Rewrite these two stories, placing them in contemporary society. Include specific ideas concerning what the man and woman do for work, what they have lost, and how they would search for that lost item.

3. Jesus told the parable of the good Samaritan to illustrate God's unconditional love for us. He chose Samaritans and Jews for the characters in His story because His audience knew that these two ethnic groups hated each other intensely and

would be very unlikely to do a kind deed for each other. Rewrite the story in modern terms as the basis for a report on the evening news. Possible details could include:

- The cities the man would be traveling to and from.
- What type of vehicle he would be traveling in.
- Who attacks him and why.
- Which people would refuse to help.
- The person who does stop.
- What type of help this concerned stranger would give.

 Focus Questions

1. What do you think the "other gods" claimed to offer that induced God's people to worship them?
2. What makes a person or a church an effective and attractive witness for God?
3. It's been said that witnessing has more to do with what you are than what you say or do. Do you agree?
4. The chosen people replaced God with human rulers and chose to follow their own desires rather than heed the messages of the prophets. Is this still a problem today?
5. How did the Jewish hatred of Romans and Samaritans affect their relationship with Christ and His teachings?
6. What are the primary causes of ethnic and racial prejudices?
7. Because of increasing violence and criminal activity on highways, is it potentially dangerous to stop and offer assistance? If someone appears to be in trouble, what safeguards should be considered?

# TIMELESSNESS

Heaven and earth are no wider apart today than when shepherds
listened to the angels' song (*The Desire of Ages*, 48).

# lesson 5

# The Bethlehem Story

**Lesson Scriptures: Matthew 1:18-2:23;
Luke 1:26-56; 2:1-39**

"T he idea of God coming to this world as a man and then all of us celebrating His birthday just doesn't make any sense to me!" This was Tom's excuse when His wife asked him to go with her and the kids to a special program at the church on Christmas Eve.

Soon after the family had gone without him, Tom was startled by a series of soft thuds against the living-room window. Stepping outside to investigate, he was surprised to see a flock of small birds huddled in the snow, shivering against the wind. To get out of the bitter cold, they were trying to fly through the windowpane.

Tom immediately felt pity for these cold, miserable little creatures. He decided he must rescue them, but he wasn't sure how. Then he remembered that the barn was warm and dry. He put on his coat and boots and tramped through the snow to open the barn door and turn on the lights. To his dismay, the birds paid no attention to what he was doing.

*They must be hungry*, Tom thought. So he went back to the house and got some old bread. Hoping to coax the birds into the barn, he began to sprinkle the pieces of bread on the snow, making a trail of crumbs from the house to the barn. But the birds ignored his efforts and stayed huddled right where they were.

Tom tried shooing them into the barn by walking

# 47

around them and waving his arms. The birds scattered in every direction—except into the barn. *These birds must see me as strange and frightening,* thought Tom. *How can I make them see that I'm their friend and*

*that it's safe to follow me? If only I could become a bird myself for a few minutes.*

Just then, as the church bells rang out an old Christmas carol, Tom remembered the text that said Jesus became flesh and lived among us. At that moment, the Bethlehem story made sense to Tom for the first time.

All heaven stood in silent awe as Jesus prepared to descend into the life of a human. Laying aside His glory, stepping down from heaven's throne to become a baby, is something we can't comprehend but only accept and appreciate.

There are those who say, "How could the God of heaven become human? It's incredible that Jesus would humble Himself like that." But the truth is, that's the way He's always been. Neither the manger nor the cross changed God. It simply revealed what He's been like all along. This is hard for us to understand. We've grown used to thinking of God as the Most Holy while failing to see Him as the Most Humble. God Himself put it this way: "I dwell in the high and holy place, with him also that is of a contrite and humble spirit" (Isaiah 57:15, KJV).

Satan did not acknowledge God's love or His willingness to humble Himself to reach us. When he rebelled against God, Satan accused God of being highhanded and self-serving. He said that God was like a big boss who made laws and gave orders but wasn't willing to give of Himself. But Jesus' humble birth in Bethlehem refutes those accusations and proves God's self-sacrificing love.

Jesus came to earth to do two things: reveal God and redeem the human race. His first task was to show us what God is like. Satan's accusations had gone unanswered since before Creation, so, vindicating God's character had to have first priority. The security and stability of the universe was at stake, and our salvation depended on God's proving Himself just and merciful.

Jesus' second task was to live as our example and die as our substitute. Jesus lived a fully human life, but without sinning.

But Jesus was not welcomed to earth as a saviour. The chosen people, who had waited over a thousand years for the coming of the Messiah, were taken by surprise. There were no elaborate preparations, no waiting dignitaries, no celebration, no flashing lights or red carpets. There wasn't even a room in a Bethlehem inn. Angels and beings from unfallen worlds watching these events must have been baffled by such indifference.

Even though Christmas is the most widely celebrated of all holidays in the Western world, the real meaning of the Bethlehem story still goes largely overlooked. What about you? What do you think about at Christmas? Do you recognize it as a celebration of God's greatest gift, or are you as indifferent as the world was two thousand years ago?

# Memory Focus

"'The virgin will be with child and will give birth to a son, and they will call him Immanuel'—which means, 'God with us'" (Matthew 1:23, NIV).

 # Into the Bible

1. Only two of the four Gospels—Matthew and Luke—describe the birth of Jesus and the events associated with it. Obtain from your teacher a copy of the worksheet "Events Surrounding Christ's Birth" on which you will identify certain aspects of the Bethlehem story as recorded in Matthew and Luke.

2. A. What do we know about Mary from the song that she wrote? Luke 1:46-55.
   B. What is the primary theme of Mary's song?

3. What indications are there that the wise men arrived quite some time after the birth of Jesus? Matthew 2:16; compare Matthew 2:11.

4. Identify what Simeon's prophecy in the temple says about the work of Jesus. What does he say about the response of the Jewish people to Jesus? About the pain and anguish that His mother would suffer? Luke 2:24-35.

5. The Bible contains biblical truths about Jesus and His first advent. The worksheet provided by your teacher will list scriptural references, and you will be asked to identify the biblical truths that are emphasized in each text.

 # Projects

1. Imagine you would be given the opportunity to interview the following people. Choose two, and prepare a list of at least five questions you would ask each individual. Then write what you think the person will say in response to your questions.
   Mary
   Joseph
   One of the shepherds
   One of the wise men
   King Herod

2. **NEWSPAPER STORY:** You are a reporter for the *Jerusalem Tribune* or the *Bethlehem Gazette*. Write a newspaper story on one of the following events:
   A. The birth of Jesus and visit by the shepherds
   B. The arrival of the wise men and the killing of the infants in Bethlehem
3. This activity is based on the events associated with the birth of Jesus. Your teacher will give you a worksheet that identifies selected chapters and pages from *The Desire of Ages* that should be used for your responses.

· · · · · · · · · · · · · · · · · · · · · · · · · · · · · · · · · · · · · · · · · · · · · · · · · · · · · · · · · · · · · · · · · · · · · · · · · · · · ·

 # Focus Questions

1. Why do you think the exact date of Christ's birth is not given in Scripture?
2. We know what Mary said to the angel when he told her she would be the mother of the Messiah. How do you think she felt?
3. Some Christians exalt Mary to a saintly status; others give her little recognition. How do you think we should feel about Jesus' mother?
4. What kind of man do you think Joseph was?
5. Why did King Herod feel so threatened by the news of Christ's birth? Why do people feel threatened today by the nearness of His second coming?
6. Do you think Christians today are better prepared for the second coming than the Jews were for the first coming?
7. How can Christians celebrate Christmas so that the primary focus is on Jesus?

# CHALLENGE

Don't let anyone look down on you because you are young,
but be an example for the believers in your speech, your conduct, your love,
faith and purity (1 Timothy 4:12, TEV).

# lesson 6

# Christ as a Teenager

## Lesson Scriptures: Luke 2:52; John 1:10-12

**H**ave you heard about the fellow who hid in a barn hayloft for thirty-seven years? Probably not, so here's his story.

Vaino Kilpinen was a young man who lived near the little town of Hameenlinna, Finland. Life was going on quite normally for him until he was drafted into the Finnish cavalry on April 20, 1928. The cavalry is that part of the army which does its fighting on horseback. Vaino's trouble was that he knew very little about horses and every time he got on one, as hard as he tried, he just couldn't stay on. He was so humiliated by continually falling off his horse that on May 18, less than a month after he had been drafted, he decided to sneak out of the camp and head for home.

Fearing he would be punished for what he had done, Vaino decided to make his home in the hayloft of the family's barn. It was in this dark and desolate place that he stayed for the next thirty-seven years. His only contact with the outside world was through his parents and a brother and sister. Five other brothers and sisters living elsewhere knew nothing of his circumstances or his whereabouts.

His food was brought to him two or three times a week, and most of his time was spent reading elementary books and making brooms and birch-bark baskets. In 1939 he tearfully watched through a crack in the barn as his father was buried in a nearby graveyard. In 1954, he

was heartbroken when he realized he had seen his mother for the very last time.

With both of his parents gone, there was nothing more to live for. Not only had life become meaningless and a great deal more difficult, there was no one to provide food, medical care, or anything else he needed. After four more agonizing years, he finally decided to leave his hiding place. His first task was to convince the astonished family and neighbors that he was actually alive after all those years of being listed as missing and presumed dead.

The strange story of Vaino Kilpinen vividly illustrates the tragedy of a wasted life. Each of us wants a life filled with meaning and purpose, a life that counts for something and makes a difference in the world. In contrast to Vaino's virtually useless existence, Jesus' life, from the cradle to the grave and beyond, was the fulfillment of God's master plan. Nothing about Jesus' life, as recorded in Scripture, was insignificant, worthless, or purposeless.

Sometimes it's hard to grasp this fact because the Bible is nearly silent about the first thirty years of Jesus' life. After Jesus and His parents return to Nazareth from Egypt, we hear nothing about Him until He appears at the Jordan River to be baptized, many years later. The only break in this lengthy silence is when the twelve-year-old Jesus appears in the temple, an event described in just a few verses.

Because the Bible tells us so little about Jesus' early years, strange speculations and legends have risen. These unbiblical tales are generally dismissed as untrue, but we're still left with the unanswered question What was Jesus really like as a child, a teenager, and a young adult? If you've wondered about the very same things, then you're going to find this study very informative and helpful.

**THE MESSIAH**

*Messiah* is a Hebrew word meaning "the Anointed One" (the Greeks translated the word as "Christ"). Few people understood what the Messiah would do when He came. Even Jesus' family believed the Messiah would come as a king who would lead the Jews in overthrowing the Romans and ending their oppression. They dreamed that the Messiah would restore Israel to the power and glory of days gone by. The Jews' attention was focused on worldly triumph, not spiritual renewal.

Jesus grew up among people who cherished these mis-

guided hopes and dreams. During this time, He came face to face with some of the most important decisions of His life. But as He watched the temple service at the age of twelve, He realized how His life would end. He knew that He was to be the sacrifice symbolized by the lamb. Was He willing to accept this role?

The decision was made when Jesus' parents found Him in the temple, and He answered their question about His behavior with the words "I must be about my Father's business" (Luke 2:49, KJV). These are the only recorded words of Jesus as a boy that tell what He understood about Himself and His life work. What was it that led Jesus to make such a commitment? Why did He turn down the opportunity to rule as a king, when everyone expected that the Messiah would come as ruler of His people? How did He discover His Father's plan and purpose for His life?

**CRITICAL CHOICES**

In these critical choices, Jesus left us an example. When we make plans for our future—choosing a career or goals to accomplish—the temptation to go for the crown (money, power, and fame for ourselves) instead of the cross (sacrifice for God and service for others) is just as real for us as it was for Jesus. To give in to personal ambition, to get the most out of what the world has to offer, is the natural choice of the selfish heart. But letting ourselves be driven by a compelling desire to "lay up— treasures on earth" (Matthew 6:19, NKJV) will surely lead to spiritual bankruptcy. Jesus said, "For what is a man profited if he gains the whole world, and loses his own soul?" (Matthew 16:26, NKJV).

When Christ is Lord of our hearts, He gives us a new, unselfish nature that takes control of our lives. Only then can we begin to choose as He chose, serve as He served, and live as He lived.

# Memory Focus

"And Jesus grew in wisdom and stature, and in favor with God and men" (Luke 2:52, NIV).

OR

"He was in the world, and though the world was made through him, the world did not recognize him. He came to that which was his own, but his own did not receive him. Yet to all who received him, to those who believed in his name, he gave the right to become children of God—children born not of natural descent, nor of human decision or a husband's will, but born of God" (John 1:10-12, NIV).

# Into the Bible

1. Read the references given below to discover insights into Jesus' early life. Write a short description for each of the following:
   A. His hometown—Matthew 2:23; Mark 6:4-6; John 1:45, 46
   B. His early occupation—Mark 6:3
   C. His parents—Luke 2:51

D. His family—Mark 6:3, 4; John 7:5

E. His growing up—Luke 2:52

F. His education—John 7:15

G. His worship—Luke 4:16; Luke 6:12

H. His appearance—Isaiah 53:2

I. His people—Isaiah 53:3; Mark 3:20, 21; John 1:11

2. What does the Bible say about how Christ's family related to Him? Did any accept Him as the Messiah?

A. Matthew 12:46-50

B. Luke 2:49, 50

C. John 7:3-5

3. Read Matthew 16:24-26:

A. What does Jesus mean when He asks each of us to deny ourselves and take up our cross and follow Him?

B. Rewrite the following statement of Jesus in your own words: "Whoever desires to save his life will lose it, and whoever loses his life for My sake will find it" (Matthew 16:25, NKJV).

 Projects

1. Let's take a closer look at the only recorded event of Jesus as a youth. Read Luke 2:41-51, as well as several references in *The Desire of Ages*—pages 78, 80, 81, 146, and answer the following questions.

A. What was Jesus doing when His parents finally found Him?

B. What was it that amazed all those who heard Jesus speak?

C. How did Jesus answer His parents' question? What was their response to what He said?

D. What two discoveries did Jesus make while in the temple on this special occasion? (See *The Desire of Ages*, 78, 81, 146.)

E. Explain what Jesus witnessed in the temple that led to His great discovery. (See *The Desire of Ages*, 78)

F. While in the temple, what questions did Jesus ask regarding the Messiah and of whom were these questions asked? (See *The Desire of Ages*, 78.)

G. Describe the answers that Jesus received to His questions and how He responded to what He heard. (See *The Desire of Ages*, 78.)

H. What did Jesus use as the basis for His beliefs about the mission and work of the Messiah? (See *The Desire of Ages*, 78.)

I. What was the attitude and reaction of the Jewish leaders to the truth as revealed to them by Jesus? (See *The Desire of Ages*, 80.)

2. In Christ's discussion with the Jewish leaders in the temple, *The Desire of Ages* states that Jesus defended His convictions regarding the Messiah by quoting from "the prophecy of Isaiah" that scriptures "point to the suffering and death of the Lamb of God" (78). Read Isaiah 53—the greatest of all Messianic prophecies in the Bible—and respond to the following:

A. What does it say about the people whom He came to save (verses 3, 6)?

B. What did Jesus learn regarding the mission and suffering of the Messiah (verses 4, 5, 7, 8, 9)?

C. Do you think Jesus was disheartened or encouraged by what He found in what Isaiah had written?

3. REPORT: There is a division among Christians regarding the family of Jesus. There are those who maintain that Christ's brothers and sisters were Mary's children, therefore, younger than Jesus. Others believe that His brothers and sisters were older than Jesus, children of Joseph from a previous marriage.

Using the *SDA Bible Commentary*, a Bible dictionary, and *The Desire of Ages*, write a short report on Jesus' brothers and sisters that would support one of the positions mentioned above.

4. Working in groups of three or four, use the worksheet "Helpful Hints for Raising Children" provided by your teacher, to help you form your personal beliefs on how children should be raised. Evaluate how your parents raised you. What changes would you make? How can Jesus' life as a youth serve as a model for raising children?

 **Focus Questions**

1. Would you say that Christ's public life and ministry are good illustrations of the kind of life He lived as a teenager?
2. Why do you think Jesus spent His first thirty years working in a carpenter's shop?
3. Why do you think the Bible reveals so little about Christ's early life in Nazareth?
4. Do you think Jesus knew that God was His real Father before His visit to the temple?
5. Why do you think the parents of Jesus did not understand His answer to their question?
6. How does your choice to serve God affect your choice of a life work?
7. How can a person discover what God's plan is for his or her life?
8. What is the importance of church worship in the life of a Christian young person?
9. How can a worship service be made spiritual and relevant?
10. How do we sometimes show that we serve self rather than serve God?

# INSURANCE

Live so that your memories will be part of your happiness *(Quips and Quotes)*.

# lesson 7

# The Word Became Flesh and Dwelt Among Us

## Lesson Scripture: Hebrews 7:23-28, NIV

**THE MIRACLE OF THE CARPENTER**[1]

It's no accident that New Mexico is called the "Land of Enchantment." Sprawling deserts spotted with sage. Purple mountains wreathed with clouds. Adobe homes hidden on hillsides. Majestic pines. Endless artifacts. A cloverleaf of cultures from the conquistador to the Comanche to the cowboy. New Mexico enchants.

And in this land of enchantment, there is a chapel of wonder.

One block south of the La Fonda Hotel in Sante Fe, on the corner of Water Street and Old Santa Fe Trail, you find Loretto Chapel. As you step through its iron gate, you enter more than a chapel courtyard. You enter another era. Pause for a moment under the sprawling branches of the ancient trees. Imagine what it was like when the Mexican carpenters completed the chapel in 1878.

Can you see the settlers stomping through the muddy streets? Can you hear the donkeys braying? The wagon wheels groaning? And can you see the early-morning sun spotlighting this gothic chapel—so simple, so splendid—as it sits against the backdrop of the desert hills?

---

[1]This story is reprinted by permission: Max Lucado, *In the Eye of the Storm* (Dallas, Tex.: Word Publishers, 1991), 135, 136, 138, 139.

Loretto Chapel took five years to complete. Modeled after the Sainte-Chapelle in Paris, its delicate sanctuary contains an altar, a rose window, and a choir loft.

Had you stood in the newly built chapel in 1878, you might have seen the Sisters of Loretto looking forlornly at the balcony. Everything else was complete: the doors had been hung, the pews had been placed, the floor had been laid. Everything else was finished. Even the choir loft. Except for one thing. There were no stairs.

The chapel was too small to accommodate a conventional stairway. The best builders and designers in the region shook their heads when consulted. "Impossible," they murmured. There simply wasn't enough room. A ladder would serve the purpose, but it would mar the ambiance.

The Sisters of Loretto, whose determination had led them from Kentucky to Santa Fe, now faced a challenge greater than their journey: a stairway that couldn't be built.

What they had dreamed of and what they could do was separated by fifteen impossible feet.

So what did they do? The only thing they could do. They ascended the mountain. Not the high mountains near Santa Fe. No, they climbed even higher. They climbed the same mountain that Jesus climbed 1,800 years earlier . . . the mountain of prayer.

As the story goes, the nuns prayed for nine days. On the last day of the novena, a Mexican carpenter with a beard and a wind-burned face appeared at the convent. He explained that he had heard they needed a stairway to a chapel loft. He thought he could help.

The mother superior had nothing to lose, so she gave him permission.

He went to work with crude tools, painstaking patience, and uncanny skill. For eight months, he worked.

One morning, the Sisters of Loretto entered the chapel to find their prayers had been answered. A masterpiece of carpentry spiraled from the floor to the loft; two complete 360-degree turns. Thirty-three steps held together with wooden pegs and no central support. The wood is said to be a variety of hard fir, one nonexistent in

62

New Mexico!

When the sisters turned to thank the craftsman, he was gone. He was never seen again. He never asked for money. He never asked for praise. He was a simple carpenter who did what no one else could do so singers could enter a choir loft and sing.

See the stairway for yourself, if you like. Journey into the "Land of Enchantment." Step into this chapel of amazement, and witness the fruit of prayer.

Or, if you prefer, talk to the Master Carpenter yourself. He has already performed one impossible feat in this world. He, like the Santa Fe carpenter, built a stairway no one else could build. He, like the name-less craftsman, used material from another place. He, like the visitor to Loretto, came to span the gap between where you are and where you long to be.

Each year of His life is a step. Thirty-three paces. Each step of the stair is an answered prayer. He built it so you can climb it. To sing.

## BEHOLD THE MAN

How do you handle some of the things Jesus said?

How would you react if someone looked you in the eye and said: "I am the way and the truth and the life. No one comes to the Father [God] except through me" (John 14:6, NIV)?

Or how about this one: Jesus, standing in front of a crowd that included His best friends and relatives, said: "Can any of you prove me guilty of sin?" (John 8:46, NIV).

If we tried that, those who know us best would say: "No problem, where would you like us to start—your big sins or just your everyday irritating little ones?"

But when Jesus asked the question, everyone was quiet.

Jesus went even further than claiming to be without sin.

Every Jew believed only God Himself could truly forgive sin. So did Jesus. And yet when He met a guilt-ridden paralytic, Jesus said: "Son, your sins are forgiven" (Mark 2:5, NIV).

What kind of man was this?

One night, Jesus and His disciples were in a life-and-death struggle. They were caught on a sinking boat in a raging storm. But Jesus didn't pray long and hard for deliverance. No. Instead, He faced the howling

storm and had a three-word conversation with it: "Peace. Be still" (Mark 4:39, KJV).

Kind of crazy, talking to the wind. Right?

Well, not if it listens. And obeys.

The storm stopped. The disciples whispered: "Who is this? Even the wind and the waves obey him" (Mark 4:41, NIV).

## WE'RE SINFUL— HE'S SINLESS

Let's look at it from another angle. The Bible says a lot of blunt things about the sinful character and corrupt moral nature of every human being. Listen to just a few examples.

"Surely I have been a sinner from birth, sinful from the time my mother conceived me" (Psalm 51:5, NIV).

"All of us have become like one who is unclean, and all our righteous deeds [notice, our righteous deeds, not our sins] are like a filthy garment" (Isaiah 64:6, NASB).

"Do not bring your servant into judgment, for no one living is righteous before you" (Psalm 143:2, NIV).

These texts make us look pretty bad. In other biblical passages, it gets even worse.

When the Bible speaks about the human heart, it pictures serious problems—a natural bent toward sin and rebellion against God. But when the Bible speaks of Jesus, it sounds a different note: "I always do what pleases him" (John 8:29, NIV).

Right from the beginning of Christ's life, the angel Gabriel told Mary: "The Holy Spirit will come upon you, and the power of the Most High will overshadow you. So the holy one to be born will be called the Son of God" (Luke 1:35, NIV).

When the Jews spoke of

"knowing" someone or something, it was intended to convey the idea of being intimate with a person or thing. Using this idea, Paul declared that on the cross Jesus could become sin for us because, unlike us, He didn't know sin. He had no intimacy with sin. John simply said that there was no sin in Him (Jesus). In Hebrews 7:26, Jesus is called "holy, blameless, pure, set apart from sinners" (NIV). Paul wrote that Jesus was tempted in every way, just as we are, but was without sin. In other words, even though He took all of our sins on Himself at the cross, He did not have any sin in Himself. God could look at Jesus and say: "This is my Son, . . . with him I am well pleased" (Matthew 3:17, NIV).

### A REAL MAN

In pagan religions, such as Hinduism or Greek mythology, there are many legends of "gods" who supposedly appear as humans. But they weren't human. They were pretending, taking on an appearance only. What about Jesus? Did He really have a flesh-and-blood body? Was He a real man?

Yes. If He wasn't, we're lost forever.

Jesus was truly human. He became a human for one primary purpose. To offer Himself as a perfect sacrifice for the sins of all humanity. To do that, He had to be a sinless and genuine human. The Creator Himself had to become a real human being to die a real death to save His lost creation. Listen carefully to what these verses from Hebrews 2 state: "Jesus . . . was made a little lower than the angels . . . so that by the grace of God he might taste death for everyone" (Hebrews 2:9, NIV).

"Since the children have flesh and blood, he too shared in their humanity so that by his death he might destroy him who holds the power of death—that is, the devil" (Hebrews 2:14, NIV).

"He had to be made like his brothers in every way, in order that . . . he might make atonement for the sins of the people" (Hebrews 2:17, NIV).

### THE SECOND ADAM

The Bible clearly says Jesus came in a flesh-and-blood body. His muscles got weary at the end of a long hike or a long day. He got tired, hungry, and thirsty. People touched Him, slapped Him, kissed Him, loved

Him, hated Him, and cared for Him. Physically, He was like you and me.

But Jesus was not like us in respect to our moral nature. Though He was tempted by sin from without, sin did not originate from within. He was physically affected by sin but not morally infected by sin.

He came in the likeness of sinful flesh to be a sin offering. Remember, the sin offering had to be unblemished, perfect, without sin. The reason Jesus could be a sin offering for us was because there was no sin in Him that required forgiveness.

Sin diminishes humanity. The fact that Jesus knew no sin means that more than anyone else, He was truly human. Sin isn't a part of true humanity. Sin is an intruder. It messes up and destroys our God-given humanity. Sin is a malignant disease, a terminal cancer that infects and "dehumanizes" us.

When Jesus takes away our corrupted nature at the second coming, we will be completely human again. Yet even now, if anyone is "in Christ" by faith, God already treats that person as a "new creation."

## WHAT WE BELIEVE MATTERS

What we believe about the moral nature of Jesus matters very much. Some people believe Jesus had a sinful moral nature, that His mind had a natural bent toward sin just like ours. If that were so, Jesus could still be our Example, but not our Saviour.

If Jesus had sin within, His sacrifice could not have saved sinners. It would be an imperfect sacrifice. Our only option would then be to save ourselves. We would need to equal His example, achieving perfect and sinless behavior in spite of our sinful nature. This would be salvation by imitation. This is impossible. The Bible teaches that our salvation is based solely on our faith in His sinless life and death for us.

We were all *ruined*, in the first Adam, by an act in which we had no part. But those who believe have been *redeemed*, in the second Adam, by an act in which we had no part. The result of one act of righteousness was justification that brings life to all people. In the first Adam, we all died (became sinners). But if we belong to

Christ, we receive the gift of eternal life through His goodness alone. To belong to Jesus is to follow Him as our Lord and to trust Him as our Saviour.

## SUMMARY

In summary, we can say that Jesus came for three purposes. First and foremost, He came to reveal God. To see Jesus is to see God; and by His life and sacrifice Jesus answered all of Satan's accusations against the character of God. He showed that God was a caring Father, full of tender love and acceptance, rather than a harsh master and severe judge.

Second, He came to be our Saviour. He came to offer Himself as a perfect and sinless sacrifice on our behalf.

Third, He came to be our Example. He came to show us what it is like to be a real person. The way He treated people and honored God shows how God wants each of us to live. It shows what God originally intended for every human being before sin messed up His plan. Even now, when we turn to Jesus, He says: Follow Me. Care as I cared. Love people the way I loved people. Be brave and live boldly for God, even as I did. Go out and do battle in enemy territory for your King.

........................................................................

# Memory Focus

" 'She will give birth to a son, and you are to give him the name Jesus, because he will save his people from their sins.' All this took place to fulfill what the Lord had said through the prophet: 'The virgin will be with child and will give birth to a son, and they will call him Immanuel'—which means, 'God with us' " (Matthew 1:21-23, NIV).

OR

"Salvation is found in no one else, for there is no other name under heaven given to men by which we must be saved" (Acts 4:12, NIV).

 # Into the Bible

1. Who was this man Jesus? Christians have claimed for centuries that Jesus was—and is—not only truly human but fully divine. On the worksheet provided by your teacher, you will be asked to identify the nature of Jesus as described in seven scriptural passages as:
   A. Truly human
   B. Fully divine
   C. Both truly human and fully divine

2. Read the listed texts, and do the following:
   A. In each passage, identify the key sin problems human beings have apart from Christ.
   B. Write a summary paragraph indicating what you think the sin problem is.
      (1) Jeremiah 13:23; 17:9          (3) Ephesians 2:1-3
      (2) Romans 3:9, 10               (4) 1 Peter 4:3

3. Jesus is identified in Revelation, chapter 1, by several titles, characteristics, and activities. Read the chapter; then, using the worksheet provided by your teacher, list the title, characteristic, or activity in the indicated verses.

4. Twelve times in the four Gospels Jesus says to an individual or group "Follow Me." Read the stories in the verses below. For each situation, write a short statement about how the person or persons responded to His call:
   A. Matthew 4:18-22
   B. Matthew 19:20-22
   C. Luke 5:27, 28
   D. John 1:43-49

...........................................................................

 # Projects

1. Read the references from books written by Ellen G. White

that are listed on the worksheet to be provided by your
teacher. Then list:

A. Satan's accusations against God.

B. The revelation of truth about God given by Jesus.

2. Jesus said: "If you really knew me, you would know my Father
   as well. . . . Anyone who has seen me has seen the Father"
   (John 14:7, 9, NIV).

   Divide into small groups, and discuss the following questions.
   Appoint someone to report your conclusions to the class.

A. What did Jesus mean when He said that seeing Him is to
   see God? Did Jesus look like God? Or was He referring to
   something other than physical appearance?

B. What personality characteristics of God do you think Jesus
   most clearly revealed?

C. In what ways did Jesus' life silence Satan's accusations about
   God?

3. Salvation by imitation is not what Scripture teaches. In
   Romans 5 Jesus is compared to the first Adam. Read Romans
   5:1, 12-19, and respond to the following questions:

A. Are we righteous before God because we achieve a
   perfection as complete as Jesus had? Why?

B. What does our status before God and our peace
   with God rest on?

····································································

## Focus Questions

1. How did the sinlessness of Jesus authenticate His humanity?
2. How does sin diminish our humanity?
3. If, as some would teach, sin is essential to being an authentic
   human, what will we be in the earth made new?
4. How is a person's belief about salvation influenced by what
   one believes about the human nature of Jesus?

# NOW OR NEVER

You cannot repent too soon, for you know not how soon
it may be too late *(Quips and Quotes).*

# lesson 8

# Won by One

## Lesson Scripture: Titus 2:11-14, NIV

**ALVATION IS A PERSON**

John Bunyan, the author of *Pilgrim's Progress,* was once deeply discouraged. He wanted to be a Christian, but it seemed no matter how hard he tried, he could not measure up. He was not good enough and was ready to give up. Suddenly, he heard a voice speak as clearly as he had heard the voice of his wife speak that morning. It said: "John, your righteousness is in heaven!" Bunyan thought that an odd idea but opened his Bible. His eyes fixed upon 1 Corinthians 1:30, where he read: "It is because of him that you are in Christ Jesus, who has become for us wisdom from God—that is, our righteous-ness, holiness and redemption" (NIV).

The light dawned. Bunyan later wrote that the only right-eousness we will ever have that is acceptable to the Father is that righteousness which already stands in the Father's presence, *the Lord Our Righteous-ness* (see Jeremiah 23:6, NIV). In other words, Jesus alone is our righteousness.

You may never have won-dered where your righteousness is. But you may have wondered about your acceptance. It's actually much the same thing. Everyone goes through times when they feel rejected and unwanted by friends, class-mates, or family.

The great question of humanity is how to find accep-tance with God and each other.

**71**

Jesus' disciples came to Him and said, "Show us the way." People are still saying, "Show us the way." During the 1991 Gulf War, the rock group Styx released a song called "Show Me the Way," which was a clear expression of this inner cry for help and meaning. Here are a few lines from the song:

Every night I say a prayer, in the hopes that there's a heaven;
And every day I'm more confused as the saints turn into sinners,
All the heroes and legends I knew as a child have fallen into clay,
And I feel this empty place inside so afraid that I've lost my faith.

Show me the way, show me the way,
Take me tonight to the river and wash my illusions away—
Please show me the way.

When the disciples of Jesus said, "Show us the way," Jesus responded, "I am *the way and the truth and the life.* No one comes to the Father except through me" (John 14:6, NIV, emphasis added).

A group of very religious people came to Jesus and asked Him a more specific question: "What must we do to do the works [plural] God requires?" They were serious about salvation and wanted to do everything right. So they said, "Give us the list, tell us what we have to do." Jesus reduced their list to one thing: "The work [singular] of God is this: to believe in the one he has sent" (John 6:28, 29, NIV). He didn't give them a long list of dos and don'ts. He told them to do just one thing, and that was to believe in Him.

The great question in being a Christian is not who we are but whose we are. God's way of salvation is not a difficult program we achieve; it is a saving Person in whom we believe! God's offer of salvation is not based on what we have done or will do for Him but on what He has done already for us in Jesus Christ.

This is what makes true Christianity unique from Buddhism, Hinduism, Judaism, Islam, New Age, or any other form of religion, including pseudo-Christianity. All of these

offer a way of self-salvation (get good enough and get saved). They teach that salvation is attained by keeping the rules, performing the correct rituals, or reaching an advanced stage of spiritual understanding.

Authentic Christianity offers salvation as the free gift of God. Absolutely free. Completely a gift. Unearned and undeserved. God freely offers *salvation as something that has already happened* to those who put their total trust in Jesus Christ. This is what the term *grace* means.

Look closely at the verbs in the following verses. They are past tense. They are describing something that has already occurred, not something that might someday happen if we are victorious enough:

"Because of **his great love** for us, God, who is **rich in mercy**, made us alive with Christ even when we were dead in transgressions—it is by grace **you have been saved** . . . through faith—and this not from yourselves, it is the **gift of God— not by works**, so that no one can boast" (Ephesians 2:4, 5, 8, 9, NIV, emphasis added).

"Join with me in suffering for the gospel, by the power of God, who **has saved us** and

called us to a holy life—**not because of anything we have done** but because of his own purpose and grace. This grace was given us in Christ Jesus" (2 Timothy 1:8, 9, NIV, emphasis added).

The good news is that God *always accepts anyone who trusts in Christ.* All who accept Christ as Lord and Saviour are saved by the finished and perfect work of Christ alone, plus nothing . . . period. We have been won by One! Our salvation rests completely on His work, and it is a work that is already finished, already perfect, and already accepted by God.

### SAVED FROM WHAT?

Why do we have to be saved by God's grace? What are we saved from? The Bible's answer is that we have to be saved from our own sin and from the wrath of God against it.

Over 650 times, the Bible talks about God's wrath. Does this mean God is irritable, prone to irrational outbursts of rage? Is God the big bad guy out to get us, and somehow Jesus stops Him?

No, God is love, and the greatest text in the Bible makes it clear that God the Father and Jesus were totally united in

their effort to save us: "***God so loved*** the world ***that he gave*** his one and only Son" (John 3:16, NIV, emphasis added). Jesus didn't die in our place to make God love us, but because God loves us, Jesus died in our place.

Then what does the wrath of God mean? It may sound strange to talk about God's great love and His wrath at the same time. But, unlike human anger, God's wrath is an essential part of His love. His anger is not directed at people but at the sin they commit.

Sin is a hostile invader in the universe. It is a destructive cancer, fatal to everything it infects. Sin creates a rebellious, self-centered spirit that causes people to deny God as their Creator and to destroy one another. It so deceives us we actually turn from life to death.

Even though we are blinded by sin, we can understand a little of God's anger. Imagine how you would feel if your mother got mugged and beat up. Then imagine how you would feel if the mugger got caught and went to court, only to have the judge say, "It's no big deal. Just say you're sorry and try not to do it again—and I'll forget the whole thing." You would be angry, and rightly so.

This is God's dilemma. He hates sin and wants to remove it from the universe. But He also loves sinners and wants us to live forever. Yet He is faced with the fact that we are all infected with sin and have all done terrible things that He cannot ignore.

God cannot change. He cannot sacrifice part of His character to satisfy another part. He is both just and merciful. He can't tell us our sins don't matter, nor does He want to punish us as our sins deserve. So what can He do?

The answer is found at the cross of Christ. God could neither sacrifice His *holiness* to His love nor His love to His holiness, so in *holy love* He sacrificed Himself for our sins.

At Calvary, God executed the punishment of death that we deserve. But instead of giving it to us, He gave it to Himself in Jesus. On the cross, God was in Christ, "reconciling the world to himself in Christ, not counting men's sins against them." He made Christ "who had no sin to be sin for us, so that in him we might become the righteousness of God"

**74**

(2 Corinthians 5:19, 21, NIV). The apostle Peter explained it this way:

"He himself bore our sins in his body on the tree, so that we might die to sins and live for righteousness; by his wounds you have been healed" (1 Peter 2:24, NIV).

Thus, God, through this one great saving act, satisfied both His love and His justice. Because of the cross, He could be both just and the justifier of the one who has faith in Jesus. At the same time He punished sin, He pardoned the sinner who turns to Christ.

Who needs this salvation? We all do, "for all have sinned and fall short of the glory of God" (Romans 3:23, NIV). And since the wages of sin is death, we all desperately need the gift of God, which is eternal life in Jesus Christ our Lord.

So why do we need salvation? Because of God's holy wrath against sin. How do we receive salvation? By God's grace alone.

| | |
|---|---|
| **G** od's | [2 Timothy 1:8-10] |
| **R** iches | [Ephesians 1:7; 2:7] |
| **A** t | [toward us] |
| **C** hrist's | [2 Timothy 2:1] |
| **E** xpense | [Hebrews 2:9] |

## WHAT IS MY PART?

No one will go into heaven singing: "Worthy, worthy is the Lamb *and me*!" We are saved only because of God's love, mercy, and grace in Christ—and for no other reason.

We do, however, have a part in our salvation. It is not to supply an adequate goodness. Christ alone gives us that. Our part is to believe in Christ—to have faith in Him as our Saviour and Lord.

The biblical concept of faith doesn't mean just agreeing with an idea. It means deep personal trust. To believe with faith in something is to trust in it completely, to bank our life on it. If we have true faith, we will be guided by it in all our relationships and actions. Seat belts can save us in an accident. Most of us believe that. But unless we decide to put one on, that belief doesn't do us any good. Faith is a personal submission to Christ.

Many people worry that they don't have enough faith. Don't worry; Jesus Himself said that faith the size of a mustard seed (a tiny seed) is enough to save us.

It is not the amount of our faith that saves us, but the

object of our faith.

"If only I had more faith, then I could be saved." No! If we have a mountain of faith, but put it in anything other than Jesus, we will be lost. But if we have only a tiny seed of faith and place it all in Jesus, we will be saved.

Neither is it the quality of our faith that saves us, but the quality of the One in whom we put our faith. Faith is not our saviour. Faith teaches us to look to our Saviour. Christ alone saves. Whenever we say "righteousness by faith," we must be clear that it is not our faith that makes us righteous. We put our faith in Christ, and He is our righteousness. Remember, the crucial question is not who we are but whose we are.

**BORN AGAIN?**

Many people feel concerned about Jesus' statement to Nicodemus: "No one can see the kingdom of God unless he is born again" (John 3:3, NIV). They are very serious words.

John Wesley used to share over and over again the need to be born again. One man, proud of his own goodness, became very irritated at Wesley. He jumped to his feet during a sermon and shouted: "Born again, born again, born again! John Wesley, why do you always preach that you must be born again?"

With a smile, Wesley looked at him and said, "Because, my friend, you must!"

What is the new birth? How does it happen? For some, it is a dramatic, life-changing encounter. For others, it unfolds as a gradually growing awareness of what God offers. For every Christian, it is an experience that deepens with time. The apostle Peter tried to explain it this way:

"Praise be to the God and Father of our Lord Jesus Christ!

In his great mercy he has given us new birth into a living hope through the resurrection of Jesus Christ from the dead" (1 Peter 1:3, NIV).

This is a helpful start, but the best place to go is straight to the source. When Jesus told Nicodemus he had to be born again, Nicodemus got very upset and said, "How?" Jesus answered him by referring to an Old Testament story:

"As Moses lifted up the snake in the desert, so the Son of Man must be lifted up, that whoever believes in him may have eternal life" (John 3:14, 15, NIV).

What did Jesus mean? In the story of the uplifted serpent in Numbers 21:4-9, the Israelites rebelled against God and cast off His protection. Into their camp in the wilderness came scores of slithering serpents filled with deadly venom. People were bitten. The venom was within. It was only a matter of time until they died. There was no human cure.

The people turned to Moses, and Moses turned to God. And God said a very strange thing: "'Make a snake and put it up on a pole; anyone who is bitten can look at it and live.' So Moses made a bronze snake and put it up on a pole. Then when anyone was bitten by a snake and looked at the bronze snake, he lived" (Numbers 21:8, 9, NIV).

There was no arguing with God. No sense in saying you didn't like His way of salvation, didn't understand it, that it did not make any sense. If any Israelite wanted to live—to be rescued from death—there was only one way. He or she had to look to live. And every Israelite who looked in faith lived!

Jesus said this is what the new birth is. Just like the Israelites of old, we have all been bitten by a deadly serpent. The venom is within. And just as Moses lifted up that bronze serpent (a likeness of the serpent, but with no venom within), so Jesus declares He must be lifted up on His cross in the likeness of sin-cursed humanity, but having no sin within.

We receive the new birth in the same way the Israelites received new life. When in faith they looked to God's way of salvation as their only hope—they lived. They were healed. They received a new start. Jesus had no sin within Himself, but He took all our sins upon Himself, so that we who have no saving righteousness within us could have all His saving righteousness placed upon us. When we look in faith at Jesus lifted up on the cross for our sins and accept that as our only hope of salvation, we are born again. By His dying for our sins and rising again, we are given new life in Him.

"Therefore, if anyone is in Christ, he is a new creation; the old has gone, the new has come!" (2 Corinthians 5:17, NIV).

It's really pretty exciting. Think of the possibilities. Jesus comes to us and says, "If you aren't happy with how you were born the first time, then let's begin again." Jesus is our fresh start. Jesus had no sin within Himself, but He took all our sins upon Himself. And we who have no saving righteousness within us have all His saving righteousness placed upon us. He loves us and accepts us with all our imperfections and then begins to change us into really caring people.

## BUT WHAT ABOUT OBEDIENCE?

Here is a very wonderful thing. We are already perfectly God's children in Christ, even though in ourselves we are not yet perfect children of God. God invites us to come to Him just as we are. When we come, He accepts us just as we are. But once accepted, we never stay just as we are. We can't. With our acceptance in Christ comes the *Holy Spirit* of Christ to help us grow into the *likeness* of Christ.

Once we accept God's total acceptance, we begin to become, by the work of the Holy Spirit within us, what God has already declared us to be.

True obedience is never the *root* of our salvation, but always the *fruit*. God doesn't save us because we obey Him, but we obey Him because He has saved us.

The theological term for this side of our relationship with God is *sanctification*. It means to be set apart for God's purpose. The minute we are *justified* (declared not guilty in God's judgment) through the blood of Christ, we are also *sanctified*, or set apart for God. The Holy Spirit begins to teach us to do God's will in everything, from the way we treat our friends to the way we spend our money or relate to our school.

**78**

We are not saved by faith and works but by a *faith that works through love.* It is the love of Christ that controls and motivates us.

"I would not work my soul to save; for that my Lord has done. But I would work like any slave—for love to God's dear Son."

It is so important to remember that the true Christian works *from* victory—not *toward* it. We are already perfect in Christ even though we are still imperfect and growing in our own experience. "Because by one sacrifice [the cross] he has made perfect forever those who are being made holy" (Hebrews 10:14, NIV).

Remember the story of the Israelites in Egypt? Think of how terrible it would have been if, when they were still slaves, Moses had come and said, "Look, here are God's Ten Commandments. If you keep them well enough, long enough, then maybe God will get you out of here."

God didn't do that. He heard their cry for deliverance and brought them out of bondage first. They had to have faith in the blood of the Lamb. When they did, God passed over them in judgment and freed them from bondage. They were a redeemed people. Before the Ten Commandments begin, you read these words: "I am the Lord your God, who brought you out of Egypt, out of the land of bondage." Only after giving such freedom did God say, "Thou shalt not . . ." (Exodus 20:2, 3, NIV). Then God led them to Sinai and said, "Now that I have freed you, follow Me."

Like them, we were redeemed by the precious blood of Christ, a Lamb without blemish or defect. Now Jesus says to us, "Follow Me."

"To run and do the Law commands—but gives me neither feet nor hands. Better news the Gospel brings, it bids me fly and gives me wings."[1]

We are not saved to sin. We are saved to serve. You cannot turn to Jesus without having your back to sin. But no one can truly obey Jesus who hasn't come to know and love Him. And no one can truly know and love Him without wanting to

[1] John Wesley

**79**

obey Him. As the hymn says: "Turn your eyes upon Jesus, \ Look full in His wonderful face, \ And the things of earth will grow strangely dim \ In the light of His glory and grace."[2]

"***Done***—therefore ***do***!" Your salvation is done through the cross of Jesus. He is the risen Lord. Therefore do His will in all things. "Trust and obey, for there's no other way / To be happy in Jesus, but to trust and obey."[3]

Every year, over a million children and teenagers take school trips to Washington, D.C., to visit the monuments. One day, a little boy walked up to a big guard at the Washington Monument, pulled a quarter out of his pocket, and said, "I want to buy that monument."

Luckily, the guard was as kind as he was big. He knelt down to eye level with the boy and said, "I need to tell you three things. First, the monument isn't for sale—you can't buy it. Second, even if it was, your quarter isn't nearly enough—you couldn't pay for it. But third, it is yours already as long as you are a U.S. citizen—now, go on in and enjoy it."

That is salvation in Christ. So, what about obedience?

It is the joyful fruit in every life where Jesus reigns as Lord and Saviour. Genuine, joyful obedience flows from a relationship of love and acceptance—not from one of fear and insecurity.

---

[2]Helen H. Lemmel, "Turn Your Eyes Upon Jesus," *Advent Youth Sing* (Hagerstown, Md.: Review and Herald Publishing Association, 1977), no.190.

[3]J. H. Sammis, "Trust and Obey," *Seventh-day Adventist Hymnal* (Hagerstown, Md.: Review and Herald Publishing Association, 1885), no. 590.

# Memory Focus

"Therefore, there is now no condemnation for those who are in Christ Jesus" (Romans 8:1, NIV).

OR

"For the grace of God that brings salvation has appeared to all men" (Titus 2:11, NIV).

# Into the Bible

1. The gospel is called the "good news" because it is almost too good to be true. The gospel is not good *advice* on how to make ourselves better, nor good *views* on what the future holds. It is the good *news* of our salvation through the finished and perfect work of Christ. Look up the following verses, and identify the part in each verse that deals directly with the idea of salvation. <u>For each verse</u>:
   - State how salvation is attained.
   - State whether the action is something already done or something still to happen.
     - A. John 3:36; 5:24
     - B. Romans 5:9; 8:1, 2
     - C. Ephesians 2:5, 8
     - D. 2 Timothy 1:8, 9

2. We often speak of God's *love*, God's *mercy*, and God's *grace*. What do these words really mean? How does the Bible define them? How has God demonstrated their meaning? Using your Bible as your only source, study the following texts. Based on what you read, in your own words write a definition of what these three words mean.
   A. God's love: 1 John 4:9, 10; Romans 5:8.
   B. God's mercy: Ephesians 2:4; 1 Timothy 1:15, 16.
   C. God's grace: Romans 6:14; Ephesians 1:7; 2:5, 8; Hebrews 2:9.

3. Many people misunderstand the idea of righteousness. They believe it is an inner goodness they have to achieve in order to be saved. In the Greek language, *righteousness* and *justification* are the same word. It is a word that means the verdict of the judge in a courtroom. It means to be declared acquitted, innocent, not guilty. Read the following verses. Summarize each verse in terms of how we do, or do not, attain righteousness.

   A. How we "DO NOT" attain righteousness (justification)

Isaiah 64:6
Galatians 2:21
Galatians 3:10, 11
Galatians 5:4
B. How we "DO" attain righteousness (justification)
Philippians 3:9
Romans 4:25–5:1
2 Corinthians 5:21
Revelation 7:14

4. In every one of his epistles, Paul comes to the point where he moves from what God *has done* for us through Christ to what He wants *to do* in us by the Spirit. Briefly describe what each of the following verses says about why we should want to seek holiness.
A. 2 Timothy 4:7, 8
B. 2 Corinthians 7:1
C. 1 John 3:1-3
D. Titus 2:11-14

........................................................

 # Projects

1. *Faith* (belief) is another key word in the Christian vocabulary. Look up the following stories or descriptions of faith, and write a phrase for each passage describing what faith means or how it is defined:
A. Mark 5:25-34
B. Luke 7:1-10
C. John 11:21-27, 40-45

2. Obedience that results only from the fear of being lost is of no value. Read the following statements from Ellen White about fear-based obedience versus obedience that springs from security and love. Write a response to the message of this quote, indicating how it affects the way you look at obedience and salvation.

"There are those who profess to serve God, while they rely on their own efforts to obey His law, to form a right character, and secure salvation. Their hearts are not moved by any deep sense of the love of Christ, but they seek to perform the duties of the Christian life as that which God requires of them in order to gain heaven. Such religion is worth nothing. When Christ dwells in the heart, the soul will be so filled with His love, with the joy of communion with Him, that it will cleave to Him; and in the contemplation of Him, self will be forgotten. Love to Christ will be the spring of action. Those who feel the constraining love of God, do not ask how little may be given to meet the requirements of God; they do not ask for the lowest standard, but aim at perfect conformity to the will of their Redeemer. With earnest desire they yield all. . . . A profession of Christ without this deep love is mere talk, dry formality, and heavy drudgery" (*Steps to Christ*, 44, 45).

 Focus Questions

1. What does it mean to "be in Christ Jesus"?
2. Explain how righteousness differs from, or is similar to, acceptance.
3. Since we are not saved by good works, are good works necessary? Explain.
4. Describe what is meant by the wrath of God.
5. Identify at least three things Jesus' death at Calvary accomplished.
6. Compare the way Israel in the desert was saved from snakebites with how we are saved from sin today.
7. Is our salvation something that is past, present, or future? Explain your response.
8. Consider how your obedience would change if motivated more by love for God than fear of being lost.

CROSSROADS SERIES

# unit

# 2

# Jesus and His Kingdom

# Jesus' Ministry

Unit two covers the early ministry and teachings of Jesus, from His baptism through the temptations in the wilderness, the choosing of the twelve, and the proclamation of a new kingdom. The Sermon on the Mount and the parables are analyzed to determine the key principles of His kingdom. The unit presents personal encounters that Jesus had with the people of His time that provided opportunity for healing and teaching and that tell the story of His saving love amid the hostility of the Jewish leaders.

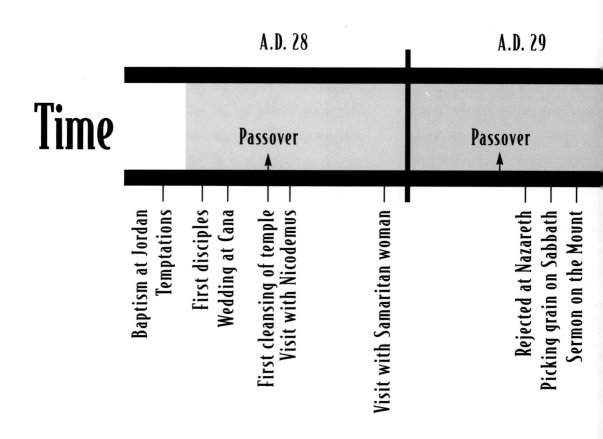

Time

A.D. 28          A.D. 29

Passover          Passover

Baptism at Jordan
Temptations
First disciples
Wedding at Cana
First cleansing of temple
Visit with Nicodemus
Visit with Samaritan woman
Rejected at Nazareth
Picking grain on Sabbath
Sermon on the Mount

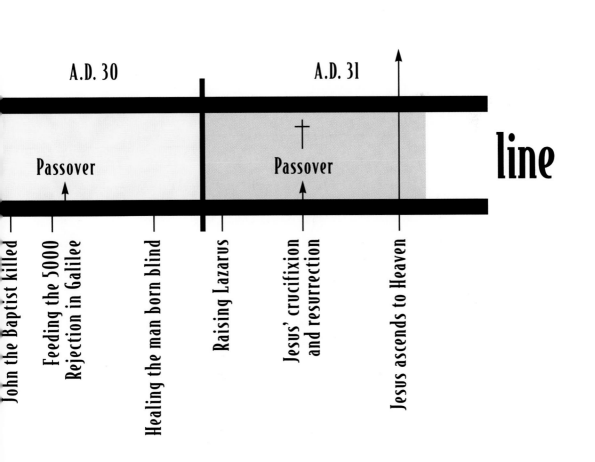

A.D. 30

A.D. 31

Passover

Passover

line

John the Baptist killed

Feeding the 5000
Rejection in Galilee

Healing the man born blind

Raising Lazarus

Jesus' crucifixion
and resurrection

Jesus ascends to Heaven

# BORN AGAIN

If being born hasn't brought you much satisfaction, try being born again

*(The Daily Walk)*.

# Baptism: A New Beginning

**Lesson Scripture: Matthew 3:13-17**

For thirty years, Jesus led a quiet life in Nazareth with His family. His day-to-day routine revolved around His home, His community, and the carpenter shop where He worked with His father, Joseph. But one day, the life of this humble, studious carpenter changed forever. We don't know how He knew that the time had come to make the change; we only know that He had been preparing for it all His life.

On the day Jesus began His public role as the Messiah, He laid down His carpentry tools, took off His work clothes, and made His way to the Jordan River. There He listened as John the Baptist urged the crowds gathered along the riverbanks to repent and be baptized. When the moment was right, Jesus stepped forward and accepted the call to be baptized.

John's preaching had attracted all sorts of people—wily tax collectors, crude soldiers, respected church leaders, repentant sinners. John had learned to look beyond their rough appearance and their various masks. He saw many sincere seekers of truth, but he also saw a lot of selfishness, anger, and greed. When Jesus stepped into the river and waded out to him, John saw something he had never before encountered—a pure soul. He must have recognized Jesus at once and was so overwhelmed by Jesus' goodness and purity

that he at first refused to baptize Him. John argued, "You should be baptizing me!"

But Jesus insisted, saying that "it is fitting for us to fulfill all righteousness," that is, to set an example in rightdoing. You see, unlike us, Jesus didn't need to be baptized, because there was "no fault in this man" (Luke 23:4, KJV). But He put Himself in our place. The Saviour of the world identified with us, showing us the steps necessary to get right with God. So He took John's arm and allowed Himself to be buried in the waters of the Jordan.

God was pleased that Jesus had taken this step. When Jesus came up from the water, He was surrounded with a supernatural brilliance, as though the sky had opened and poured all its light on the place where Jesus stood. Jesus knew that this was God's way of anointing Him for His ministry—God's stamp of approval on the next phase of His life.

## A BRIEF HISTORY OF BAPTISM

Baptism is a Christian rite that most of us have either been through or look forward to. Except for a few hours in baptismal class, we spend very little time thinking about how this rite originated or just what it means.

John the Baptist did not invent baptism. From history and stories outside the Bible, we know that converts to Judaism were immersed in water as a sign of their separation from heathen ways. From the Old Testament, we learn of ceremonial washings that symbolized spiritual cleansing. These were in David's mind when he wrote, "Wash me thoroughly from mine iniquity . . . wash me and I shall be whiter than snow" (Psalm 51:2,7, KJV).

The early Christians had just one form of baptism—complete immersion in water. In fact, in Greek, the language most early Christians spoke, the very word *baptizo* means "to immerse." To these believers, baptizing by sprinkling would be like trying to go swimming in a teacup.

It was later, after all the apostles had died, that changes began to creep into Christian practice. One group of Christians decided that the only proper way to baptize was to dunk the candidate three times. Another group decided that a

little sprinkle on the head would be more than enough. Others insisted that true baptism had to take place in running water.

But the most significant change in baptism had to do with what it meant. What was the purpose of baptism? Was it a public testimony of a change that had already taken place in the believer's heart? Or was it baptism itself that changed a person's life? Was baptism really necessary for salvation?

Some Christians dealt with all these questions by introducing the idea of "holy water." Priests or holy people would bless the water itself, believing that this gave it sacred power. A person baptized with holy water would have his sins washed away even if he hadn't repented of them! This made baptism a sacrament rather than an ordinance. That is, baptism became an act that all by itself gave a person salvation, not an ordinance that represented the salvation God had already given.

If baptism was a sacrament,

it was natural to believe that salvation wasn't possible without it. This led to the notion that it was best to baptize babies as soon as they were born rather than risk having them die unsaved.

Baptism is "into Christ Jesus." When we are baptized, we accept Christ's death for our sins—in our place; and His holy life becomes our righteousness before God. Catch the symbolism: He dies—we go into the water. He is buried—we are immersed. He rises—we come up from the water to a new life of obedience in Christ (see Romans 6:1-11, 16-18).

 **Memory Focus**

"Therefore we were buried with Him through baptism into death, that just as Christ was raised from the dead by the glory of the Father, even so we also should walk in newness of life" (Romans 6:4, NKJV).

 **Into the Bible**

1. Read Acts 2:38, 41. Put in your own words the best reason for a person being baptized.
2. When considering baptism, a person must accept both its symbolic significance and its life-changing experience. Study Romans 6:1-11, 23, and answer the following questions:
   A. According to Romans 6:5, what does baptism symbolize?
   B. What is accomplished for the believer in Christ, according to Romans 6:3, 4, 23?
   C. How is the believer able to overcome sin? Read Romans 6:6, 11.
3. When is a person ready for baptism? Write a short paragraph, using these verses as a guide: Mark 16:16; Acts 16:28-33.

 **Projects**

1. Make a poster to publicize John the Baptist's crusade at the Jordan River. You are his agent in Jerusalem, and your job is to attract people to John's call for repentance and baptism.
2. Jesus commanded that we should be baptized in the name of "the Father, the Son, and the Holy Spirit." Identify one specific role each One plays in leading a sinner to salvation.

3. Read the list of questions in the Baptismal Vow for those who want to be baptized into the Seventh-day Adventist Church. Your teacher will give you a copy. Are they all equally important? Explain your answer.
4. Under what circumstances could a person be saved without baptism? Use Mark 16:15, 16 to help you formulate an answer.

 Focus Questions

1. What is a good reason for being rebaptized?
2. How do you explain the fact that being baptized seems to change some people's lives very little, if at all?
3. How would you help someone who wants to be baptized but has a genuine fear of water?
4. Seventh-day Adventists don't baptize babies; instead, they dedicate them. Explain the difference.
5. Baptism is an outward act that symbolizes and reinforces an inward decision. Does our society have any other similar rituals?

# MISCHIEF

When temptation knocks, our imagination usually answers (Unknown).

# lesson 10

# Temptation: Sin's Calling Card

**Lesson Scriptures: Matthew 4:1-11;
Mark 1:12; Luke 4:1-13**

In the burning desert sun, a lone figure follows a faint trail across the sandstone cliffs high above the Jordan Valley. He looks back over his shoulder and mops the sweat from his brow. The valley below him is no longer visible. Ahead of him is only a barren landscape of sand, boulders, lizards, and scrub junipers. Suddenly, he feels sick with loneliness. How will he survive out here? Still, some inner voice urges him on.

He is Jesus of Nazareth, being "led by the Spirit into the desert" (Matthew 4:1, NIV). Just yesterday, He was baptized in the Jordan River. But before He begins His full-time ministry, He goes into the desert to do battle with His chief adversary, Satan.

Matthew says Jesus went into the wilderness "to be tempted of the devil." He was doing exactly what the Spirit was leading Him to do. Surrounded by legions of devils and wild beasts, He was still in the safest place in the world— the center of God's will.

Satan always times his attacks to catch us at the lowest ebb of our spiritual and physical energies. When Moses was old and weary, Satan tempted him to lose his temper and the right to lead his people into the Promised Land. When Elijah was exhausted and scared, Satan overwhelmed him with despair. When Esau was famished, Satan talked him into selling his birthright.

For forty days in the desert,

Jesus fasted and prayed. Some of us may have fasted for a day or a weekend, but going without food for forty days is more than we can imagine. After almost six weeks of fasting, Jesus had gone beyond hunger; He was close to death. He looked weak and rejected, so unlike the Son of God. And here, at this weakest moment, the devil saw an opening.

### ROUND ONE

As Jesus lies propped against a boulder, suddenly a "being" robed in light descends from heaven. The "angel" picks up a round, flat stone the color and size of a loaf of pita bread. He approaches Jesus and suggests that he has been sent from heaven to assist the Son of God but isn't quite sure that he has found Him. Then he suggests: "If you are the Son of God tell these stones to become bread" (Matthew 4:3, NIV).

Jesus senses a trap. If you are the Son of God? Why "if"? Back at the Jordan River, God had promised, "This is my Son" (Matthew 3:17, NIV). Why would an angel of God doubt that now?

Jesus' faith rallies. Even if He is close to death, He is the Son of God. He won't doubt His divinity, and He won't use it to save Himself, either. He came to this world to face dangers and temptations and to triumph over them by depending totally on God. Through parched and swollen lips, He tells the tempter, "It is written: man does not live on bread alone, but on every word that comes from the mouth of God" (Matthew 4:4, NIV). The Word silences the devil.

Grab hold of that. If we will rely on the power of the Word and not on ourselves, "our only questions will be, What is God's command? and what His promise?" (*The Desire of Ages*, 121).

### ROUND TWO

Thinking that Jesus might be overwhelmed by a show of strength, Satan scoops Him up and sets Him atop the highest pillar of the temple. In the first temptation, Satan asked Jesus to prove His divinity through a show of power. Now Satan asks Him to do it through an act of "faith." "OK," he says, "You wouldn't work a miracle to feed Yourself because You have faith in Your Father to feed You. Fine. Here's Your chance to show Your faith in a spectacular way. Jump off this pillar, and show how God takes care of a son as loyal as You."

Jesus didn't bite. He would not imperil His life in order to give evidence to Satan. He answered, "You shall not tempt the Lord your God." What He meant was, I won't take flagrant risks and presume God will come to My rescue.

When we walk in the ways of God, we can count on the protection of angels. Through common sense alone, we can't avoid all dangers and risks, but we can avoid the obvious ones— traveling with a drunk driver, walking alone at night, playing on the edge of a precipice. We are stewards, or caretakers, of our bodies, minds, and souls. We must know the difference between trusting God and daring Him.

### ROUND THREE

The world can look wretched or desirable, depending on the "camera" angle. For his third temptation, Satan gives Jesus a panoramic view of earth, but he keeps his "lens" trained on the scenic vistas. Poverty, squalor, corruption, and pollution are not part of his script or shooting schedule. It is all spacious skies and amber waves of grain.

Satan suggests that all of this can be had cheap. "Just think, Jesus. No suffering, no death on a cross. Just a quick bow at my feet, and presto! It's all Yours." The scene spreads before Him, a beautiful world filled with beautiful people. For a moment, at least, He is reminded of Eden and filled with longing.

Glossing over evil is still a strategy Satan uses well today. Tobacco ads show attractive athletic people having outdoor adventures, not operations for lung cancer or landscapes ablaze with forest fires. Alcohol is associated with romance and sociability, not disease and family violence.

Those who follow God must learn to see the truth behind alluring lies. Jesus knows that the scene spread before Him isn't reality, and it isn't Satan's to give away. In spite of sin, Jesus, not Satan, is the rightful ruler of all He surveys. "Jesus said to him, 'Away from me, Satan! For it is written: "Worship the Lord your God, and serve him only.' " Then the devil left him" (Matthew 4:10, 11, NIV).

**97**

Satan has to obey the order to flee. He slinks away, determined to make Jesus' life on earth as bitter as possible. Meanwhile, angels come to Jesus, giving Him food and the assurance that heaven is pleased with His victory.

"Hold on to the good. Avoid every kind of evil" (1 Thessalonians 5:21, 22, NIV). How do you hold on to good and avoid evil? How did Jesus become exposed to evil without catching the disease of sin? It's a constant struggle but here are some helpful guidelines.

## 1. BELONG TO JESUS

There are many ways for dealing with addictions, avoiding failures, and overcoming temptation. But all of these efforts will fail if a person does not surrender his or her life to Jesus. Jesus told His disciples, "I am the vine; you are the branches. If a man remains in me and I in him, he will bear much fruit; apart from me you can do nothing" (John 15:5, NIV). With Jesus you can meet temptation with a sense of security and acceptance—even if you make mistakes.

## 2. KNOW THE WORD

In His struggles with the devil, Jesus didn't rely on His debating skills or even on His own words. His answer was always "It is written."

Knowing the Word is knowing the difference between right and wrong. "I have hidden your word in my heart that I might not sin against you" (Psalm 119:11, NIV). This was the

key to Jesus' victory, and it is a key to ours. A mind filled with God's Word sees clearly the devil's lies for what they are.

## 3. STAY IN TOUCH WITH GOD

Beating temptation takes more than a brief prayer. It flows out of practicing the presence of God—sensing Him right at our elbows throughout the day. This makes a tremendous difference in how we live. Can you imagine telling a lie if God were seated at the table with you? Would you throw a fit on the ballfield if God were the umpire? Would you say something cutting or crude if God were listening to your conversation?

## 4. EXERCISE YOUR FAITH

Jesus kept His faith alive by acting on it. He trusted God and believed God loved Him. "My food . . . is to do the will of him who sent me," Jesus said (John 4:34, NIV). That kind of faith leads to obedience. It is "faith expressing itself through love" (Galatians 5:6, NIV).

## 5. COOPERATE WITH GOD

Is the secret of victory to just "let go and let God"? Or are we supposed to struggle against evil? Ellen White said that each of us must be a "co-worker" with Christ in the work of fighting temptation (*Testimonies for the Church*, 4:33).

The key is to cooperate with God. God doesn't give us victories over sin whether we want them or not; nor do we earn them by our own heroic, independent efforts. We cooperate by praying, studying the Bible, and keeping our minds and bodies fit for the struggle. God will impress our minds and urge us in the right direction, but He won't make our choices for us. We must still weigh the evidence and decide whom we will serve.

## 6. DON'T MAKE EXCUSES

It's so easy to blame someone or something else for our shortcomings: poverty, bad parents, poor teachers, hypocrites in the church. God knows all about the influences that have shaped us. He doesn't hold us personally accountable for our genes or all the ills of society. But sinful acts are a choice, and God expects us to use all the gifts He's given us to make the right choices.

It would have been easy for Jesus to complain to God, "Look, aren't You expecting just a bit too much from someone who grew up in Nazareth? Have You seen My neighborhood? Have You seen how My own brothers treat Me?" But such excuses never entered His mind. He focused on His mission and relied on the power of God to defeat every temptation.

## 7. EXPECT VICTORY

If you believe you're doomed to a life of sin, then you'll probably be an easy mark for Satan. You must believe that Jesus can "keep you from falling" and does "present you faultless" before God (Jude 24). Jesus' life and death made a way of escape that is open to us if we depend on Him.

## Memory Focus

"No temptation has seized you except what is common to man. And God is faithful; he will not let you to be tempted beyond what you can bear. But when you are tempted, he will also provide a way out so that you can stand up under it" (1 Corinthians 10:13, NIV).

 # Into the Bible

1. Write a Bible study on how to overcome temptation by using the texts listed below. Assume you are giving this study to a student who has asked you for advice. Beside each text, write down appropriate comments you would make to your friend.

   | | |
   |---|---|
   | Revelation 3:20 | Psalm 119:11 |
   | 1 John 5:4 | Ephesians 6:10-17 |
   | James 4:7 | Romans 12:21 |
   | Matthew 26:41 | 1 Corinthians 10:13 |

2. Read Hebrews 4:14-16 to discover how Jesus as our High Priest helps us overcome temptation. In your own words, describe four reasons why Jesus' role as High Priest is important.

3. Hebrews 4:15 states: "We have one [Jesus] who has been tempted in every way, just as we are." How could this be? Use the texts listed to answer the question.

   A. What do John 1:1, 14 and Philippians 2:5-8 say about the humanity of Christ?

   B. Besides the temptations in the wilderness, Jesus met other temptations. Put in your own words the temptations Jesus faced as described in the following texts:

   Matthew 21:6-11
   Matthew 26:39
   Luke 4:16-30

   C. Hebrews 4:15 reveals that although He was tempted, Jesus was without sin. The following texts support belief in the sinless nature of Jesus. Read the texts, and write the idea of each.

   John 1:1
   2 Corinthians 5:21
   1 Peter 2:24
   1 Peter 3:18
   Hebrews 7:24, 26

**4.** The Bible seems to reveal three common ways that we are tempted. These are given in 1 John 2:16. Use the worksheet provided by your teacher to identify the temptations that came to Eve and Christ and the basic issue in each temptation.

# Projects

**1.** Temptations come from a variety of sources: (1) hereditary tendencies, (2) habits, (3) environment, (4) popular culture, (5) other people, (6) Satan himself, (7) thoughts from within. List ten common temptations, and match them with the seven possible sources listed above.

Example:  **Temptation**        **Source**

           Stealing      3 - Environment
                         6 - Satan

**2.** Satan not only tempted Jesus, he carried Him physically to the top of a high tower. What are the limits of Satan's power in our lives? Use the Bible and the writings of Ellen White as sources, and prepare a report.

**3.** In the first five chapters of his Gospel, Matthew compares experiences in the life of Christ with events in the history of God's people. Matthew focuses on the Exodus from Egypt and shows that where the children of Israel failed, Christ succeeded. You will be asked to do the following on the worksheet your teacher will give you. Read the texts listed, and indicate the experience from the life of Christ that is a comparison with an experience from the history of God's people during the Exodus.

 **Focus Questions**

1. Did the fact that Jesus was divine make temptation easier or harder for Him to resist?
2. Does what we eat and drink have any effect on our spiritual health?
3. Why was an angel of light a natural disguise for Satan?
4. How can you use Jesus' methods of resisting temptation when you are tempted to watch a violent or sexually explicit movie or video, engage in gossip, or neglect your spiritual life?
5. Jesus ordered Satan to go away, and Satan went. Do we have that authority today?
6. Is it ever right to do wrong for "good" reasons? Would you lie to protect a friend? What about people who make money in questionable or unjust ways, then give a lot of it to the church?
7. People engage in a variety of harmful activities that we call sins, but what is the basic problem in the nature of men and women from which these sins arise?
8. Who was tempted more severely? Adam and Eve? Christ? or you and I? Why?
9. How can a person determine whether a supernatural event is from God or Satan?
10. Satan not only tempted Jesus but carried Him physically to the top of a high tower. What limits do you think God imposes upon Satan's access to our lives?

# STANDING TALL

Only those who kneel before God are prepared to stand up to the world

*(Quips and Quotes).*

# lesson 11

# The Twelve Jesus Chose

**Lesson Scriptures: Luke 5:1-11; John 1:35-51; Mark 3:13-19; Matthew 10:5-42**

t would be an exciting thing to find an old yearbook for the "First Discipleship School, class of A.D. 31," complete with portraits of the class members, their teacher, and snapshots of class activities. The Bible gives us a few tantalizing glimpses, but our human curiosity always wishes there were more.

Class membership was somewhat unsettled for the first couple of years, with some members attending part time. Probably sometime in the summer of A.D. 29, however, Jesus began calling selected ones to full-time discipleship. Eventually, twelve were ordained and became known as apostles—"ones sent forth."

It can be a challenge to keep the identity of the twelve apostles (disciples) straight. There are two each with the names James, Simon, and Judas. There are two, perhaps three, sets of brothers. Sometimes they are called by their first names; sometimes by a surname. Some figure prominently in the Gospel story; some are not associated with even one incident in the life of Jesus beyond their ordination.

You will find four lists of the Twelve in the New Testament: Matthew 10:2-4; Mark 3:16-19; Luke 6:14-16; and Acts 1:13. Following is a brief sketch of each. You will meet some of them again, a bit more "up close and personal," as you continue your study of the life of Christ.

## PETER

In all four lists, Peter's name appears first, indicating that the writers thought of him as a leader and spokesman (self-appointed at times, to be sure) for the group. His parents named him Simon, but Jesus gave him a new name, *Petros*, meaning "rock" or "stone" in Greek. For that reason, he is often called Simon Peter.

It takes quite a list of adjectives to describe Peter—both his positive and negative traits. Most of us would probably have called him an unpredictable extremist. He could be loyal and courageous, but he could also be weak and cowardly. He could swing from generous to selfish, from sensible to reckless, from faithful to doubting.

Jesus called Peter and his business partners, James, John, and Andrew, from their fishing operations on the Sea of Galilee. Peter was married. It must have been hard for him to leave his family in the care of others while he followed an unknown rabbi on his preaching tours.

Peter was one of three disciples privileged to witness the resurrection of Jairus's daughter, the Transfiguration, and Christ's agony in Gethsemane. He became a leader in the Christian community in Jerusalem and a pioneer in breaking through race barriers to take the gospel to the Gentiles.

A thorough conversion on the day of Christ's crucifixion transformed the old Peter into a great preacher and the author of two New Testament epistles. Peter closed his ministry in Rome, where he was crucified about A.D. 67, upon the order of Emperor Nero.

## JAMES

It's not always easy to keep track of James, the son of Zebedee, because the New Testament refers to so many others named James. They include another disciple, James the son of Alphaeus; James, a brother of Jesus; and James, father of the disciple Thaddaeus. James is the Greek form of a popular Jewish name, Jacob.

James, the son of Zebedee, was in the fishing business with his father and brother, John, on the Sea of Galilee when he was called to be a disciple. Jesus nicknamed James and John the "Sons of Thunder," undoubt-

edly because of their quick tempers and vengeful spirit. These young men may not have been as poor as most of the disciples, since their father had hired servants (see Mark 1:20). John was well known by the high priest (see John 18:16), a possible indication that the family had some social standing.

It is generally agreed among scholars that this James was not the prominent church leader spoken of in the book of Acts, nor the one who wrote the epistle of James. He was executed on Herod's orders about A.D. 44 (Acts 12:1, 2), the first of the Twelve to be martyred.

### JOHN

John is thought to be younger than his brother James and may have been the youngest of the Twelve. Probably quite athletic, he tells how he outran Peter as they raced to the tomb on the resurrection morning (see John 20:4).

Like his brother, John was proud, self-promoting, and combative. But beneath all that, Jesus could see one who was basically sincere and loving. Ellen White says that "in the life of the disciple John true sanctification is exemplified" (*The Acts of the Apostles,* 557); that is, his life is a good illustration of how a close association with Jesus can change someone from a "Son of Thunder" to "John the Beloved."

For raw courage, no disciple stands taller than John. He was the only one who braved the dangers of the judgment hall during Jesus' trials; he is the disciple who stood by the cross while the others shivered in fear in the upper room.

John wrote one of the four Gospels, the book of Revelation, and three epistles. He was imprisoned for a time on the Island of Patmos by the Roman emperor Domitian. He is believed to be the only one of the Twelve who did not become a martyr.

### ANDREW

His name means "manly." He is another of the four fishing partners. He was one of the disciples of John the Baptist who transferred allegiance when Jesus was introduced as the Lamb of God.

Andrew is probably remembered best for his example in showing his faith. After spend-

ing a few hours with Jesus, he was off in search of his brother Peter and brought him to the Saviour. Shortly before the crucifixion, he helped arrange a meeting between Jesus and a group of Greeks. He is the one who brought the boy to Jesus with a lunch that was used to feed five thousand.

Andrew is seldom mentioned by the Gospel writers, overshadowed, no doubt, by his talented, more assertive brother. Tradition says that he was put to death in Greece on a cross in the shape of the letter X, known today as St. Andrew's cross.

### PHILIP

His hometown was Bethsaida, on the northeastern shore of the Sea of Galilee. Since that was also the home of Peter and Andrew, the three of them could have grown up together. His name has an unusual meaning—"fond of horses."

Philip is distinguished as the first to whom Jesus said, "Follow Me." He immediately set to work, bringing his friend Nathanael to Jesus.

Like Thomas, Philip had trouble believing what he couldn't see. He failed to trust Jesus in the feeding of the five thousand. After Jesus had spent years showing His disciples what His Father was like, it was Philip who said, "Show us the Father" (John 14:8, NIV).

Philip is last seen in the upper room with the other disciples just before Pentecost (see Acts 1:13).

### NATHANAEL

His hometown was Cana. For some reason, John is the only Gospel writer who calls him Nathanael; the rest call him Bartholomew.

Nathanael is best remembered for his response when Philip urged him to come and meet Jesus of Nazareth: "Can anything good come from there?" (John 1:46, NIV). Because Jesus showed that He had seen and known him before Philip called him, Nathanael readily acknowledged Him as the son of God. He was the "Honest Abe" of the disciples. "An Israelite indeed, in whom is no guile [deceit]" (John 1:47, KJV), Jesus had said.

### MATTHEW

He is also referred to as Levi. He was called from his

duties as tax collector while stationed at Capernaum. The fact that he was a hated "publican"—one who worked for the Roman government—must have filled his life with misery and loneliness. He must have read hope and forgiveness in the face of Jesus. He didn't hesitate. When Jesus called, he "arose and followed him." He wrote the Gospel of Matthew. Nothing is known of his later life and work.

## THOMAS

John is the only Gospel author who tells us anything about Thomas, also called Didymus. Both names mean "twin." Even though he is called the doubter, he had the capacity to be courageous and loyal, volunteering to follow his Lord to the death (see John 11:16). Some scholars think he worked in Parthia and Persia; some say he went to India, where, even to this day, there are "Thomas Christians."

## JAMES THE LITTLE

He may have had "the less" or "the little" attached to his name because he was younger than the other James or because he was short. He is also known as the son of Alphaeus. Since Matthew's father was also named Alphaeus, there is a possibility they were brothers.

## THADDAEUS

He was also known as Lebbaeus or Judas, the son of James. When John refers to him, he is careful not to confuse him with Judas Iscariot (see John 14:22).

## SIMON THE ZEALOT

He is described by one writer as "the uncompromising foe of the imperial authority." The zealots were a Jewish patriotic party that waged fanatical underground resistance against

Roman rule. They were also called "daggermen" (Sicarii).

Simon did not maintain his connection with any such organizations after he chose to follow Jesus. His selection does indicate that Jesus' family of disciples were a diverse, even colorful, group of men.

## JUDAS ISCARIOT

Judas is included along with Peter, James, and John as the four who were to act a leading part in the events of Christ's life. As Jesus' betrayer, he chose to play an unhappy and tragic part.

Judas was a native of Judea and therefore probably the only disciple who was not a Galilean. Ellen White says that Judas was not invited personally by Jesus to join the "inner circle of disciples" (*The Desire of Ages*, 293). Judas believed Jesus was to be king of an earthly kingdom, and he wanted to secure a position of power for himself in that new kingdom.

The other disciples were excited about Judas joining them. He had administrative abilities. He was articulate, discerning, and professional in appearance. Jesus, however, did not encourage him. He called Judas's attention to His poverty, hoping to discourage his worldly ambitions. Judas persisted in his desire to be included, so Jesus ordained him along with the rest.

When Judas joined the group, he stood on a "level playing field." Like the rest, he came with his assets and liabilities. From that point onward, he heard the same sermons, saw the same miracles, joined in the same witnessing ventures as the other eleven. But his response was not the same. He did not accept Jesus' efforts to change him.

Judas could have been listed among the chief apostles, but his name has become a byword for all that is deceitful and selfish. On the very day that Jesus was nailed to the cross to bring salvation to all, Judas died without hope—on another tree.

After Jesus' resurrection and ascension to heaven, the eleven remaining apostles met and after study and prayer cast lots to find a replacement for Judas Iscariot. The lot fell to Matthias, one who had been with the disciples from the beginning of Jesus' ministry.

• • • • • • • •

When we look at the apostles, a number of questions can be asked about the selection process. Why Peter? How did Thomas qualify? What did Jesus see in James? Were these men the very best available in the whole country?

Jesus selected men without much formal education. His disciples needed to be teachable. He was introducing radical new concepts—new ways of thinking about the plan of salvation. There was much to learn and much to unlearn.

Most of the disciples were poor, but this does not mean that people with money are excluded or even less desirable. Jesus needed men who were not looking for security in a materialistic, secular world. He alone would be their security. He called them to a single-minded obedience, warning them that "no man can serve two masters" (Matthew 6:24, KJV).

These unknown men provide proof of what the Master Teacher can do with those who dedicate their talents to Him. Some became authors whose books and letters have been read by billions, and some became great preachers and soul winners, but all were given power to heal the sick and cast out demons. The names of tens of thousands whom the world calls great will be forever forgotten; the names of these humble men will be inscribed on the foundations of the New Jerusalem.

### "SO SEND I YOU"

"When Jesus had ended His instruction to the disciples, He gathered the little band close about Him, and kneeling in the midst of them, and laying His hands upon their heads, He offered a prayer dedicating them to His sacred work. Thus the Lord's disciples were ordained to the gospel ministry" (*The Desire of Ages*, 296).

Jesus enrolled His disciples in a school that was more than a series of classroom sessions; they were to learn by doing. As they traveled from place to place, Jesus revealed to them the healing power of the kingdom of God, how to face demons and human hostility unafraid, and how to see in each scared face a child of God. It was hard work but exciting and satisfying.

Jesus knew that He would not always be with them. They

needed experience in working on their own. He sent them out by twos to the towns and villages. His instructions to them contain valuable principles for us all.

1. They were to go with a partner (see Mark 6:7). In this way they could encourage one another, pray together, and correct each other's mistakes.
2. Their message was to be simple and positive. "The kingdom of heaven is at hand" (see Matthew 10:7, KJV). They were not to be dogmatic or argumentative or use high-pressure tactics. "Wise as serpents, and harmless as doves" (verse 16), they were to search for receptive hearts (verse 14).
3. They were given power to perform both physical and spiritual healing. We, too, are to care about the physical and emotional needs of those around us. This opens hearts to God's forgiveness.
4. They were to begin their work with "the lost sheep of the house of Israel" (verses 5, 6). On this first tour, they were to go where Jesus had gone before and made friends. In our day, our most important circles of influence are still our family members and friends.
5. They were to expect opposition and persecution (verses 16-31). The religious leaders hated, tortured, and killed the Messiah. "A student is not above his teacher" (Matthew 10:24, NIV). Whatever the cost, we are to share the truth in love and not be afraid of being laughed at or ridiculed.
6. They were to be compassionate and courteous to all. To be kind to the quiet, the rejected, and the lonely is the mark of real courage.

"In simple trust like theirs who heard, Beside the Syrian sea, The gracious calling of the Lord, Let us, like them, without a word, Rise up and follow Thee."
—John Greenleaf Whittier, *Seventh-day Adventist Church Hymnal*, no. 480.

 **Memory Focus**

"Anyone who does not take his cross and follow me is not worthy of me. Whoever finds his life will lose it, and whoever loses his life for my sake will find it" (Matthew 10:38, 39, NIV).

OR

"There is no limit to the usefulness of one who, by putting self aside, makes room for the working of the Holy Spirit upon his heart, and lives a life wholly consecrated to God" (*The Desire of Ages*, 250, 251).

 **Into the Bible**

1. Read through Matthew 10:1, 16-31. Imagine that you, like the disciples, have been sent into a city to go from door to door to spread the gospel. From the Scripture passage, write five sentences that tell what Jesus said that can give you courage and success when witnessing to others.
2. A. Read the following texts; then write a summary for each that explains Jesus' title as "the Prince of Peace."
    (1) Isaiah 9:6
    (2) Luke 2:14
    (3) John 14:27
   B. Read Matthew 10:34. Jesus said that He did not come to bring peace, but the sword. If the sword represents conflict, list four conflicts that resulted when Jesus came into this world or when He comes into our homes and into our lives.
   C. Write a paragraph analyzing the paradox (apparent contradiction) of Jesus as the Prince of Peace but bearing a sword. Use the information from items 2A and 2B to help you write this paragraph.

3. Read the following verses, and make a list of the characteristics marking true disciples of Jesus:
   A. Matthew 10:37
   B. Matthew 10:38
   C. Matthew 10:42
   D. Luke 14:33
   E. John 8:31
   F. John 13:35
   G. John 15:5, 8
4. Analyze the account of "the big catch" in Luke 5:1-11. Make a list of the lessons you think Jesus was trying to teach through this miracle.

 # Projects

1. Write a biographical sketch of one of the disciples. Base it on what you can learn from the Bible, the Spirit of Prophecy, and other sources, but use your imagination to fill in the blanks.
2. Jesus chose men who had, for the most part, very little formal schooling. List the advantages and disadvantages of this in terms of the kind of persons Jesus was looking for.
3. Jesus sent His disciples out two by two. Organize a witnessing activity in which your class members work in teams of two. When you are finished, discuss the advantages of such an approach.

 **Focus Questions**

1. Jesus instructed His disciples to "heal the sick, raise the dead, cleanse those who have leprosy, and drive out demons" (Matthew 10:8, NIV). Why do you think these activities are not prominent in the work of Seventh-day Adventists today? Is there reason to believe that they will be in the future?
2. Why were some of Jesus' disciples closer to Him than others?
3. When He sent the disciples out to do missionary work, Jesus used the expression "Shake the dust from your feet." Is there any parallel to this in doing Christian work today?
4. The disciples forsook *all* to follow Jesus (see Luke 5:11). What did they actually forsake? Was there a trade-off? Is less required of disciples today?
5. If Jesus cared for all the disciples, why was John called "the disciple Jesus loved"?
6. If Jesus came into your life today and asked you to leave everything and follow Him, what would you do?
7. What does it mean to go into all the world and make disciples?
8. Why do you think Jesus had twelve disciples?
9. Are being baptized and becoming a disciple the same?
10. In what ways may one's education be a barrier to becoming a follower of Jesus today? How can it be a help?

# PERCEPTION

Sorrow is a great educator. You can see farther through a
tear than through a telescope (Unknown).

# lesson 12

# Good News Proclaimed

## Lesson Scriptures: Luke 1:5-25, 57-80; John 2:1-22

There are different ways God's message can be proclaimed and different ways we can respond to it. The word *gospel* generally means "good news," but that doesn't mean that people are always glad to hear it. Depending on who we are and what we value most in life, the news that God is among us can be cause for rejoicing or cause for fear and despair.

News can be proclaimed in different ways too. Remember when you were little and your mother had to call you to supper? Sometimes she barely had to say anything. The odors wafting from the kitchen were all the message you needed. Other times she had to call you over and over to get your attention away from something else. And sometimes she had to shout to get you to do something you didn't especially want to do.

This lesson looks at three instances of proclaiming the gospel. In the first, John the Baptist has to repeat his message over and over. Some people accept it willingly and some don't. In the second example, Jesus' action is the message, and the people rejoice in response to it. In the third, Jesus has to shout the message that God had come and must be listened to, and the people flee in terror. The stories may seem very different from each other, but remember—in each case, God is sending a message, and His people must respond accordingly.

117

John knew that the Messiah had already been born—the Son of God was already among them. He knew what this meant for him. The waiting and preparing were over. The time for proclaiming had come.

John was no ordinary young man, and he knew it. Like Isaac, he was a miracle baby born to elderly parents. God had specially selected John's parents and his name and given strict instructions on how he was to be raised. He was to be a vegetarian, and he was never to touch alcohol. Instead of being filled with wine and rich foods, he was to be filled with the Holy Spirit, who would anoint him for a special work.

John's special work was to prepare the way for Jesus. In today's terms, John was Jesus' advance man. These days, when a VIP visits a town hall or shopping mall, it isn't the simple, spontaneous event it appears to be. Weeks before, advance teams scour the area, making sure the place is clean, secure, and filled with photogenic crowds.

In somewhat the same way, before the Messiah appeared, John had to help the people prepare their hearts. His mes-sage was simple and direct: "Repent, for the kingdom of heaven is near" (Matthew 3:2, NIV). When the Messiah comes, he said, your hearts must be ready to receive Him, not barricaded by selfishness and worldliness. John hit them between the eyes. He called the Jewish leaders who came to hear him a "brood of vipers."

How in the world could such a message be good news? Well, being called a viper isn't good news, but being forgiven for such wickedness is. And sin-ners who really want to be for-given know they must repent. That's why thousands flocked to hear John preach, in spite of his hard words, and many were converted and baptized.

## A WEDDING MIRACLE

Read about the life of Jesus, and you see the gospel unfold-ing in many different ways. Sometimes, to teach the people, He barely had to speak at all.

After His grueling ordeal of being tempted in the wilder-ness, Jesus made His way back to Galilee and met with His dis-ciples. There He heard the news of a wedding in His family and quickly went to Cana, where His mother, whom He

had not seen in nearly two months, was helping with the preparations.

In Jesus' day, weddings were not thirty-minute ceremonies followed by a small reception where you might get a bite of cake and a few mixed nuts. It was a huge affair that would continue around the clock. Fifty or sixty guests might have to be fed for three or four days. It had all the elements of a hostess's nightmare.

Jesus' mother may have been serving as wedding coordinator for her relatives. In any case, when the wine ran out before the party was over, she knew that it was a serious breach of hospitality and felt responsible for getting a new supply. At this anxious moment, she went to Jesus and said simply, "They have no wine" (John 2:3, KJV).

You may wonder why Mary would turn to Jesus with such a problem. He had just returned from the arduous wilderness experience. Mary knew this, of course. But she noticed something else—a new look of purpose and power that had not been there before. Coming to Jesus with her dilemma showed that even though she didn't

fully understand His mission, she believed He was special. Jesus didn't quickly agree to help, but she didn't give up. Turning to her servants, she said, "Do whatever he tells you"

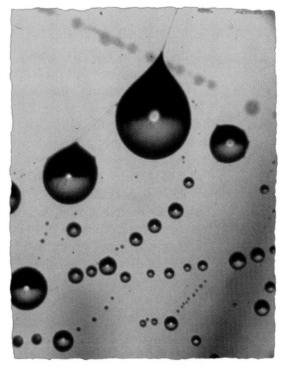

(John 2:5, NIV). And Jesus did respond to her faith in Him. "It was to honor Mary's trust, and to strengthen the faith of His disciples, that the first miracle was performed" (*The Desire of Ages*, 147).

Jesus ordered the servants to fill six large stone jars with water, then to draw some out and serve the steward of the feast. The steward was amazed at the fine quality of the wine, telling the bridegroom that the best is customarily served first, not saved until the feast is nearly over. The Bible says, "His disciples believed on him [Jesus]" (John 2:11, KJV), and so did His mother and probably most of the wedding guests. This first miracle dramatically proclaimed that God did indeed walk among His people.

## A LESSON IN REVERENCE

Does love ever need to shout? Of course it does. A parent shouts at a child about to run into the street after a ball. A neighbor shouts a warning when she sees smoke coming from a friend's house. In dire circumstances, shouting is an appropriate expression of love.

Does God ever need to shout? Not often, perhaps. But when He can't be heard any other way, God will shout. It happened at the Passover in the spring of A.D. 28. Jesus and His disciples had traveled ninety miles on foot from Capernaum to Jerusalem, along with throngs of other pilgrims.

When they arrived at the capital city, they made their way to the temple, the great center of worship for all Jews.

At the doors of the temple, Jesus stood transfixed, shocked by the sights, sounds, and smells that greeted Him. "There could be heard sharp bargaining, the lowing of cattle, the bleating of sheep, the cooing of doves, mingled with the chinking of coin and angry disputation" (*The Desire of Ages*, 155).

For worshipers who lived far from Jerusalem, bringing a Passover sacrifice from home was not permitted by the temple authorities. They demanded that the people buy temple lambs "with temple shekels." So the people were forced to buy a dove or small animal from someone who sold them in or near Jerusalem. Over the years, the merchants who sold this livestock had pushed their stalls closer to the temple grounds, until now they were crowded right into the outer courtyard.

Adding to this confusion and filth was the hubbub of the money-changers. The priests required that all business having to do with the temple be transacted with specially minted money called temple shekels. Many pilgrims arrived in

Jerusalem with foreign money that had to be exchanged. As in today's money markets, the exchange rate fluctuated, usually to the great benefit of the money-changers.

Jesus stood in the doorway and took in the whole scene. It looked and sounded like an ordinary bazaar, not a house of worship. A righteous anger overwhelmed Him. Picking up a small knotted whip, perhaps from one of the animal keepers, He marched into the temple with a zeal and severity He had never shown before. He didn't strike anyone with the whip, but the people got the message loud and clear. Tables tipped over; coins rang on the stone floor; animals and their keepers fled out the side doors. But even in the noisy chaos, all heard the voice of Jesus shouting, "Take these things away! Do not make My Father's house a house of merchandise!" (John 2:16, NKJV).

God's message may come to us as an urgent message repeated day after day, as a wordless reminder of God's goodness and providence or as a wake-up call to clean up our acts and do the right thing. God will send whatever message we need at the moment we need it. Our job is to respond appropriately: to repent, to rejoice, to live for God.

# Memory Focus

"It is written in Isaiah the prophet: 'I will send my messenger ahead of you, who will prepare your way—a voice of one calling in the desert, "Prepare the way for the Lord, make straight paths for him" ' " (Mark 1:2, 3, NIV).

 Into the Bible

1. Read the following Bible texts, and describe what Jesus and the Old Testament prophets had to say about John the Baptist.
   A. Isaiah 40:3
   B. Luke 1:76
   C. Malachi 3:1
2. Isaiah had prophesied six centuries before the Baptist's birth that John the Baptist would "prepare the way for the Lord" (Isaiah 40:3-6, NIV). Do the following:
   A. Identify three ways John prepared people to receive Jesus (Matthew 3:1, 6, 11).
   B. Identify three ways John described or identified Jesus (John 1:27, 29, 33, 34).
   C. Explain the meaning of John 1:29.
3. Read the following texts, and explain what principles or aspects of reverence or irreverence are given in these four incidents.
   A. Leviticus 10:1, 2, 8-10
   B. 2 Kings 2:23, 24
   C. Luke 19:45-47
4. The Scriptures contain spiritual principles that relate to reverence. Use the worksheet provided by your teacher to indicate the spiritual principle and key thought for the texts that are listed.
5. From what you have learned in doing questions 3 and 4, write a three- or four-sentence description stating what you believe are the essential aspects of reverence.

 Projects

1. *Repentance* means "to turn around," signifying a change of heart. Explain the relationship of repentance to receiving

salvation in Christ.

2. Was the wine Jesus made at the wedding alcoholic or not? Read what the *Seventh-day Adventist Bible Commentary* has to say, and summarize your findings.

3. Solve this Bible math problem: About how much wine by our measure did Jesus make? How many servings is that? How many guests would that serve at three servings each? Why do you think Jesus provided such a superabundance?

 # Focus Questions

1. In what way does the character of the parents determine what their children become?

2. Can the gospel be preached without calling people to repentance?

3. Jesus' answer to His mother, "Woman, what does your concern have to do with me?" seems abrupt and disrespectful. How do you explain this? (See John 2:4, NIV, and *The Desire of Ages*, 146, 147).

4. Jesus liked being among all kinds of people. What can Christians learn from His example?

5. Jesus is most often described as loving and gentle. How does His cleansing of the temple fit with that? Can a meek and gentle person still be forceful and courageous in defense of what's right?

6. Why do you think Jesus began His public ministry by cleansing the temple?

7. How does the way we worship affect our spiritual growth?

# REVELATION

And Christ became a human being and lived here on earth among us and was full of loving forgiveness and truth (John 1:14, TLB).

# lesson 13

# A Ministry Misunderstood

## Lesson Scripture: John 1:10-12, TLB

lthough he made the world, the world didn't recognize him when he came. Even in his own land and among his own people, the Jews, he was not accepted. Only a few would welcome and receive him. But to all who received him, he gave the right to become children of God. All they needed to do was to trust him to save them" (John 1:10-12, TLB).

### SOME PEOPLE REALLY ARE MESSED UP #1

No doubt we wouldn't have been as messed up as the people who were "looking" for the coming of the Messiah (Christ) about two thousand years ago.

Of course, there were texts about Him coming as a king and restoring Israel to the days of glory. But those were based upon the Jews really following what God had already revealed to them. It's called conditional prophecy. If the people don't live up to the conditions, they shouldn't expect the prophecy to be fulfilled the way it was spelled out with the conditions.

And how could they miss those clear passages in the book of Isaiah, a major prophet, that referred to a suffering Messiah who would die for the people rather than set up an earthly kingdom for them. It truly is amazing how people will blind themselves so they see only those parts of Scripture they want to follow.

The religious leaders probably deserve some of the blame. The people had come to expect these leaders to give them the truth. After all, they had studied it more than other people. Certainly they could be trusted.

They did have certain problems regarding the promises that required some explanations. For example, how could a king be born to the Jews when the Jews had no royal family? Perhaps the religious leaders stood in the place of a royal family, so the Messiah would come from the line of the most significant religious leader's family.

But even among the religious leaders there was a split. The Sadducees seemed to have a little better understanding of how the system operated. They also seemed smarter, so they were probably more apt to be correct. But the other religious leaders, the Pharisees, seemed so dedicated, so spiritual.

And then there were so many false Messiahs (false Christs) who came and went that some figured the hype about Jesus would soon die out after His crucifixion. It's really not surprising that so many people didn't catch on that He was the Messiah at His first coming.

Although the religious leaders were notified of the coming of the Messiah from the wise men, only Herod responded to the news. And while angels personally gave the news to shepherds, who saw it for themselves and told others, they were lower-class people. Who would really want to follow them? And committed followers of God by the names of

Simeon and Anna responded with ecstasy when Baby Jesus came to the temple. But they were very old, and even the local priest didn't notice anything that would show that Jesus was the Messiah.

Apparently, the people were really messed up in Christ's day. Those who seemed most likely to discover the Messiah (Christ) missed Him, while those most unlikely to find Him did just that.

## SOME PEOPLE REALLY ARE MESSED UP #2

Jesus is coming again. We call it the second coming of Christ. Seventh-day Adventists carry their eager anticipation of this event right in their name—Adventists—the coming of Christ. We believe that He will come in a way similar to the way He left. Although this time, it will be with power and great glory.

But a lot of people really are messed up on this second coming of Christ. Some are still looking for the first coming of the Messiah. They're expecting a rejuvenation of one ethnic group rather than all people. They would paraphrase John 3:16 as, God so loved my ethnic group, that He gave His only begotten Son, that my ethnic group would not perish, but be given international dominance.

There are others who look for Jesus to set up a Christian kingdom as some had hoped at His first coming. The second coming will include greater political support, which expands beyond ethnic barriers to include Christians from all ethnic and national groups. Then Christians will have supremacy over atheists, secular humanists, and New Agers. Instead of streets of gold, Jesus will sponsor a major infrastructure program so there won't be any potholes in our asphalt highways. The mansions He was supposed to build for us will simply be remodeled high-rise condos.

Many Christians have given up on the idea that Jesus will ever return. His promise of a return is spiritualized into a warm feeling some people experience when they become Christians. Because they also tend to believe that when a person dies, they go to heaven, there isn't such an urgency for a second coming of Christ. Why does He need to come to earth when we just go to be with Him after we die?

A non-Christian variation of this is the concept of righteousness by works in which your behavior will be rewarded after you die. Reincarnation says that you will return to earth as a higher or lower life form, based on your goodness during your previous life. So be kind to ants, since they may be relatives who have come back to try and work their way to a higher existence. If you get to be good enough, some believe you will actually attain a godlike status. You become your own christ.

Many of the TV evangelists today subscribe to a belief called the secret rapture. It's based on a variant interpretation of Daniel 9:27, revived and made popular about one hundred years ago. With an unusual twist of prophetic interpretation, seven years of prophecy are placed after the second coming of Christ. The followers of Jesus are secretly snatched away from this world and taken to heaven. Seven years later, Jesus returns to take additional people to heaven. Those who can go to heaven at the end of the seven years are those who got serious about their commitment to Christ once they real-

ized that they were left behind during the secret rapture. They will have had to survive seven years of "tribulation," or a seven-year time of trouble that those who were secretly raptured got out of. This nonbiblical viewpoint of last-day events has a nice psychological appeal—be true to Jesus, and you won't have to go through times of trouble. But it doesn't quite fit with many of God's followers in the past, like Shadrach, Meshach, and Abednego.

But even those who believe in the secret rapture aren't in agreement as to when this secret event really occurs. Many place it before this agreed-upon seven-year "tribulation." But others say that the secret rapture happens in the middle of the seven years. As you might expect, some believe the secret rapture occurs at the end of the seven-year "tribulation." Some serious, intelligent, religious people have this all figured out. It's just that they don't agree.

At least that's clear enough now! At least we aren't as messed up as the people in Jesus' day were. At least we will be able to recognize Christ when He comes. Won't we?

 **Memory Focus**

"We know God has spoken to Moses, but as for this fellow, we don't know anything about him" (John 9:29, TLB).

OR

"'What are we going to do?' they asked each other. 'For this man certainly does miracles. If we let him alone the whole nation will follow him—and then the Roman army will come and kill us and take over the Jewish government. . . . Let this one man die for the people—why should the whole nation perish?'" (John 11:47-50, TLB).

 **Into the Bible**

1. On the worksheet your teacher will give you, write a summary of each of the Old Testament passages that describe the promise given to the Jewish people about the coming Messiah who would rule as king.
2. On the worksheet your teacher will give you, list the descriptions in Isaiah 53:3-10 that refer to the coming Messiah as one who would serve, suffer, and die for the sins of humanity.
3. Jesus came to save people from their sins (see Matthew 1:21). On the worksheet provided by your teacher, write a statement that summarizes the response of various people to the teachings and ministry of Jesus.
4. On the worksheet provided by your teacher, indicate how some persons responded to the events that occurred on the Sabbath as described in selected passages of Scripture.
5. Every society has persons whom some classify as "lowlifers" or "scum." Using the references listed, you are to identify four types of people who were considered "lowlifers" in the days of Jesus. Indicate how Jesus treated these people in contrast to

the way most people treated them. Use the worksheet provided by your teacher for your answers.

 Projects

1. On a sheet of paper, write a response to the question "Why did Jesus come to earth?" Then ask two students and two adults why they think Jesus came to earth. Record their responses. Be prepared to share the responses you receive with the class.
2. Divide into small groups of two to four students, and identify facts that help in deciding whether Jesus was the Messiah.
   A. Place the facts in two lists.
      (1) Identify five things Jesus did that proved He was the Messiah.
      (2) Identify five things Jesus did that caused some to think that He was not the Messiah.
   B. For each of the events or actions that some used against Jesus, indicate why they were wrong in their interpretation.
   C. Develop a master list from the small-group lists of the events or actions that supported Jesus' claim to be the Messiah.

3. Survey five people who are not members of your church, using the following two questions:
   A. Jesus was rejected and crucified when He came two thousand years ago. If He had waited and come today, do you think He would be rejected?
   B. Why or why not?

Be prepared to discuss the results of your survey with the class.

**4.** Read one of the following three chapters from The *Desire of Ages.* Based on your reading, write a response to the question, Why was Jesus misunderstood and rejected?

    A. Chapter 31     "The Sermon on the Mount"
    B. Chapter 42     "Tradition"
    C. Chapter 59     "Priestly Plottings"

 # Focus Questions

1. How could so many people misunderstand Jesus?
2. Why did so many people follow Jesus and then reject Him later?
3. Why do people reject Jesus today?
4. What would it take for you to accept Jesus?
5. Upon what do you base your understanding of Jesus? What is the accuracy of your source(s)?

# REFLECTION

Treat other people exactly as you would like to be treated by them—
this is the essence of all true religion (Matthew 7:12, Phillips).

# Religion Made Plain & Simple

**Lesson Scriptures: Matthew 5:48; 6:31-33;
Luke 6:32-35**

NAUTHORIZED VEHICLES PARKED IN THIS LOT WILL BE TOWED AT OWNER'S EXPENSE!!! It couldn't have been more clear, especially to those who were clear about it. What was not clear was how two people could be so clear and yet very different in what they understood the sign to read.

The owner of the parking lot had discovered an "unauthorized vehicle" parked in his lot. So he called the tow truck and had it removed. When the owner of the car finally located his car that had been towed, there was quite a debate regarding who was going to pay for the towing of the vehicle.

The owner of the car admitted that he was not authorized to park in that particular lot. But, he reasoned, the sign spelled out that the owner of the parking lot would pay for any towing that he decided to carry out. Such a claim was promised on the sign posted in the lot. Therefore, the owner of the parking lot should pay for the towing.

The owner of the parking lot had posted the sign not only to prevent unauthorized vehicles from parking in his lot but also to warn and inform offenders that if they did park an unauthorized vehicle in his lot, their vehicle would be towed, and the owner of the car would have to pay for it. The sign spelled that out.

The owner of the tow truck

simply wanted to be paid. But the owner of the car was threatening a lawsuit if his car wasn't released. The owner of the parking lot had never paid for the towing of an unauthorized vehicle, and he wasn't about to start doing it. But going to court would cost him more than the $85 towing fee. Couldn't somebody explain what the sign meant?

The message was clear: UNAUTHORIZED VEHICLES PARKED IN THIS LOT WILL BE TOWED AT OWNER'S EXPENSE!!! But which owner—the owner of the car or the owner of the parking lot? It would be unusual for the owner of the parking lot to pay for this. But that must have been why three exclamation points were placed at the end of the words, countered the car owner. This had the makings for a lawyer's heyday to get the car owner off on a technicality.

While both owners could argue over the meaning of the sign, the sign wasn't much help because it couldn't talk. The sign carried the message, but some observers either misunderstood or chose to see things from a different perspective.

Most teens have mastered the art of getting off on a technicality. For instance, your parents may ask if you were at the mall last night. If you don't want them to know that you were AND you don't want to lie, you can think to yourself, *No, I wasn't at the mall, I was standing outside the mall,* or *No, I wasn't at the mall, I was in the Taco Bell inside the mall,* or *No, I wasn't at the mall (all night), I was at Joey's house (before I went to the mall),* etc. You don't give the entire message because your parents wouldn't fall for it, but it's a way to technically avoid the truth (at least in your own mind).

How specifically must things be spelled out for you? If your mom wants to preserve some special food for the weekend, do you need to be told to stay out of the brownies, stay out of the food, or stay out of the kitchen? Or do you need to be told anything? Wouldn't you be able to figure that out on your own?

When the children of Israel came out of slavery in Egypt, they were accustomed to being told exactly what to do. It's no wonder that God not only gave them the Ten Commandments, but a host of other laws as well. They were beginning a new society and needed lots of

details for circumstances they would face.

God could have just said, "Love me and love each other." But most of the people wouldn't know how to live that out in every situation. So God spelled it out for them. Many people have seen that even the Ten Commandments, as broad as they are, can be summed up as love to God (commandments 1 to 4) and love to each other (commandments 5 to 10).

In fact, when asked what was the greatest commandment in the Law, Jesus responded, "Love the Lord your God with all your heart and with all your soul and with all your mind. This is the first and greatest commandment. And the second is like it: Love your neighbor as yourself. All the Law and the Prophets hang on these two commandments" (Matthew 22:37-40, NIV).

When Jesus quizzed an expert in the law regarding the greatest commandment, the expert tried to wiggle out on a technicality by further questioning, "Who is my neighbor (Whom I should love as I love myself)?" (Luke 10:29, NIV). Jesus decided to spell it out by means of the parable of the good Samaritan.

The Jews had become quite adept at wiggling out of things due to technicalities. God had told them to remember to keep the Sabbath holy. But He had not told them all the ways to do that (or not to do that). So they invented growing lists of what could and couldn't be done, as

well as all possible exceptions to these lists. But when the Lawgiver came, they found out that He didn't keep their laws.

Even today, many people continue with a very limited and literal understanding of what God has revealed. When God spoke and wrote "Don't murder," they believe that it only means you can't physically destroy a person. But they fail to capture the spirit of the message that includes destroying a person through gossiping, ignoring, or constantly putting people down.

In the Sermon on the Mount, Jesus took the limited and literal understandings of what He had revealed in Old Testament times and expanded them to include the possibilities of living by the spirit of the law instead of merely the letter of the law. Living by the letter of the law is doing the minimum required—just to get by. It hardly captures the fullness of living in the spirit of "more and more" rather than "is that enough?"

Considering the fact that Jesus desires a relationship with us, do you think He desires us to get by with just a minimum amount of time with Him, or would He prefer for us to enter the spirit of "more and more"? Which attitude would you want from someone who is a special friend?

· · · · · · · · · · · · · · · · · · · · · · · · · · · · · · · · · · · · · · · · · · · · · · · · · · · · · · ·

 # Memory Focus

"There must be no limit to your goodness, as your heavenly Father's goodness knows no bounds" (Matthew 5:48, NEB).

 # Into the Bible

1. So many people seek happiness in so many different ways. Happiness, however, seems to come as a by-product of other efforts. Jesus provided the prescription that would bring happiness several different ways. The beginning of the Sermon on the Mount focuses on eight things that bring "blessing" or "happiness." Write each condition (blessing) in your own words and the resulting blessing/happiness found in Matthew 5:3-12. You may prefer to consult *The Seventh-day Adventist Bible Commentary*, volume 5, for additional input. Record your responses on the worksheet your teacher will give you.

2. Perhaps the best-known sermon of Jesus is the one referred to simply as the Sermon on the Mount, found in Matthew 5 to 7 (the parallel passage is Luke 6:20-49). Most of what Jesus presented was based on the Old Testament, except the people hadn't quite understood it the way He presented it. Read the following Old Testament passages, and find their corresponding part in the Sermon on the Mount as recorded in Matthew 5 to 7. Then explain how Jesus expanded the literal, but limited, Old Testament understanding. Record your responses on the worksheet your teacher will provide.

3. On the worksheet provided by your teacher, some of the key passages from the Sermon on the Mount will be listed. You are to read the passages, write what you believe is the principle (main lesson) of each passage, and give an example of how the principle can be applied to your life.

4. Read Matthew 7:12, and explain the importance of what is often called "the golden rule."

 # Projects

1. Try living out the principles of the Beatitudes for twenty-four hours (see Into the Bible 1). Keep a log of how this works, such as times when it's difficult, times it seems to pay off, times it doesn't seem to pay off, times you forgot, etc. Be prepared to discuss your experience in small groups in class. Pray about it before you even give it a try. It takes supernatural assistance—God's help!

2. Forgiveness is more easily talked about than practiced. Ask seven different people the four questions on the worksheet that will be given to you by your teacher. See if there are any trends in the answers you receive. Be prepared to discuss the results of your survey in class.

3. Two students can volunteer to do the skit "If God Should Speak." (Your teacher will provide copies of the skit.) This can be done for class, for a Sabbath School program, or even a church service or school chapel program.

4. Get a copy of your school's student handbook or a copy of the rules concerning class attendance and student conduct (discipline). Schools generally include principles (the "spirit of the law") and standards or rules (the "letter of the law"). Standards or rules should be based on principles. On the worksheet provided by your teacher, do the following:

   A. Identify the standards or rules regarding class attendance and dress in your school.

   B. Identify statements that you think are the principle(s) that form the basis for the standards or rules.

 **Focus Questions**

1. Which Beatitudes seem the easiest to apply to our lives? Which ones are difficult? Why?
2. What is the difference between not doing wrong and doing right?
3. Why do you think Jesus ended this sermon with the parable of the two builders?
4. If Jesus said lusting after a person is the same as "doing it," should a person just go ahead and carry through on their thoughts since they're guilty anyway?
5. Why do rules in sporting events have to be spelled out in such detail?
6. Why are there so many law books for attorneys and judges?

# IDENTITY

Every soul is as fully known to Jesus as if he were the only one for whom the Saviour died (*The Desire of Ages*, 480).

# Personal Encounters With Christ

## Lesson Scriptures: John 3:1-21; 4:1-42

Imagine that you could have a private meeting with Jesus this evening. Would you want to meet with Him? What would your opening line be? And what would you say after that?

Or what if the circumstances were different? What if Jesus simply came across your path today, without warning, and started a conversation with you? What would be His first question to you? What would He want to talk about?

Since Jesus created each person as a unique individual, it's reasonable to expect that He can also relate to people in equally different ways. Consider two very different encounters with Jesus in successive chapters in John. The first deals with Nicodemus (John 3) and the second with a Samaritan woman (John 4).

### HOW JESUS REACHED OUT TO NICODEMUS

Nicodemus initiated contact with Jesus, yet Jesus didn't let him control the entire conversation. Jesus picked up on Nicodemus's calling Him "Rabbi," which means "teacher." In response, Jesus began to teach Nicodemus about salvation.

To begin with, He told Nicodemus that he needed to be born again. Nicodemus played dumb, not because he didn't understand what Jesus meant, but because he did understand, yet didn't want to believe it.

The Jewish understanding

of salvation was that a person needed to be a Jew to be saved. If you weren't a Jew, you could be baptized (born again) to become a Jew and, thereby, be saved.

Nicodemus was not only a Jew, but he was a Pharisee (a seriously religious Jew) and a member of the Jewish ruling council called the Sanhedrin. But Jesus challenged him by stating that in spite of his wonderful position and record, he needed a completely new start, to be "born again," in order to be saved. It's not surprising that Nicodemus responded with, "How can this be?" (John 3:9, NIV).

Jesus followed up His inquiry with a slight chastisement. "You are a great teacher in Israel, and you don't know this? . . . You do not believe me when I tell you about the things of this world; how will you ever believe me, then, when I tell you about the things of heaven?" (John 3:10, 12, TEV). In other words, you're a great teacher, but you don't seem to grasp even the basics of what I'd like to share with you.

Jesus continued by telling Nicodemus that salvation is not a matter of being a Jew, but it is available to whomever believes in the Son of Man. "Just as Moses lifted up the snake in the desert," Jesus said, "so the Son of Man must be lifted up, that everyone who believes in him may have eternal life" (John 3:14-16, NIV).

Accepting Jesus as the promised Messiah was a bit too much for Nicodemus to handle at the time, but he didn't reject the message. He simply needed more time to process it. To accept Jesus as the Messiah would mean that he would lose all he had gained as one of the Jewish leaders.

Yet in the Sanhedrin he began to indicate his growing allegiance to Jesus (see John 7:45-53). When he saw Jesus crucified, he remembered the nighttime conversation three years earlier in which Jesus had spoken of the Messiah being lifted up on a cross for the salvation of all. This led him to confess openly his faith in Jesus and to care for Jesus' body following the crucifixion (see John 19:38-40).

## HOW JESUS REACHED OUT TO A SAMARITAN WOMAN

Jesus' interaction with the woman at the well was quite dif-

ferent. As an indication of how important she was to the people of her day, we don't even know her name. While most people went to draw water from the well at morning and evening, she went at noon. Five failed marriages and living with a sixth man reflect a shattered sense of self-worth.

Because the background and situation contrasted sharply with Nicodemus, we wouldn't expect Jesus to present salvation in the same way to her. He didn't. Jesus initiated the conversation, and He did so by asking a question. More specifically, He asked for her help. "Will you give me a drink?" (John 4:7b, NIV).

Have you ever been in a situation with a stranger in which you saw each other but neither one of you spoke? There was a mutual silence that neither one of you broke. Jesus didn't let that happen. He asked a question, and He asked for help. How would you respond if a stranger of the opposite sex, from an ethnic group that acted superior, asked you for help?

Her response was, "You are a Jew and I am a Samaritan woman. How can you ask me for a drink?" (John 4:9b, NIV). What do you suppose her tone of voice was? Try reading her response with a tone of surprise. Read it again with a tone of spite. Read it another time with a tone of hope. Read it a fourth time with a tone of confusion. What do you think her tone was?

Jesus' tactics were to create curiosity as the dialogue continued. Jesus offered living water.

The Samaritan woman could see He didn't have the necessary equipment to draw water. She pointed out her spiritual heritage of being in the line of Jacob. The Samaritans were descendants of Jacob, as were the Jews. The difference was that the Samaritans had intermingled and intermarried with pagans, with a resulting mixture of various religious beliefs. The Jews kept their national heritage pure through marriage and their religious practices free from paganism.

Jesus instructed the woman to go and get her husband.

She replied that she didn't have a husband.

Jesus gave her information that no stranger would have known about her.

She perceived that He must

be a prophet and launched into a theological discussion of the controversy between Samaritans and Jews.

Jesus, a Jew, told her that salvation came from the Jews. He then told her that He was more than a prophet. He was the Messiah—the One who gives salvation.

Think back over this entire conversation. The stranger she had been talking with was God! With no thought of why she had come to the well in the first place, this woman raced back to town and, despite her reputation, recruited the people of the town, not only to go to Jesus and invite Him to stay with

them, but to put their faith in Him as well (see John 4:39-42).

How ironic that the disciples, the ones Jesus was training to tell others about Him, didn't recruit a single person from the town. But the Samaritan woman, a social outcast, brought out the whole town!

## WHAT'S THE DIFFERENCE?

Talk about opposites! Nicodemus was a respected spiritual leader of the Jews. The Samaritan woman was a despised, unnamed, immoral ingredient in a small Samaritan town. When it came to salvation, Jesus presented a seemingly impossible challenge to Nicodemus: "You must be born again." But for the woman at the well, He offered a free drink of living water. It's almost as if Jesus came to afflict the comfortable and to comfort the afflicted. Comfortable Nicodemus took approximately three years to fully respond to the offer of Christ, while the Samaritan woman accepted Christ's offer immediately.

Part of the gospel presentation to Nicodemus contains perhaps the best-known verse of the Bible, "For God so loved the world that he gave his only

begotten son, that whosoever believes in him should not perish, but have everlasting life" (John 3:16, KJV). The illustration of the snake being lifted up in the wilderness (see John 3:14) was nothing new to Nicodemus. But having the Messiah crucified and providing eternal life to those who would "look and live" certainly was not what Nicodemus expected. Nicodemus, who did not sense his tremendous need because of his privileged position, heard from the lips of Jesus the good news (gospel) that because of God's love for all humanity, everyone whose only hope rests in Christ's sacrifice for sins is given eternal life.

### WHAT ABOUT YOU?

Are you more like Nicodemus or the Samaritan woman? Are you in a privileged position? Do you want salvation as an exclusive package for you, but not for "everyone who believes"? Or are you more like the Samaritan woman who is ready and eager to accept the living water Jesus offers to you right now? Would you be more likely to say Yes to Jesus if salvation was presented to you in the way it was presented to

Nicodemus or to the Samaritan woman? Why?

Consider several people in your class. If you were to present salvation to each of them individually, with which ones would you use the method Jesus used with Nicodemus? With which ones would you follow the presentation He made to the Samaritan woman? What are the differences between the two presentations?

### TRYING IT OUT

How can you know just how to present Jesus and His plan of salvation to an individual? Jesus knew what people were like, what made them tick (see John 2:24, 25). You can too. John the Baptist was dependent on promptings and insights from the Holy Spirit. But he also studied people to determine the best way to reach their hearts with the message of salvation (*The Desire of Ages*, 102).

A lazy excuse of just letting the Spirit move you is inadequate. Consider many ways of meeting the needs of people with the good news of salvation. In the next few days, we'll consider some other examples besides Nicodemus and the Samaritan woman.

**145**

# Memory Focus

"They said to the woman, 'We no longer believe just because of what you said; now we have heard for ourselves, and we know that this man really is the Savior of the world' " (John 4:42, NIV).

OR

"The Son of Man came to seek and to save what was lost" (Luke 19:10, NIV).

# Into the Bible

1. Based on John 3:1-21 and John 4:4-42, complete the worksheet "Nicodemus and the Samaritan Woman" that your teacher will provide. This will prepare the way for class discussion on these two Bible characters and their encounters with Jesus.
2. Based on John 8:2-11, complete the worksheet "Jesus Wants You" that your teacher will provide. This will give an overview of how Jesus reached out to the woman caught in adultery.
3. Based on John 9:1-41, complete the worksheet "Jesus Wants You" that your teacher will provide. This will help you understand how Jesus ministered to a man blind from birth.
4. Based on Mark 10:17-31, complete the worksheet "Jesus Wants You" that your teacher will provide. This will show how Jesus met people personally through His contact with the rich young ruler.
5. Based on Luke 19:1-10, complete the worksheet "Jesus Wants You" that your teacher will provide. This activity will help you understand how Jesus reached out to Zacchaeus.
6. A. Identify the person named in each of the following texts, and state Jesus' requirements for each of the three persons who wanted to become one of His followers.
   (1) Luke 8:26-39
   (2) Luke 18:18-30
   (3) Luke 19:1-10
   B. Which requirement(s) would Jesus be most apt to present to you? Why? Why not other ones?

 **Projects**

1. Interview at least four different people from the categories listed below. Identify ways in which Jesus has drawn them to Himself.
   A. An adult
   B. A new convert
   C. A classmate
   D. A teacher
   E. An elementary student
   F. A pastor
2. Develop a role-play for a group of two to six students in which a gospel presentation is made. Determine the setting and the roles for the various participants, as well as the method you think would be most effective for reaching the other person(s) in the role-play. After the group has practiced sufficiently, present your role-play to the class, to the entire school, and/or for a Sabbath School program. Observers should discuss the methods of presenting salvation following the presentation.
3. Working in small groups, develop a list of suggestions that could be used as guidelines when witnessing to others. Then during the next week, apply at least one suggestion in witnessing to one person.

 **Focus Questions**

1. What beliefs are critical when sharing the gospel with someone?
2. How would Jesus go about showing the gospel to students at your school?
3. Why do some people find it difficult to accept Christ as their personal Saviour?
4. Do you think it's easier for teens or adults to accept the gospel? Why?

# PRIORITIES

If your troubles aren't big enough to pray about,
then they certainly aren't big enough to worry about *(Quips and Quotes)*.

# Prayer: The Openness of God

**Lesson Scripture: Matthew 6:5-15, KJV**

From his bed, Greg could switch off the light in his room. But he couldn't switch off the tangle of voices in his head. He lay back on his pillow and stared toward the ceiling.

The confusion of the day returned. He knew that registering for his first semester in college would be difficult, but this was impossible. It wasn't that no one would help him. Everyone he talked to knew exactly what he should do. But each one thought he should do something different!

Personally, Greg didn't know what he wanted to do. He sighed and closed his eyes. He could still hear their voices.

"You really must sign up for Computer Science. First, you need to take Introduction to Programming, then . . ."

"Biotechnology is the fastest-growing job area. Sign up this semester for Biology 101, then . . ."

"If I were you, I'd take Fine Arts. It opens up worlds of possibilities. Start with Ancient Literature now, then . . ."

Greg shook his head. *I got advice from almost everyone today,* he thought. *Who else could I ask?* Then another thought struck him, and he wondered why it hadn't occurred to him sooner.

*I guess I could ask God. But,* he wondered, *would God listen to me? And would He help?*

With these thoughts tumbling through his mind, Greg started a simple prayer. "God, I'm confused. I don't know . . ."

Then he drifted off into a dream. He was back at registration.

"Over here, young man! Sign up here for Prayer 101." Greg turned toward the college advisor. "Learn all about prayer—what to say, when to pray, and how to get the answers you need."

Greg turned away, but the room was filled with advisors trying to sign him up.

"Everyone needs Intro to Prayer," the man at the closest table explained.

"Learn the basics of praying: how to fold your hands, when to kneel, how to pray over your food. A must for every young Christian!"

"Desperation Praying is what you need," another announced, pointing to the textbook. "Topics include: Panic Prayers, Promises You Should Never Make, and How to Make God an Offer He Can't Refuse."

"Every serious student needs Advanced Praying 401," a voice proclaimed. "Learn the value of fasting and praying. Learn how to stay on your knees for hours without permanent leg damage. Learn the secret of 'praying without ceasing.' "

When Greg's eyes snapped open, he was even more confused than before. He slid to his knees beside the bed and prayed. "God, I don't know if I'm doing this right, but I need help. Please show me what to do."

Then he slipped under his covers and drifted back to sleep.

### THE DISCIPLES' PRAYER

Will God really help you with problems if you ask? How should you ask? Is there a certain way to pray? Have you ever been confused about prayer?

A lot of people are confused about prayer. Some see prayer as a kind of vending machine—you say the right words, push the right buttons, and what you want pops out at the bottom.

Some people seem to think that prayer is their opportunity for another sermon. They are supposed to be talking to God, but most of what they say seems to be aimed at the people who are listening to the prayer.

To others, prayer takes the form of a chant, kind of like a cheerleader's. Usually, they are past the "God is great, God is good," or "Now I lay me down to sleep" stage, but their prayers are basically a repeat of the same words every time.

The disciples were confused about prayer too. Jesus didn't seem to pray in the formal way they had been taught, but obviously, His prayers were answered. So they asked Him to teach them to pray. What He taught them was what we call the Lord's Prayer. It really should be called the Disciples' Prayer, since they were the ones learning to pray.

Since Jesus taught His disciples to pray that way, does that mean that we have to use that same prayer when we pray?

No. Jesus wasn't spelling out a formula to memorize. He was telling His disciples what was important to say in a prayer. He was teaching them what prayer was all about. And we can learn the same thing.

Prayer is about relationships. And Jesus starts off this prayer with a new idea for the disciples. It's not the "Supreme Being" or the "Master of the Universe," although those titles would be correct. It's not "Lord God Almighty" or "Most High God," as they might have been used to saying. It's "Our Father." Someone whom we know. Someone who loves His children no matter what.

*Our Father which art in heaven, Hallowed be thy name.*

God is our Father, someone with whom we can talk and have a relationship. Not only is He willing to communicate with us, He is anxious to. But He is not only our Father, He is the Holy King of heaven. We have the privilege of speaking on intimate terms with the most powerful, most holy Being in the universe.

It's like being invited to hang out in the Oval Office of the White House. You're not there to order the President around; you're just there because he likes to listen to you and you know he can help you with your problems.

*Thy kingdom come. Thy will be done in earth, as it is in heaven.*

These sentences remind us of two things that should hang over every Christian's life like an umbrella:

1. We want God's plan, the best possible choice in any situation, to be followed, and

2. This world is coming to an end someday soon, and God's kingdom will be set up.

*Give us this day our daily bread.*

God will supply our needs. This part of the prayer includes more than just food. God knows we need daily doses of friendship and love too.

When we pray the way Jesus taught us, we are reminded not only of how much we should depend on God, but also of how much He loves us.

*And forgive us our debts, as we forgive our debtors.*

The meaning of these words is clear. Not only do we need forgiveness, but we need to forgive others. The next two verses after the Lord's Prayer in Matthew 6 spell it out. If we forgive others who wrong us, then our Father in heaven will forgive us. If we don't, He doesn't.

This isn't just a rule God made up. It has to do with attitude. A person who will not forgive is not in an attitude to receive forgiveness. They'll never really believe that God could forgive them if they can't forgive another.

*And lead us not into temptation, but deliver us from evil:*

In today's words, we would say, "Protect us from temptation; give us the power to escape sin." If we pray, we can

have the strength to deal with temptations that would blow us away otherwise.

*For thine is the kingdom, and the power, and the glory, for ever. Amen.*

Finally, a reminder that there is no end to God's power or His kingdom and that He has invited us to share in both. The primary purpose of prayer is to focus our eyes on Calvary and remember, "If God is for us, who can be against us? He who did not spare his own Son, but gave him up for us all— how will he not also, along with him, graciously give us all things?" (Romans 8:31, 32, NIV).

## WHY BOTHER TO PRAY?

What difference does it make whether or not you pray? After all, God knows what you are thinking anyway. He knows what you need. Why pray?

The purpose of prayer is one of the most misunderstood aspects of being a Christian. We like to think that when we pray, it does something to God. The truth is, when we pray, it does something to us. Prayer doesn't bring God down to us; it brings us up to Him.

It goes back to that idea

**152**

that prayer is about relationships. When we choose to pray, to communicate with God, we are choosing to grow a relationship. A person can only have a real relationship with God, with spiritual life and energy, by actually talking to God. And that doesn't mean reciting verses back to Him or chanting the same old words all the time. It means saying something about our real lives, about things that really matter to us.

Prayer is opening your heart up to God as you would to a friend. It means talking about the things that really matter to you. It means sharing your dreams and your anger. You cannot hurt God by expressing honest feelings. You can only hurt Him by pretending to feel good or pretending to be religious, or worse, by not speaking to Him at all.

But how can you have a relationship with a friend who doesn't actually speak to you?

You've heard those radio talk shows that ask people to phone in. They get to ask some famous or interesting person a question or make a comment, and then they hang up and listen to the DJ or his guest respond to it.

Prayer is a little like that. You can talk to God and ask Him questions. But then you have to sit back and wait for a response. God doesn't usually speak out loud to us. We have to wait and watch and listen.

That's what makes Bible study and quiet meditation

such an important part of being a Christian. When we are concentrating on God's words in the Bible or thinking about God and His plans for us, He can speak to our minds. Sometimes, it's just a thought or an impression. Sometimes, the words of a friend answer a question we prayed about. Often, the words of Scripture say exactly what we need to hear.

In those ways, God speaks to us and responds to our

prayers. We miss His answers if we feel we are too busy to sit and quietly think or too busy to spend time with His Word, the Bible.

For prayer to make a real difference in our lives, there are five things we need:

1. We need to recognize that we need God's help. If we don't feel a need for help, we won't ask. Asking doesn't change God's mind about helping us; it changes our attitude about receiving His help.

2. We need to start clearing the path between us and God. If other things come first or keep us away from Him, then our first prayers should be for His power to clear those things away.

3. We need to have faith, to believe that God can and will help us. Sometimes it seems impossible to really believe. But if all we can do is truly want to believe God, then He will give us faith.

4. We need to forgive others. Then our attitude will allow us to accept God's forgiveness and help.

5. We need to hang tough with God. We don't succeed in prayer by praying harder or longer. We only succeed by having patience and determination to keep talking to God, no matter how we feel or what others think.

A growing Christian wants to pray in faith. It's not a give-me-what-I-need-now prayer. It's a here's-what-I-need prayer that trusts God to take care of things in the way that He sees best.

God always answers the prayer of faith. Sometimes He says Yes. With some requests, He always answers Yes. A prayer for help in understanding spiritual truth or a prayer for more faith is always answered Yes. And in many other cases, God sends the solution to a problem right away.

Sometimes, God answers No to a prayer of faith. You wouldn't agree to buy a big ice-cream cone for your little brother after he had eaten two bags of greasy popcorn just before he goes on a roller coaster. As much as he might think he wants the ice cream, you know what will probably happen when his stomach loops the loops around with the roller coaster.

In the same way, God sometimes knows better than to give us what we ask for. He knows what will only bring us trouble. So sometimes He says No. And if we knew what He knows, we'd be happy He did.

Often the answer to a prayer is Wait. God's plans and His timing are far better than ours. The growing Christian can trust God to work things out at the best possible time.

The secret to a Christian's peace of mind is knowing that God can be trusted to work things out for the best and leaving it all in His hands.

A real prayer life is what makes the difference between a happy Christian and someone who's just going through the motions. Too many Christians seem miserable about the things they believe and are determined to make sure others are also. Knowing that you can really talk to God and that you can really trust Him is what being a Christian is all about.

 ## Memory Focus

"Our Father which art in heaven, Hallowed be thy name. Thy kingdom come. Thy will be done on earth, as it is in heaven. Give us this day our daily bread. And forgive us our debts, as we forgive our debtors. And lead us not into temptation, but deliver us from evil: for thine is the kingdom, and the power, and the glory, for ever. Amen" (Matthew 6:9-13, KJV).

 Into the Bible

1. Jesus had a lot to say about prayer in Matthew 6. Read through verses 5 through 8, and answer these questions:
   A. Where do the hypocrites pray?
   B. Why do they pray there?
   C. Does this mean we shouldn't pray in public? What does it mean?
   D. Where should we pray?
   E. Why should we pray there?
   F. How do the heathen pray?
   G. Why do they pray that way?
   H. Why do we not need to pray as they do?
2. Each of the following verses mentions an important ingredient to having a strong prayer life. Read each reference, and write down the ingredient mentioned.
   A. Matthew 7:7
   B. Hebrews 11:6
   C. Matthew 6:14, 15
   D. Colossians 4:2
   E. Jude 20
3. The Bible contains many stories of people who prayed and how God answered their prayers. Read the texts indicated on the worksheet provided by your teacher; then, for each, do the following: record who prayed, what they prayed for, and how God answered their prayer.

 Projects

1. The Lord's Prayer in Matthew 6:9-13 is not a chart to learn; it is a pattern to teach us how to pray. Read the prayer in three different translations. Consider the meaning of each verse (refer to the lesson if you need help). Then write your own

paraphrase of the Lord's Prayer. Personalize it so that it becomes your own prayer.

2. Do many people seem to misunderstand prayer? Would it be helpful if there really were courses on prayer, like those in the story at the beginning of the lesson? Individually or in groups as assigned by your teacher, make a list of five prayer courses you think most people at your school could use. Include a name for the course and a description of what should be taught.

3. Keep a prayer journal for two weeks on the form your teacher will give you. Each time you pray, list on that form the following information:
   A. What I told God I was thankful for.
   B. What I told God I needed or needed help with.
   C. How I think God responded.

 # Focus Questions

1. Is there a certain correct way to pray? Explain.
2. What does it mean to say, "Prayer is about relationships"?
3. Since God knows what you're thinking anyway, what difference does it make whether or not you pray?
4. Can your relationship with God really be like a friendship? How is it the same? How is it different?
5. The lesson gave five things we need in order for prayer to make a real difference in our lives. Which do you think is the most important? Why?
6. What is a prayer of faith?
7. How can a Christian be just as happy with a No answer to a prayer as with a Yes answer?
8. How is prayer related to a Christian's peace of mind?

# PRESENCE

**Have no fear about tomorrow. God is already there** *(Quips and Quotes).*

# Miracles: Wonders of God

**Lesson Scriptures: Mark 2:1-12;
John 9:1-41**

NTRODUCTION
"Let me see if I got this straight, Simeon," the Pharisee said. "You've been blind all your life, and suddenly you can see. You expect us to believe that?"

"It happened last Sabbath. I was standing there on the street, begging, when a man named Jesus rubbed mud on my eyes. He told me to go wash it off. When I did, I could see."

"Now, you know very well that the man who did this cannot be from God, since he did it on the Sabbath," one man flatly stated.

Another one was not so sure. "But if he's not from God, where does he get this power to do good?"

"It could be a trick of the devil," the Pharisee said. "What do you think, Simeon?"

"I think he's from God," Simeon said with cautious conviction.

Frowning, one of the other Pharisees shook his head. "I'm not convinced that this man was ever really blind. Let's ask his parents."

Simeon's parents were called in, and the inquiry began. "Is this your son? The one who was born blind?"

"Yes."

"So how do you explain the fact that now he can see?"

Dad whispered to Mom, "We must answer this very carefully. If we say that we believe Jesus healed him, then they will say that we are followers of Jesus and throw us out of the synagogue. Don't say anything.

I have a plan."

Turning to the Pharisees, he said, "We know he is our son. We know that he was born blind. We know that he can now see. But we don't know how it happened. Ask him; he is old enough to speak for himself."

So they called Simeon back in. "You must swear to tell us the truth!" the Pharisee shouted. "We know that the man who healed you is not from God. He doesn't even keep the Sabbath. Admit it. He is from Satan! He is a sinner."

With unshakable conviction, Simeon stood his ground. "I don't know if he was from God or from Satan. But there's one thing I do know. I was blind, but now I can see."

"What magic did he do?" a man asked. "How did he cure you?"

"I've already told you that, and you wouldn't listen. Why do you want me to tell you again? Do you want to become his disciples too?"

A ripple of angry scoffs and cynical laughter bathed the room. "Simeon, you must be a disciple of his already. But we are disciples of Moses, and we know how to keep the Sabbath. And we know a fake miracle

when we see one." The Pharisee threw up his hands.

"Fake?" Simeon shouted. "I can see! This man opened my eyes. No one has ever been cured of blindness. He has to be from God! Only God could do this."

The Pharisees sat smugly as one of them insultingly replied, "You were born blind because you are a sinner. Are you trying to teach us? Gentlemen, I move that we throw this fellow out."

Do miracles really happen? If they ever happened in the past, do they still happen today? And if they do, how can we know who caused them?

If you look up the word *miracle* in the dictionary, you would find that the definition includes the following: anything that cannot be explained by common sense, experience, or the scientific method; an extraordinary, anomalous, or abnormal event brought about by superhuman agency.

In other words, something happened here that we don't understand and can't explain. There are basically four attitudes or beliefs people hold about miracles.

1. There are no such things as miracles. So-called "mira-

cles" can be explained as coincidences or exaggerations of the facts. Everything that happens can be explained in clear scientific terms. For example, the star over Bethlehem was simply a comet that happened to be in the sky at that time. From the east, where the wise men were, it may have appeared to be over Israel.

2. Miracles are rare, completely unexplained, and impossible to comprehend. This would include the creation of the world and the incarnation of Jesus, when God became a human. Most other "supernatural" events can be explained if all the facts are known and the distortions of time and enthusiasm are taken into account. For example, the walls of Jericho falling down could be explained as the result of an earthquake that occurred in the area at that time.

3. Miracles are direct acts of God that alter natural law. To help His people or to save someone, God steps in and changes what would normally happen. For example, feeding five thousand people with a few loaves and fishes is impossible, unless God overrides natural law.

4. Miracles are direct acts of God in harmony with higher laws that we don't know about or understand. For example, when the first airplanes flew, some called them "bewitched tools of the devil." After all, the natural laws they knew about were based on the premise that objects heavier than air could not fly. (The law of gravity makes objects fall.) But, obviously, there were other natural laws that hadn't been discovered yet. In the same way, when Jesus raised Lazarus from the dead, He used a law that restores life, a law that we don't know about or understand.

Seventh-day Adventists believe that while God sometimes works in a supernatural way (above and beyond the natural realm), He never acts in a way that violates His moral laws. We believe that the universe is constructed around laws that reflect God's character and love. So when miracles occur, and we believe they do, they happen as God acts in harmony with higher laws.

## MIRACLES—INSIDE AND OUT

To a Christian, miracles aren't limited to someone being healed from a disease or surviving a car crash. In many cases, the miracle is not so much the event itself as it is the effect that event has on the minds of the people involved.

Michael, who had left his Christianity behind years ago, was involved in a serious car accident. The patrolmen said it was a miracle that he came out alive. That day, Michael rededicated himself to God. Since then, he has faithfully tried to follow God's plan for his life.

So which is the miracle? What happened to Michael during the car wreck or what happened to him afterward?

Christians recognize God's ability to perform not only physical miracles but spiritual ones as well. A broken home healed by God's love; a selfish, sinful life converted by the power of the gospel; a bitter child who is finally able to forgive an abusive parent—any one of these is as much a miracle as Peter walking on water!

Another example is the story in Mark 2:1-12. When a large crowd in the home where Jesus was talking prevented four friends from getting their paralyzed friend to Jesus, they cut a hole in the ceiling and lowered him down. Of course, this interrupted the meeting. Jesus saw how strongly the four men believed that He could heal their friend. And He knew the paralyzed man was feeling

intense guilt because his lifestyle had led to this disease and his condition. How amazed the man must have been when he heard Jesus say, "Your sins are forgiven."

The Jewish teachers of the law were astounded. *Teacher, you can't do that*, they thought. *Nobody can forgive sins except God.*

Knowing what they were thinking, Jesus said, " 'Which is easier: to say to the paralytic,

"Your sins are forgiven," or to say "Get up . . . and walk"? . . . "The Son of Man has authority on earth to forgive sins.' " Then turning to the paralyzed man, Jesus said, " 'I tell you, get up, take your mat and go home.' He got up, took his mat and walked out in full view of them all. This amazed everyone and they praised God, saying, 'We have never seen anything like this!' " (Mark 2:11, 12, NIV).

## THE MAN BEYOND THE MIRACLE

Each of Jesus' miracles had a purpose. John's Gospel calls them "signs" that pointed to Jesus. The miracles helped those who were healed or resurrected. But, as the above story of the paralytic shows, the real purpose of the miracles was to draw people to Jesus. This concept of "miracles as signs pointing to Jesus" helps us understand why there were so many miracles at the beginning of Jesus' ministry. Because miracles catch people's attention and stir up curiosity, the early miracles of Jesus' ministry announced the coming of the Messiah. God was breaking into the world, changing the water of legalism into the wine of the gospel. Jesus was restoring the Sabbath to a day of healing and freedom instead of a day of restriction and confinement. These were some of the ways miracles pointed to Jesus. This is why the religious leaders became so angry with Jesus and were so offended by His actions. Miracles involved faith—faith in Jesus.

Unfortunately, too many of the people turned away from faith. They were attracted to the signpost (miracle) but never came to Jesus. They saw the signs, but they didn't get the message. Their trust in themselves prevented them from truly knowing the Man beyond the miracle.

## MIRACLES FROM ANOTHER SOURCE

Not all miraculous, supernatural occurrences are caused by God. Satan can produce counterfeit miracles. He understands natural laws that human beings have not even imagined.

A good example of Satan's miraculous powers is the story in 1 Samuel 28. When King Saul visited the witch of Endor, he asked to speak to the prophet Samuel. The witch called up a spirit who told Saul

he would die the next day.

Was it really the spirit of Samuel? No, it was a supernatural trick performed by Satan. Since Saul had turned away from God, he was open to Satan's deceptions. So Satan, or one of his evil angels, appeared to be Samuel and pushed the king over the edge mentally.

Satan continued to work demonic miracles in Jesus' time. Jesus healed many people who were possessed by demons. Jesus warned that this would continue to the end. "False Christs and false prophets will appear and perform great signs and miracles to deceive even the elect—if that were possible" (Matthew 24:24, NIV). Since genuine miracles point to Jesus, Satan does everything in his power to turn people away from Christ.

So, how can we tell the difference between God's miracles and those performed by Satan?

Fortunately, one of the gifts of the Holy Spirit given to the church is the ability to distinguish between spirits, to tell whether someone works with God or with Satan (see 1 Corinthians 12:10). And we have these guidelines to help us decide.

1. Do the ones performing miracles believe in Jesus as the Saviour and Son of God? First John 4:1-3 says that they must if they are from God.

2. Do they live according to God's law? First John 2:4 says that anyone who claims to follow Jesus without following His law is a liar. Test everything (1 Thessalonians 5:21). Compare people's words and their actions to the teachings of the Bible. God is not going to send someone to do His miracles who, at the same time, disregards His Word.

3. Base your decision and your beliefs on your own study of Scripture (1 Peter 3:15). Don't settle for what someone else tells you the Bible says.

Suppose a friend of yours tells you about a faith healer who claims to even heal people with AIDS. The healer says that God sent him to heal people and to teach them that sex is an act of love and should be shared freely without guilt. What if his miracles were real and people really were healed? Would you be able to believe this person was from God?

**164**

## DEMANDING A MIRACLE

Although Jesus did many miracles, the Jewish leaders refused to believe that He was the Messiah, the One sent from God. To test Him, they demanded a miracle. "Other prophets have done miracles to prove they were from God. Do one for us now if you really are from God," they said.

Jesus just sighed and shook His head. Miracles had been happening all around Him since His birth, but they refused to recognize them. He said to them:

" 'You know how to interpret the appearance of the sky, but you cannot interpret the signs of the times. A wicked and adulterous generation looks for a miraculous sign, but none will be given it except the sign of Jonah.' Jesus then left them and went away" (Matthew 16:3, 4, NIV).

In unconditional love, Jesus provided one last miracle—the greatest of all—His death and resurrection. He was God on a cross reaching out to embrace lost humanity. It was He—the Saviour who conquered death, emptied a tomb, and has turned graveyards into rest stops. No wonder the disciple John concludes, "These are written that you may believe that Jesus is the Christ, the Son of God, and that by believing you may have life in his name" (John 20:31, NIV).

# Memory Focus

"He said to the paralytic, 'I tell you, get up, take your mat and go home.' He got up, took his mat and walked out in full view of them all. This amazed everyone and they praised God, saying, 'We have never seen anything like this!' " (Mark 2:10b-12, NIV).

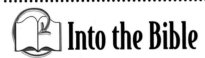

# Into the Bible

1. The prophet Elijah participated in the incredible miracle on Mt. Carmel, when God miraculously sent fire from heaven to burn up a sacrifice, the altar, and even the water around it. Read the following texts, and describe what happened after the events on Mt. Carmel.

A. 1 Kings 19:1-5. Write a description of Elijah's condition.
B. 1 Kings 19:5-9. Describe what miracle God worked for Elijah.
C. 1 Kings 19:5, 6, 9. How does Elijah respond, and why?
D. 1 Kings 19:11, 12. What are three of the powerful forces of nature that God used to reveal Himself?
E. God finally revealed Himself to Elijah in a gentle whisper. At this time, when Elijah was depressed, God spoke to him through a whisper, not a miracle. Why do you think God chose this approach?
F. List three ways God might whisper to you in your life.

2. Read Luke 8:26-39. Answer the following questions.
   A. What miracle takes place in this story?
   B. What does this story teach you about the character of Jesus and the character of Satan?
   C. What does the experience of the pigs teach us about the end result of devil possession?
   D. When they saw what Jesus had done, what did the people ask Jesus to do? Why do you think they asked Him to do this?
   E. What did Jesus tell the healed man to do?
   F. What do you think Jesus wants you to do about what He has done in your life?

3. Study these miracles of Jesus. Write down the response of those who witnessed each event.
   A. Mark 1:21-28       D. Mark 6:53-56
   B. Mark 1:40-45       E. Mark 7:31-37
   C. Mark 3:1-6         F. Mark 10:46-53

4. Summarize what each of these verses says about discerning whether or not miracles are from God.
   A. 1 John 2:4, 5
   B. 1 John 4:1-3
   C. 1 Thessalonians 5:21
   D. 1 Peter 3:15

 **Projects**

1. Examine some modern-day examples of people who claim to be used by God to perform miracles. Do the following:
   A. Locate stories in newspapers, magazines, etc., that describe what are reported to be modern-day miracles from God.

B. Analyze each "miracle," using the guidelines provided in this lesson to discern whether the miracle is genuine.

C. Share the stories and your conclusions with the class.

2. Interview someone, or read about someone, who believes they have witnessed a miracle, or tell about a miracle you have witnessed. Give the reasons why you, or they, think it was miraculous. Why do you, or they, believe God performed the miracle?

3. Divide the class into small groups. Each group can act out one of the following miracles. Each group should emphasize why this miracle took place.

A. The paralyzed man (Mark 2:1-12)

B. The invalid at Bethesda (John 5:1-15)

C. The widow's son raised (Luke 7:11-17)

D. The demoniac in the synagogue (Mark 1:21-28)

4. The transformation in the life of a person who becomes a Christian is a miracle too. What evidences should there be of this miracle of conversion?

 # Focus Questions

1. Do miracles still happen today?

2. Why do you think Jesus did more miracles at the beginning of His ministry than at the end?

3. What do you think most Seventh-day Adventists believe about miracles?

4. Which is the greater miracle: changing a person's heart or healing his or her body?

5. How can being forgiven be the same as being healed?

6. Why does Satan have power to do miracles?

7. Why wouldn't Jesus work a miracle when the leaders asked for one?

8. Can a "fake" healer be used by God to perform a genuine miracle if the person involved has faith in God?

9. Why do you think God sometimes miraculously heals one person but does not heal another one, even though they both have faith?

10. Why do you think the Gospel of John uses the term *signs* to refer to miracles? In what ways are miracles like signs?

11. Why do you think Jesus sometimes told people not to tell anyone about a miracle He performed, such as the experience in Mark 5:43?

12. How long does faith that is based solely on miracles last?

# VALUES
### A task worth doing and friends worth knowing make life worth living
*(Quips and Quotes).*

# lesson 18

# Parables: The Windows of God

## Lesson Scriptures: Matthew 18, 20, 22, 25; Luke 10, 12, 14, 15, 18

**AY I HAVE YOUR ATTENTION?** The sanctuary doors opened slowly. Every head turned to catch a glimpse of the radiant bride, swathed in satin and lace, clutching her father's arm as they began their walk down the aisle.

Mrs. Casey, the organist, opened the appropriate stops and played the first majestic bars of the familiar wedding march. Everyone in the audience silently hummed along.

As the bride and her father neared the podium, the groom stepped forward and took the bride's arm in his own. With this ritual exchange completed, they turned to the minister, and the wedding proceeded the way all weddings do—a vocal solo, lighting of candles, homily, vows, kiss, presentation of the new couple, recessional. No surprises. Just a familiar rehearsal of a well-known ceremony.

Or so everyone thought.

When the ushers dismissed the last row of guests, Mrs. Casey turned off the organ and gathered up her music and went to the back of the church to the little booth where her husband was manning the PA system. "Well, that went off without a hitch, didn't it?" she asked in an offhand way.

"You must be kidding!" Mr. Casey said. "I still can't believe he said that."

"What on earth are you talking about?" his astonished wife asked.

"The minister. Didn't you hear what he said?"

"Hear what?" Mrs. Casey's anxiety was keeping pace with her curiosity.

"Come here. I'll show you." Mr. Casey started rewinding the tape he had just made of the wedding service. "I may be mistaken, but I'm sure I heard the minister say something he never meant to say. Now listen," he said when he found the right spot in the homily.

"And now, Rachel and Dan," the minister said, "do you promise, in the presence of these thine enemies, to love . . ."

Mr. Casey pressed the stop button. Suddenly he and his wife found themselves giggling uncontrollably over the minister's unwitting fusion of the marriage vows with the twenty-third Psalm. When they thought about it, it was an easy mistake to make, especially if you're nervous. The truly amazing thing was that only one person seemed to notice it.

You can hardly blame the audience for not pricking up their ears at this simple slip of the tongue. After all, they'd heard the exchange of wedding vows a hundred times before. Each one of them could probably recite the entire service word for word.

Instead, their minds were engaged elsewhere, even as their faces expressed rapt attention: *Isn't that flower girl darling? I wonder if my husband signed the guest book. I've got to find out when the term paper is due. That bridesmaid must be six inches taller than her escort. No one's getting me into a tux for my daughter's wedding. I sure hope they have something to eat at the reception.*

People in Jesus' time were no different. Placed in familiar situations, they put their minds in neutral or heard what they wanted to hear. When it came to messages from the Lord, they thought they had heard it all and had nothing to learn. They could listen to John the Baptist or Jesus for hours on end and never comprehend what they heard.

"You will be ever hearing but never understanding; you will be ever seeing but never perceiving. For this people's heart has become calloused; they hardly hear with their ears, and they have closed their eyes. Otherwise they might see with their eyes, hear with their ears, understand with their hearts and turn, and I would heal them" (Matthew 13:14, 15, NIV).

Repent? You must mean someone else. I'm one of the chosen people, a son of Abraham. What do you mean, "It is right to do good on the Sabbath"? Don't you know the laws? Your kingdom is not of this world? Then you can't be the Messiah.

To cut through all these preconceived ideas and capture His audience's attention, Jesus had to use radical methods.

Most often, He used parables to open a window into God's kingdom and let a little light into dark, closed minds.

When Jesus spoke to people about the kingdom of God, He had to use common words and images from everyday life—things from their world to explain things of His world. In its most basic form, a parable is a story illustrating a principle of God's kingdom in language anyone can grasp.

Jesus also knew that everyone loves a story. So as He taught, He told stories, using situations, objects, and characters His listeners would be familiar with. Not only could they identify personally with what He was saying, but in the future, His words would echo in their minds whenever they saw bread rising in the oven, when they passed a field of mustard plants waving in the breeze, or when they watched a farmer sowing wheat on a hillside.

Parables forced Jesus' audience to think, because the meaning behind a parable is not immediately clear. You have to work it over a bit to understand fully. How is the kingdom of heaven like a mustard seed?

How is it like a lost coin?

Jesus' parables had one other function too. Among the crowds listening to Him wherever He went were His enemies. Good, Sabbath-keeping, tithe-paying church leaders, but enemies just the same. Jesus knew that some of His hearers were not there to find truth but to find fault. Through parables, Jesus could teach without giving these spies any reason to accuse Him. Instead of saying something inflammatory like, "There will always be evil people in the church," He could tell the para-ble of the enemy who plants weeds in a wheat field. By the time His enemies figured out He was talking about them, He often would be someplace else.

Jesus' parables come alive and ring with truth today, just as they did when they were first told. They cut through our short attention spans, our ready-made notions, our shallow beliefs, and open a window on the kingdom of God. If we open our minds to them, they still have the power to plant mustard seeds of faith in the stony ground of our hearts.

# Memory Focus

"Jesus spoke all these things to the crowd in parables; he did not say anything to them without using a parable" (Matthew 13:34, NIV).

# Into the Bible

1. This activity covers ten parables of Jesus in the order in which He gave them. You are to read the parables and complete the worksheet provided by your teacher.
2. The Sower and the Seed. Read Matthew 13:3-23. Use the worksheet provided by your teacher to record details about the groups described in the parable.

3. Read Matthew 13:24-30, 36-43—the Wheat and the Tares.
   A. Identify the central meaning.
   B. What trick is played on the sower?
   C. Why doesn't the landowner weed his field?
   D. What happens to the wheat?

 **Projects**

1. Rewrite one of Jesus' parables in modern English.
2. Write your own parable to illustrate a spiritual truth. Use these suggestions if you need to:
   A. graduation is like the second coming
   B. taking a test is like handling temptation
   C. friendship is like a relationship with Jesus
   D. garbage is like sin

3. A. Write out a parable or a short story that you have heard during a religious service.
   B. Summarize what you think was the main lesson the parable or short story was trying to teach.

 **Focus Questions**

1. Do you think it was easier in biblical times to focus people's minds on spiritual matters? Is it easier today? Why?
2. If Jesus came to your school for a Week of Spiritual Emphasis (Week of Prayer), do you think you would find His parables interesting? Why or why not?

CROSSROADS SERIES

# unit

# 3

# Jesus and His People

# Jesus' Ministry

Unit three deals with the later ministry of Jesus' life and the mounting rejection by the Jewish leaders and people. The reasons for their rejection and misunderstandings are analyzed in light of their interpretation of Scripture and national heritage.

The unit examines how the feeding of the five thousand and the confession of Peter became the turning point in Christ's ministry. It also examines how the raising of Lazarus marked the beginning of the end.

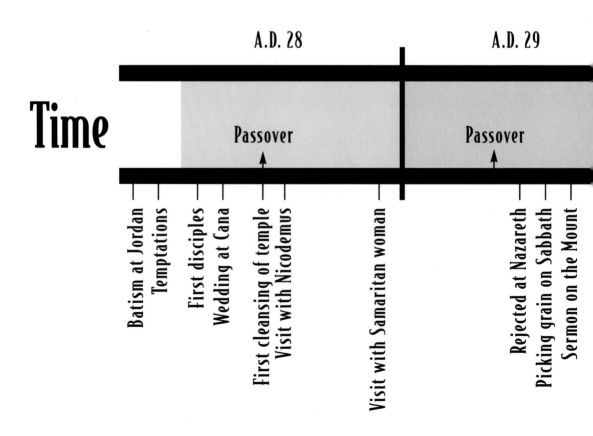

A.D. 28

A.D. 29

## Time

Passover

Passover

Batism at Jordan

Temptations

First disciples

Wedding at Cana

First cleansing of temple

Visit with Nicodemus

Visit with Samaritan woman

Rejected at Nazareth

Picking grain on Sabbath

Sermon on the Mount

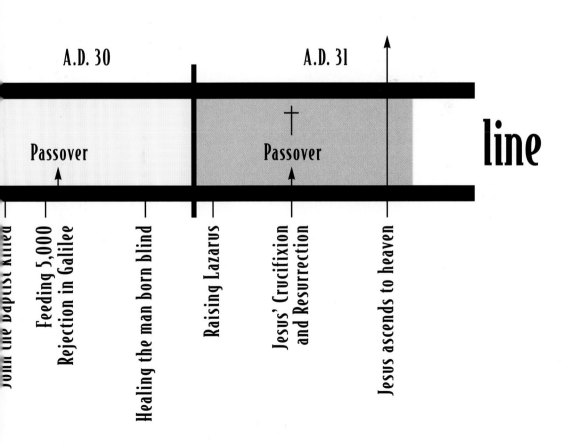

A.D. 30

A.D. 31

Passover

Passover

line

John the Baptist killed

Feeding 5,000
Rejection in Galilee

Healing the man born blind

Raising Lazarus

Jesus' Crucifixion
and Resurrection

Jesus ascends to heaven

# TODAY

The best time to do something worthwhile is between yesterday and tomorrow (Unknown).

# lesson 19

# The Turning Point

**Lesson Scriptures: John 6:1-69;
Matthew 16:13-28**

Picture this. Leaning on a cane, an old man walks toward an open grave. His gray hair is matted, his wrinkled face drawn with anxiety. He stands at the edge of the grave and looks back on the long pathway of his life. He recalls that when he was young, he came to a fork in the road. Now, when it is too late, he knows that one road led to prosperity and the other to failure and disappointment. He knows that he chose the wrong road, and in bitter anguish he cries out, "If only I could be at the crossroads again!"

His cry awakens him from sleep. He sits up and stares at his hands, which are not wrinkled with age. His hair is not tangled and gray. There isn't a cane in sight. When this young man realizes it was just a bad dream, he shouts, "Thank God, I'm still at the crossroads!"

It isn't just in dreams that we come across forks in the road. We encounter them daily, some big and some small, each time we make a decision. If we are wise, we will remember that there are no small decisions, only ones that look that way at the time.

Jesus had His share of crossroads—His temptations in the wilderness, His struggle in Gethsemane—and so did His disciples. There must have been many times when their faith was tested by the nagging question "Is this really the Messiah?"

Perhaps the most crucial

turning point for all of them came on a secluded hillside near the city of Caesarea Philippi, north of Galilee. As Jesus was talking with His disciples, He suddenly confronted them with a very direct question: "Who do men say that I, the Son of Man, am?" (Matthew 16:13, NKJV). Jesus regularly asked His disciples thought-provoking questions; this might have been just one more of the same. To understand why this question represented a turning point in Jesus' ministry and in the disciples' faith, we need to look at some of the events that led up to it.

A few months earlier, Jesus had taken His disciples to a quiet place along the eastern border of Galilee. He needed to rest and spend time alone with them. But when the people heard where Jesus had gone, they followed Him, bringing their sick to be healed. The Bible says that when Jesus saw the vast throng, He felt compassion for them, forgot about His need for rest and privacy, and began to heal the sick (see Matthew 14:14).

Hours later it was getting dark and the crowds were hungry, the disciples urged Jesus to send them all home. But again, Jesus showed compassion. He performed a miracle and fed a crowd of over five thousand by multiplying a boy's lunch of five barley loaves and two small fishes. There was so much food, the disciples collected twelve baskets of leftovers when everyone was done (see John 6:1-14, NIV).

This is the only miracle recorded in all four Gospels. That shows how significant it was in Jesus' ministry and in the minds of His followers. Jesus had wanted to spend time alone with His disciples, teaching them about the real spiritual nature of His ministry and the work they had to prepare for. Instead, He spent most of the day meeting the needs of a multitude of near strangers. Still, it didn't keep Jesus from teaching His disciples a valuable lesson; it just took a little longer.

What Jesus wanted His disciples to learn from the miracle of the loaves and fishes was to depend on God rather than on themselves. They had to see that they alone couldn't satisfy the spiritual and physical needs of the people. They could lead the sick to Jesus for healing. They could bring Jesus the boy's

lunch. But they couldn't do the healing and feeding by themselves. God alone can heal, transform, and save.

But the disciples, and the multitude who were fed, misunderstood what happened that day. When they saw the sick healed and the hungry fed so miraculously, they were dazzled by the earthly, political potential of such power. Caught up in a frenzy, they tried to force Jesus to be their king. Even the disciples were caught up in this misguided conspiracy. They imagined throwing the Romans out of their country and installing themselves in positions of power in a Jewish kingdom where Jesus reigned as king.

Jesus knew what the disciples and the crowd were plotting and took immediate action. He realized that they had listened for months to everything He had said without understanding for a moment that His mission was spiritual, not political. So He sent the crowds home and told His disciples to get in their boat and sail to the other side of the Sea of Galilee. When everyone was gone, He went up into the hills by Himself to pray for the power to finally get through His followers' prejudices and ambi-

tions and make them understand that His mission on earth would end in a way they could hardly imagine. He prayed for the Holy Spirit to broaden their minds so their faith would not fail them when events spun out of their control.

The next day, after a night of dramatic miracles at sea, Jesus spoke to His followers again and explained the meaning of what they had witnessed. When they asked Him why He wouldn't be their king, "Jesus answered, 'I tell you the truth, you are looking for me, not because you saw miraculous signs but because you ate the loaves and had your fill. Do not work for food that spoils, but for food that endures to eternal life, which the Son of Man will give you. On him God the Father has placed his seal of approval.'

"Then they asked him, 'What must we do to do the works God requires?'

"Jesus answered, 'The work of God is this: to believe in the one he has sent . . . I am the bread of life. He who comes to me will never go hungry, and he who believes in me will never be thirsty. . . . For my Father's will is that everyone who looks to the Son and believes in him shall have eternal life, and I will raise him up at the last day' " (John 6:26-29, 35, 40, NIV).

When the people realized that Jesus' goal was spiritual, not to reward them with power and riches, they quickly lost interest. Many turned away and stopped following Him. The twelve disciples reassured Jesus that they had faith in Him and would never abandon Him, but it was obvious to Jesus that their faith was shaky. If the events of the last two days had rocked their faith, Jesus thought, what would happen when the really terrible test came? How would they feel when they saw clearly that Jesus' work would culminate in His death? Jesus knew that their hopes for honor and power in an earthly kingdom had left

them unprepared for the shocking events just ahead.

In the next few months, as He prayed for His disciples and agonized over their future, Jesus must have realized He'd reached a turning point in His ministry. It was time to shake His disciples out of their unrealistic hopes and confront them with what it really meant to follow the Messiah. It was time to prepare them for a death on the cross, not a reign on the throne. Which brings us back to where we started—a secluded hillside north of Galilee, where Jesus asked that crucial questions, "Who do men say that I, the Son of Man, am?" (Matthew 16:13, NKJV).

In the scripture study with this lesson, you will discover what Jesus revealed to the disciples for the first time and their astonished reaction. You will also examine what this means to us today. Perhaps we still have mistaken ideas about Jesus' work and His will for our lives. Maybe we're just as unclear about these things as the disciples were. Maybe we still have a lot to learn, just as they did. Who knows? Maybe this lesson can be a turning point for us too.

 **Memory Focus**

"Then Jesus said to his disciples, 'If anyone would come after me, he must deny himself and take up his cross and follow me. For whoever wants to save his life will lose it, but whoever loses his life for me will find it' " (Matthew 16:24, 25, NIV).

OR

"I tell you the truth, he who believes has everlasting life" (John 6:47, NIV).

 **Into the Bible**

1. Matthew 16:13-28 records what happened when Jesus asked His disciples the crucial question about who people said He was. Read these verses, and answer the following questions:
   A. How did the disciples answer Jesus' question about who people said He was?
   B. What did Jesus ask next, and what was Peter's reply?
   C. When Peter said that Jesus was "the Christ," Jesus responded by making three points. What were they?
   D. What unusual warning did Jesus give His disciples?
   E. What startling news did Jesus reveal to His disciples for the first time?
   F. How did Peter react to Jesus' shocking announcement? What was Jesus' reply to Peter?
   G. A week before He died, Jesus told His disciples once again of His impending suffering and death. How did they react that time? See Luke 18:31-34.
   H. What did Jesus clearly declare to His disciples?
2. When Jesus stated in Matthew 16:17-19 that He would build His church on a rock, what was He referring to? Among Christians, there are three generally accepted explanations:
   (A) The rock is *Peter*, spokesman and leader of the disciples.

(B) The rock is Peter's *declaration* that Jesus was the true Son of God.

(C) The rock is a symbol of *Jesus*, Saviour and Redeemer of the world.

All three of these explanations can't be true, but it's possible that more than one of them is correct. Read the following Bible texts, and discover for yourself what Moses, David, Luke, Paul, and Jesus have to say about "the rock" on which the church is grounded. Do the following:

A. Briefly explain or summarize each of the texts.
B. State which of the three explanations of the "rock" these texts support.
   (1) Deuteronomy 32:4
   (2) Psalm 18:2
   (3) Acts 4:8-12
   (4) 1 Corinthians 10:1-4
   (5) 1 Peter 2:4-8

 Projects

1. There are several pivotal events in Christ's ministry that lead up to the turning point. None is more significant than the feeding of the five thousand and its aftermath. In fact, the Bible says that following this episode, "many of his disciples turned back and no longer followed him" (John 6:66, NIV).

   You are a reporter for the *Jerusalem Times* newspaper. You have heard the exciting news about the feeding of the tremendous crowd in Galilee. You have been assigned to write a follow-up article to this most unusual incident. What you hear, see, and feel is recorded in John 6:25-52 and serves as the basis for your newspaper article. You may find the following questions helpful in putting together your story.

A. What do you discern as the main reason for the people seeking after Jesus?
B. What do you think are the key questions that the people are asking Jesus? How does Jesus reply?
C. In trying to explain His work, to what does Jesus compare Himself?
D. Why do you think the people reacted so negatively to what Jesus said? What do you see as the primary problem for the misunderstanding that occurred between Jesus and the people?
E. What are your personal conclusions to what you have heard and witnessed?

2. Summarize the Roman Catholic position on the "rock" of Matthew 16:17-19. Use the *SDA Bible Commentary*, volume 5, as a resource.

 Focus Questions

1. Why did Jesus ask His disciples who they thought He was?
2. Why was feeding the five thousand such an important miracle?
3. What did Jesus mean when He called Himself "the Bread of Life"?
4. What does it mean to deny yourself and "take up your cross and follow" Jesus? Why would you deny yourself? How can you do that and still have a wholesome self-esteem? What is the best motivation for denying yourself?
5. What did Jesus mean when He said that if you save your life, you will lose it, and if you lose your life for His sake, you will find it? How does Matthew 16:26 answer this question?
6. Can you think of modern examples of people who have gained the whole world, or at least a big chunk of it, but lost their souls in the process? Why do people choose such a lifestyle?

# GREATNESS

The measure of a man's greatness is not the number of servants he has but the number of people he serves *(Quips and Quotes)*.

# Formula for Greatness

**Lesson Scriptures: Matthew 18:1-6;
Mark 9:33-37; Luke 9:46-48;
Mark 10:35-45; Matthew 20:20-28**

**PHARISEE:**

Lord, over by the palm tree stands a genuine unwashed sinner. It's Levi-Matthew, publican from Capernaum, a stinking tax collector. He is a robber, thief, and collaborator with the Roman enemy. He represents all that is wrong with Your church, all the sinfulness You're coming to wipe away and clean out.

I pray You'll clean it away soon, for the stench of sin pollutes this house that bears Your name.

Lord, when I look at him, I am overwhelmed with the good life You have given for me to enjoy.

Every Monday and Thursday, I, as You have encouraged, drink only a little water, leave off all food, and pray to You thrice each hour. These are the days of my greatest pleasure. *Lord, You are good to me.*

When I receive my weekly payment and holy bonus from the Sanhedrin, I, as you have required, return exactly 10 percent to you as tithe. I also freely give an additional 3.724 percent to cover temple maintenance, widow feeding, poor-student scholarships, and candle wicks. That leaves an adequate amount for me and my family. *Lord, You are so good to me.*

Sovereign Lord, please accept my deepest, sincerest appreciation for Your great goodness to me. Instead of making me into a broken sinner like Levi-Matthew, You have made me holy. Your worthy

**187**

ambassador. Yes, Lord, You have chosen me as recipient of Your greatest blessings.

I congratulate You on the wisdom of Your choice.

*Lord, You are good to me.*

living. Waiting for Your goodness to fill the vacuum created by my sinful spirit. Calling for You to replace my desperation with Your smile of hope.

I have enjoyed being separated from You, living independently, powered by the strength of my own selfishness. But I enjoy it no longer—for I have seen You. And in Your glory I have seen the desperate uselessness of my life today and the delightful possibilities of tomorrow.

I bring the only gift You can accept from me, my need.

I pray for You to exchange that need for Your merciful acceptance. And I thank You for transforming me into Your servant, Your child.

*Lord, please, be good to me.*

**PUBLICAN:**

Father, I am unnerved by the whispers of hatred fluttering about me and so have come to You for safety. My clothes are poor, my smile is weak, and my life broken. But, Lord, Your love overwhelms me and draws me to You.

I stand here begging to be washed with Your mercy. Pleading for Your healing hands to cleanse the filth of my

The parable of the Pharisee and the tax collector makes clear God's estimate of true greatness. He commends the tax collector for sensing his need and begging for mercy. But, clearly, God is not pleased with a proud, egotistical heart, because it feels no need of Him. What is God's teaching on the subject of greatness? What does it take to be great in God's eyes? As we accept God's evalu-

ation of us in Christ, He sets us on the high road above human pride and self-centeredness.

There is another wonderful story about real greatness so well known among early Christians that all three Synoptic Gospels record it (Matthew 18:1-6; Mark 9:33-37; Luke 9:46-48). It's the story of bickering disciples vying for position, contrasted with the humility of a little child. There is Jesus, always in control, always saying what the disciples did not expect and yet most needed to hear. And there are the disciples—twelve men, constantly bewildered, usually saying all the wrong things, often acting like little kids, probably behaving as we would if we were in their place.

Meanwhile, Jesus' heart is heavy. He's trying to get through to His disciples the all-important issue of why He came to our world—to die for our sins. He desperately needs to communicate to them this news, so terrible and at the same time so wonderful, that He must suffer before He would (and we could) enter His glory. But the disciples' minds are set on an earthly, physical kingdom, and all they can think

about is money and fame and power.

Nearly every person in the world desires one of these three things, sometimes openly, sometimes secretly. The disciples were no different. They wanted the sort of greatness the world values. As they watched Jesus display divine power in His miracles; produce thousands of dollars' worth of food with a single, simple prayer; command the respect of thousands of people; and, with power they had never witnessed before, even bring the dead back to life; they had the same vision of grandeur and greatness we would have had if we had been in their places. They dreamed about their own rank and privilege in this new kingdom. Who would be vice-president? How about the secretary of defense?

Often the disciples would lag behind Jesus as they walked from village to village, and conversation would turn from the marvelous words and deeds and person of Jesus to rivalry and rank—who was the greatest among them? Their interest was in a physical kingdom of worldwide renown and the personal prestige that would fol-

low. Not until the other side of the cross would the disciples finally understand that Jesus' physical kingdom would not be ushered in until His second coming. It would be in heaven that streets would be paved with gold and there would be no more pain. But the kingdom that Jesus ushered in at His first coming was spiritual. What does that mean?

In Christ's first coming, God has provided complete forgiveness, peace with God, "every spiritual blessing in Christ" (Ephesians 1:3, NIV). When God gave us Christ, He took all heaven, wrapped it up in one gift, and gave it to us. Jesus came "to serve, and to give his life as a ransom for many" (Matthew 20:28, NIV).

The disciples wanted the physical dimension of God's kingdom more than the spiritual, while He wanted to give them both. But first things first. And in God's system of salvation, the spiritual kingdom precedes the physical, the cross before the crown.

## Memory Focus

"Not so with you. Instead, whoever wants to become great among you must be your servant, and whoever wants to be first must be your slave—just as the Son of Man did not come to be served, but to serve, and to give his life as a ransom for many" (Matthew 20:26-28, NIV).

# Into the Bible

1. Read Luke 18:9-14 about the Pharisee and the publican (tax collector) who went up to the temple to pray. Rewrite their prayers in your own words. The rewrite must assume that the prayers are being prayed in a Seventh-day Adventist church in modern times.

2. In Matthew, Mark, and Luke, Jesus uses a child to illustrate greatness in His kingdom. Read Matthew 18:1-5; Mark 9:33-37; and Luke 9:46-48, and answer the following questions:

   A. According to Matthew 18:1-5, why did Jesus use a child as an example to answer the disciples' question, "Who is the greatest in the kingdom of heaven"?

   B. In your opinion, what are three positive characteristics of a child that reveal the characteristics of a person considered great in God's eyes?

   C. What were the disciples arguing about? Mark 9:33, 34; Luke 9:46.

   D. How did Jesus' use of a child illustrate His statement that if anyone wanted to be first, he would have to be last and serving all others? Mark 9:35-37; Luke 9:47, 48.

3. Read Matthew 20:17-28, and answer the following questions:

   A. What did Jesus say was the reason He was going up to Jerusalem?

   B. What request did the mother of James and John make to Jesus on their behalf?

   C. Explain the meaning of the cup Jesus referred to. Matthew 26:39 may help.

   D. How did the Gentiles relate to other people?

   E. What did Jesus say was the main characteristic of a great person?

   F. How did Jesus apply the principle of service to His own life and death?

 # Projects

1. Select three people of Scripture whom you admire the most, and write a private prayer that those people might have prayed to tell God how they felt about life. (For example, Moses on Mt. Nebo probably would have thanked God for the chance to lead the Israelites, climb Sinai, meet Joshua, and have Zipporah as a wife. He probably would have also marveled at God's greatness and love, while asking forgiveness for his own failings. The main point of his prayer, however, would have been an appeal for God to show special grace to the unruly mob at the base of the mountain. His prayer would have shown humility, meekness, and love.)
2. Identify three people among your acquaintances who are successful by the world's standards, yet who seem to have effectively avoided pride in their lives. Ask them how a person can become successful without becoming egotistical and full of pride. What did you discover? Report your findings in writing or in a report to the class.
3. In your imagination, choose a career or profession you would like to pursue. Then write a short essay identifying those characteristics of true greatness that you believe are essential for success in your life's work.

## Focus Questions

1. What made the Pharisee's prayer so ugly?
2. What made the publican's prayer so beautiful?
3. What determines the "look" of your prayers? How can you pray with beauty?
4. Is it possible to compliment someone without making them feel egotistical pride?

**193**

# TRANSLATION

Jesus is God spelling Himself out in language that man can understand
(Unknown).

# lesson 21

# The Jewish Advantage

**Lesson Scriptures: Matthew 21:33-46;
27:15-25**

NTRODUCTION
"You must be crazy!"

Benjamin just looked at James. "I'm just telling you what it says. Read it yourself," he said.

James was still sputtering. "Maybe that's what you think it says. But it can't. If the sacred writing of the prophet really predicted that the Messiah would appear this year, everyone would be talking about it."

"Then what does it mean?" Benjamin persisted. "If you start when the prophet Daniel says to start and add seven weeks and sixty-two weeks, you come out to this year."

"So who's the Messiah then?" James asked. "The new high priest? Rabbi Gamaliel? You?"

"No. I don't know."

James patted his friend on the back. "Then that's how I know you're wrong. If this was the year of the Messiah, then the Messiah would be here. There is no Messiah, so you must be wrong."

"Then what does it mean?" Benjamin asked again. "When an almost five-hundred-year-old prophecy points to this year, I want to know what it means."

"Let's ask Rabbi Gozer."

They approached the older man as he began his daily walk. "Rabbi, isn't it time for the Messiah according to the prophecies of Daniel?" Benjamin asked.

"What? What's this talk about the Messiah?"

"The prophecy of the seventy weeks, in Daniel. Doesn't it

say that the Messiah will appear very soon now? We've been trying to figure it out," Benjamin explained.

"Yes, the prophecy does talk about the Messiah," the rabbi answered slowly.

Benjamin shot a quick glance at James. "But I'm afraid you youngsters may be taking it a little too literally."

"That's what I tried to tell him, Rabbi," James agreed.

"Then what does it mean?" Benjamin asked.

The rabbi took his time answering. "The promise of the Messiah is given to give us hope for the future, my young friend. The Messiah is coming, but we cannot tell when. The prophecy is there to encourage us to watch for Him."

Benjamin's shoulders slumped. "Then what are we watching for? Will there be a sign or another prophecy?"

"No one can be certain. But be sure that the priests and leaders will be watching for signs. When the Messiah comes, we will announce it to the whole country. To the whole world."

"Rabbi," James asked timidly, "what about that new teacher I've heard about? Some

people say he's the Messiah."

Rabbi Gozer looked puzzled. "New teacher? Where is he from?"

"Nazareth."

Rabbi Gozer was disgusted. "I wouldn't own a dog from Nazareth. Stay away from such rabble. Nazareth, indeed." With that, he turned and walked away, muttering to himself.

Benjamin grinned sheepishly. "OK, I guess I was wrong. Where do you want to go now?"

"Let's go over to the temple courtyard. I heard that yesterday some guy went crazy and practically destroyed the market. Maybe he'll come back."

### SECTION I

Have you ever wondered why the Jewish people were so unprepared for Jesus? Couldn't they see that this man who went around healing people and talking and teaching was no ordinary human? Didn't their Old Testament Scripture point to the time of the coming of the Messiah? Let's take a look at one particular prophecy that was well known by the Jewish people during Christ's time.

The Jewish people studied Daniel's writings. Daniel was an important official in both

Babylon and Medo-Persia while his people were in captivity. Nearly seventy years had gone by since Jerusalem had been destroyed by Babylon. Daniel and his countrymen longed for freedom and the opportunity to go back home.

In Daniel 9:1-18, we find Daniel praying, pleading for God's mercy and forgiveness toward His rebellious people. Daniel knew that the release of the people depended on their repentance and renewal before God.

While he was praying, God sent Gabriel with an answer. This mighty angel answered even before Daniel finished his prayer. Gabriel showed Daniel what is known as the "seventy-week prophecy" (see Daniel 9:24-27). Actually, Daniel got more than he bargained for.

it also announced the coming of the Messiah into their midst.

The seventy-week prophecy was to begin when the Jews were freed from captivity. During the passing of these seventy weeks (490 years) of time, the Jews were asked to demonstrate that they were in harmony with God's plan for them as His chosen people. This time period was divided into two sections—sixty-nine weeks (483 years) and one week (seven years). At the end of the sixty-nine weeks, the Messiah would appear. During the middle of the final week, He would die as the sacrifice for human sin.

Is all of this a little confusing? Let's retrace some history.

King Artaxerxes of Medo-Persia issued the final decree that allowed the Jews to return home in 457 B.C. When you go

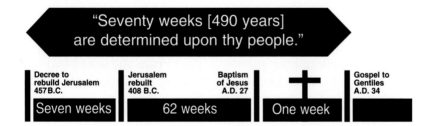

"Seventy weeks [490 years] are determined upon thy people."

| Decree to rebuild Jerusalem 457 B.C. | Jerusalem rebuilt 408 B.C. | Baptism of Jesus A.D. 27 | | Gospel to Gentiles A.D. 34 |
| --- | --- | --- | --- | --- |
| Seven weeks | 62 weeks | | One week | |

This prophecy not only assured the Jews that they would return to and rebuild their homeland,

forward 483 years, you arrive at A.D. 27 (the old calendars did not include the year 0). The

Jews who studied the prophecy should have been looking for the Messiah about that time. In A.D. 27, Jesus began preaching and teaching. And just as the prophecy said, three-and-a-half years later, in A.D. 31, Jesus was crucified.

When Jesus died, the Jewish nation had very little time left to accept and follow God's plan. Sadly enough, by A.D. 34, the Jewish priests and leaders had stoned Stephen to death for preaching about Jesus and had begun to kill or imprison others who did the same. In rejecting the messages the disciples preached, the Jewish leaders sealed the rejection of Israel as God's people, and the gospel began spreading to other nations.

Could the Jewish people have known when to look for the Messiah? Yes. So why didn't they?

A few were looking for Him. The shepherds outside Bethlehem were talking about the coming Messiah when the angels appeared and announced His birth. The wise men from the East weren't even Jewish, but they recognized the time and the signs of a King's birth.

Why were the majority of the Jewish people unprepared?

1. They were too busy with other things to be concerned. There was too much happening on the job or at school. They were satisfied with weekly trips to the synagogue and willing to let the priests and leaders worry about things like a coming Messiah.

2. They depended on the scribes and rabbis to tell them how to live and what to believe. So it was easy to depend on the rabbis and leaders to study and tell them when the Messiah would appear.

Since they were confused about what the Messiah would do and were willing to let others tell them what to think and believe, they failed to see that the time for the Messiah had come. They failed to recognize the Person the world had been waiting for since the Garden of Eden.

**SECTION II**
If someone visited a hospital and healed every sick person there, it would be a big news

story. If someone broke up a funeral by raising the dead person to life, it would be headline news! Don't you think that even if the Jewish people were not looking for the Messiah around A.D. 27, someone who went around teaching, healing, and raising people from the dead would get their attention?

Jesus did get a lot of attention. Thousands of people followed Him from place to place. Everywhere He went, great crowds waited. People even took the roofs off houses just to be near Him! So why was He not accepted as the Messiah?

The truth is, many people did believe He was the Messiah. At least for a while. But they expected something different from the Messiah. They wanted someone who would become King and General and lead them against the hated Roman soldiers. They wanted someone to set Israel up as the most powerful kingdom on earth.

The disciples had a plan for the Messiah as an earthly ruler. And Jesus just wasn't following it. They were always arguing about who would be the greatest in the new kingdom. James and John even had their mother ask Jesus to let

them be His closest advisors! Judas didn't betray Jesus because he hated Him and wanted Him to die. He was trying to force Jesus to take over the government and set up His kingdom. But Jesus wasn't acting according to plan. If the disciples, who were with Jesus

constantly, were that confused, you can imagine how confused others were.

There's another reason why people turned away from Jesus: they weren't sure that He was God. In John 6, after He fed five thousand people with a little boy's lunch, the enormous crowd crossed the Sea of

Galilee to follow Him. But it seems that they mostly wanted another free lunch. When Jesus began to talk about who He really was, the Son of God, the crowd began to melt away. Even though they had seen His miracles and had eaten the food He created, many never listened to Him again.

Many people didn't accept Jesus because the priests and leaders didn't. These leaders, called the Pharisees and Sadducees, were in control of both the synagogues and the Jewish government. They controlled what people could and couldn't do on Sabbath, who they could or couldn't be friends with, and how they should act toward the Romans.

It's the same old story. "Wouldn't the church leaders be the first to know, if He really is the Messiah? I guess we'll just have to trust their judgment."

Why didn't the leaders accept Jesus? Wasn't He just what they had been watching for? Wasn't He just what the nation needed?

No. They were looking for something different also. They wanted a Warrior King to break the Roman chains that held their nation down. Many

Pharisees hoped that one of their rabbis might be the Messiah, destined to lead their people to battle.

But when Jesus appeared, the Sadducees were in the comfortable position of controlling the government and religion of the people. They had a working relationship with the Romans that gave the Jewish leaders power over the people. If Jesus really was the Messiah, He would have come to them first and shared His plans to deliver the nation.

Since Jesus didn't do that, since He insisted on disobeying their rules and regulations and challenging their authority, they were convinced that He was a major problem to their authority.

The truth is, they felt threatened. If the people listened to Jesus, they would no longer listen to the rabbis and priests. They were losing control and power. Jesus was taking over as leader.

It was a power struggle they were determined to win. They couldn't perform miracles. And they couldn't out-debate Him or trick Him into saying the wrong thing. So they began plotting Jesus' death.

Whatever advantage the Jewish nation had was lost. They had allowed their own ideas about the Messiah to cloud their minds. The people grew accustomed to letting others make their decisions about religious things. And the leaders grew accustomed to controlling people's lives and refused to give up that power and authority.

As God's special people, they failed one last time. God's last attempt to reach them as a nation failed. As individuals, however, some Jewish men and women accepted Jesus as the Messiah and turned the world upside down with the message of God's love.

So what about you? Are you allowing others to think for you? Are you depending on your parents or teachers or pastor to watch for signs of the end? Are you letting others tell you what the Bible says, or do you read it to discover truth?

Make good use of the advantages you have been given. Be ready to give reasons for "the hope that is in you." God is looking to you to proclaim the message of Christ's soon return. If each accepts the challenge, we will fulfill God's plans for us.

# Memory Focus

" 'This is the covenant I will make with the house of Israel after that time,' declares the Lord. 'I will put my law in their minds and write it on their hearts. I will be their God, and they will be my people' " (Jeremiah 31:33, NIV).

# Into the Bible

1. A. Read Daniel 9:3-19, and describe the main concerns of Daniel's prayer.
   B. From reading this prayer, explain whether the Jews had

changed from Daniel's time to Christ's time.

    C. How did their attitudes affect their readiness for the coming of the Messiah?

**2.** Read the texts listed on the worksheet that will be provided by your teacher, and identify the reasons why many of the Jews rejected Jesus as the Messiah.

**3.** Read Matthew 21:33-46.

    A. Make a list identifying the principal characters in this parable and whom they represent.

    B. What is the conclusion of this parable (verse 43)?

    C. How does Jesus' parable describe the attitude of the Jewish leaders?

**4.** Jesus wasn't the only one whom the priests wanted to kill. Read John 12:9-11. Who else was marked for death? Why did they want him dead?

 # Projects

**1.** From the narrative, list the reasons why the Jewish people were unprepared to recognize and accept Jesus as the Messiah.

**2.** Place yourself in the story of John 6. You've seen Jesus feed five thousand. You've seen Him heal people who had been crippled since they were born. But you've heard the Pharisees and leaders say that He is a fraud, an imposter. You know they don't approve of Jesus, and you've listened to them since you were a child.

    When Jesus talks about being from heaven and wants you to give up everything and follow Him, what does He mean? Write your response to His invitation.

**3.** The following is a role-playing activity. The class will be divided into three groups. One group is to play the part of Jews in Jesus' time who have decided to follow Him. The second group will be those who have agreed with the priests and leaders that Jesus is a fraud. The third group is undecided about Jesus.

In this role-play, both of the decided groups will try to convince the others to join them. Select one or two key stories in Matthew, Mark, Luke, and/or John as the basis for your arguments. The following are suggestions.
A. Triumphal entry and cleansing of the temple. Matthew 21.
B. Jesus feeds five thousand. Mark 6:30-44.
C. Jesus casts out a devil. Luke 11:14-28.
D. Jesus raises Lazarus. John 11:38-57.

 # Focus Questions

1. Could the Jews have known when the Messiah would appear?
2. What events marked the end of the Jews as God's chosen people?
3. Why did so many Jews fail to realize the time of Christ's coming?
4. What were the people and leaders looking for in a Messiah?
5. Why were the priests and leaders really opposed to Jesus?
6. Could it be time for Jesus to return now? What do you see as the greatest signs that indicate the nearness of Christ's return?
7. What are the reasons why Christians today might not realize the time of Christ's return is near?

# COMMITMENT

People don't care how much you know until they know how much you care
(Unknown).

# lesson 22

# A Time to Rejoice

## Lesson Scripture: John 11; 12:1-19

Things don't always turn out as we think they should. Even in the Bible, we often find confused and disappointed people. Christ's most dramatic miracle, the raising of Lazarus from the tomb, blossomed out of the ashes of bitter disappointment.

Lazarus was the brother of Mary Magdalene and Martha. He suddenly took sick. Though his condition was critical, the sisters weren't worried too much as they bathed his fevered forehead. Surely their friend Jesus would heal their brother.

"So the sisters sent word to Jesus, 'Lord, the one you love is sick.' When he heard this, Jesus said, 'This sickness will not end in death. No, it is for God's glory so that God's Son may be glorified through it' " (John 11:3, 4, NIV). Then John tells us that Jesus loved Lazarus and his sisters, so He waited two more days where He was.

Wait a minute! If Jesus loved Lazarus and his sisters, why did He wait around for two days when He could have come and healed him? During that mysterious delay, the unthinkable happened. Lazarus died.

Jesus broke His promise! That's the way it seemed. He said the sickness would not end in death, yet Lazarus died.

You probably know what it's like to have a dream shattered. Maybe you prayed that your parents wouldn't get divorced, and they did anyway. Or you prayed that your best friend

## 205

wouldn't move away, and he did anyway. You prayed that you would be chosen as a member of the team but didn't make it. So you found yourself wondering, What good does it do to pray? What use are God's promises?

That's how Mary Magdalene and Martha must have felt when they wrapped up their brother's lifeless body and laid it in the tomb. Where was Jesus when they needed Him most? And what about His promise?

After burying their brother Lazarus, Mary and Martha sat around the house and cried their hearts out. Then the news came that Jesus was headed their way. Brokenhearted though they were that Christ had apparently broken His promise to heal Lazarus, He was still their only hope. Only with His help could they face the future.

"Then Martha, as soon as she heard that Jesus was coming, went and met Him, but Mary was sitting in the house. Then Martha said to Jesus, 'Lord, if You had been here, my brother would not have died. But even now I know that whatever You ask of God, God will give You' " (John 11:20-22, NKJV).

As she poured out her grief to Jesus, Martha managed to express some faith. Even though Lazarus was dead, she knew Christ still could perform a miracle and raise him from the grave. Then, remembering how long he had been dead—four days now—her faith took a plunge again. Brushing off any hope of seeing her brother anytime soon, she told Jesus, "I know he will rise again in the resurrection at the last day" (John 11:24, NIV).

Jesus had some explaining to do. "Martha," He said, "the resurrection isn't merely some future event. The resurrection is a person. Look at Me."

"I am the resurrection and the life. He who believes in me will live, even though he dies; and whoever lives and believes in me will never die. Do you believe this?" (John 11:25, 26, NIV).

Jesus wasn't denying the reality of death. He was denying its power to claim anyone who has faith in Him. Since Christ Himself is the Lord of life, death to Him is just like sleep. Even more easily than you might wake up your roommate to get ready for breakfast, Jesus will awaken His faithful ones from death.

Martha's mind, suffocating from grief, was slow to catch what Jesus wanted to do. When He commanded that the stone of the tomb be rolled away, she protested: "Lord, by this time there is a bad odor, for he has been there four days" (John 11:39, NIV).

Jesus warned her, "Did I not tell you that if you believed you would see the glory of God?" (John 11:40, NIV).

You've heard it said, "Seeing is believing. I'll believe it when I see it." That's not the way it is with God. It's the other way around. Jesus told Martha, "If you believe, you will see." Believing comes first. Then we will see God at work in our lives. He may not fulfill all our expectations, but everything He does is always for our good.

Something big was going to happen, something really big, if Mary and Martha would only believe. Helplessly but hopefully, they hung their faith on the promise of Christ.

"Then Jesus looked up and said, 'Father, I thank you that you have heard me. I knew that you always hear me, but I said this for the benefit of the people standing here, that they may believe that you sent me.'

When he had said this, Jesus called in a loud voice, 'Lazarus, come out!' The dead man came out, his hands and feet wrapped with strips of linen, and a cloth around his face. Jesus said to them, 'Take off the grave clothes, and let him go' " (John 11:41-44, NIV).

Picture that incredible scene! Relatives and friends hugging Lazarus, shouting and jumping for joy. Amid all the excitement, Jesus slipped away with His disciples.

The Lord didn't break His promise that Lazarus's sickness would not end in death. Death was just an interruption of life in Christ. The happy ending of the whole scene was resurrection and restoration.

Imagine the faces of the crowd around the tomb as Lazarus, still wrapped like a mummy in his white grave clothes, shuffled out of the dark tomb! The Bible says many eyewitnesses put their faith in Jesus. Not everyone, though.

[The Sanhedrin was the ruling council of the Jewish nation, comprised of leading Pharisees (strict conservatives) and elite Sadducees (wealthy and sophisticated liberals). Normally bitter rivals, these two groups found common cause in doing away with Jesus.]

"Then the chief priests and the Pharisees gathered a council and said, 'What shall we do? For this Man works many signs. If we let Him alone like this,

everyone will believe in Him, and the Romans will come and take away both our place and nation.' Then from that day on they plotted to put Him to death" (John 11:47, 48, 53, NKJV). Amazing unbelief!

When Jesus raised Lazarus to life, He sealed His own death warrant in the minds of His enemies. The religious leaders hated Him before and desired His death, but now they were more determined than ever to murder the Messiah.

## SIMON'S BANQUET

With the religious leaders growing increasingly insecure about Christ's success, His days on earth were numbered. He had less than a week to live when a Pharisee named Simon invited Him over for a banquet. Ignoring the danger involved, Jesus agreed to attend. Something unexpected happened when an uninvited visitor crashed the party. It was Mary Magdalene, sister of Lazarus. When respectable people got together for social occasions, Mary wasn't on the guest list. As a young woman, she had gotten herself into trouble. Perhaps to save the reputation of her family, she moved far away from Bethany to the town of Magdala on the southwestern shore of Galilee, where she only plunged deeper into sin. She was trapped in sin without hope for a better life.

Then one bright morning, she met a man who was different. He didn't lust after her,

nor did He condemn her like the so-called righteous people did. Jesus looked past her sin and saw her soul longing for peace of mind and freedom from guilt. Mary responded to His mercy and became a faithful disciple.

Mary yearned to express her appreciation. She wanted to do something really special that the Lord would never forget. Taking a year's wages, she splurged on a bottle of rare perfume. Showing up uninvited at Simon's feast, she tiptoed over to where Jesus was eating, broke open the flask, and poured the precious liquid on His feet.

As the fragrance filled the room, dinner guests stopped chewing their food. They saw Mary kneeling at the feet of Jesus. Simon the Pharisee did not appreciate having dinner interrupted by someone he condemned as an awful sinner. He considered himself an honorable man, a vigorous defender of God's law. He claimed to represent the best that the religious establishment had to offer. Mary, with her history as a prostitute, represented the worst the world had to offer.

Actually, according to Jesus, even immoral people are closer to the kingdom of God than hypocritical legalists who feel no need of a Saviour. You see, none of us are good enough to stand before the holy law of God. The Bible says, "There is none righteous, no, not one" (Romans 3:10, NKJV).

Even the most faithful among us still fall far short of God's glorious ideal. The only hope any of us has is to honestly admit our sinfulness and ask God for pardon through the blood of Jesus.

During the feast at Simon's house, Christ warned the proud Pharisee he needed to experience forgiveness, just as Mary Magdalene had. Jesus said that the one who is forgiven much loves much. That makes sense, doesn't it? And on the other hand, one who has but little sense of forgiveness also has but little love for God.

While everyone else at the banquet criticized Mary, Jesus looked at her and said, "Your sins are forgiven" (Luke 7:48, NKJV). Then He added, "Your faith has saved you. Go in peace" (Luke 7:50, NKJV).

The patient mercy of Jesus was Mary's salvation. He didn't

cast her off. Seven times He reclaimed her from the demons fighting for control of her life, until she found lasting deliverance.

Jesus wants to do the same for each of us today. Maybe you struggle with a sin you can't overcome. You've made all kinds of promises to God, but all your sincere resolutions are like ropes of sand.

Don't be discouraged—God still loves you. If you have honestly entrusted your life to Him, He counts you perfect in Christ even when you fall. Jesus said, "The spirit is willing, but the body is weak" (Matthew 26:41, NIV). In other words, God knows when we have a willing spirit of repentance and really do want His help. He doesn't get discouraged with us, so why should we get discouraged with ourselves? What matters is not how many times we fall but whether we are willing to get picked up.

## A JOURNEY IN TRIUMPH

Just five days before His crucifixion, Jesus entered Jerusalem as the successor to David's throne, riding in royalty toward the temple. "A very large crowd spread their cloaks on the road, while others cut branches from the trees and spread them on the road. The crowds that went ahead of him and those that followed shouted, 'Hosanna to the Son of David!' 'Blessed is he who comes in the name of the Lord!' 'Hosanna in the highest!' " (Matthew 21:8, 9, NIV).

Children and teenagers led the parade. The religious authorities didn't like the noise of the happy crowd praising Jesus on their way to the temple. "When the chief priests and the teachers of the law saw the wonderful things he did and the children shouting in the temple area, 'Hosanna to the Son of David,' they were indignant. 'Do you hear what these children are saying?' they asked him. 'Yes,' replied Jesus, 'have you never read, "From the lips of children and infants you have ordained praise"?' " (Matthew 21:15, 16, NIV).

Jesus didn't lose His temper when attacked by His critics. Neither did He make apologies for what He knew to be right. Instead, He calmly explained, "You can't stop My people from celebrating. " 'I tell you,' He replied, 'if they keep quiet, the stones will cry out' " (Luke

19:40, NIV). The triumphal procession had to happen in order to fulfill an important Old Testament prophecy about the Messiah (see Zechariah 9:9). But there was another reason why the people couldn't be restrained from shouting their praises: In the heart that is secure in Jesus, it's impossible to quench the spirit of celebration.

# Memory Focus

"Then Jesus said, 'Did I not tell you that if you believed, you would see the glory of God?' " (John 11:40, NIV).

# Into the Bible

1. Did Jesus really break His promise that Lazarus would not die? (John 11:4.) Explain your answer.
2. One of the favorite promises of many Christians is Romans 8:28. Read the text, and do the following:
   A. Rewrite the text in your own words.
   B. Relate a personal example in which God actually turned a bad experience into a result that was for your ultimate good.
3. Read John 12:4-8.
   A. What was Judas's complaint regarding Mary's act of anointing Jesus' feet?
   B. Why was his complaint not justified?
   C. What was Jesus' reaction to Judas's complaint?
4. Jesus had a special message for Simon at the feast in his home. Read Luke 7:40-50, and do the following:
   A. Identify the main characters in the story.
   B. Describe their attitudes toward forgiveness.

5. What are the limits of spiritual security? The Bible says it's possible for believers once saved to forfeit their salvation. Look up three of these texts, and write down the reasons why believers can lose salvation.
   A. John 6:60, 66
   B. 1 John 2:4
   C. Psalm 66:18
   D. Matthew 24:13
   E. 2 Peter 2:20, 21
   F. 2 Peter 3:17, 18
6. Jesus wanted to shake up Simon and encourage Mary. Read the story in Luke 7:40-50, and identify the following:
   A. Simon's attitude toward Mary.
   B. Mary's attitude toward Jesus.

 Projects

1. Interview two senior citizens, and record on paper how a major disappointment in their earlier years actually turned out for the best.

2. Using your Bible; a concordance; the *SDA Bible Dictionary*, pages 689 and 690; the *SDA Bible Commentary*, volume 5, pages 764-767; and *The Desire of Ages*, pages 558-563, write a short biographical sketch on the Mary who anointed Jesus' feet at the feast of Simon.

 Focus Questions

1. If Jesus knew that He was going to raise Lazarus, why did He weep at his tomb?
2. What does the experience of Lazarus tell us about the claim of modern faith healers that God will heal everyone who has faith?
3. If God knows what is best and promises to work all things for good in His own time and way, why should we even pray?
4. When we give our hearts to Jesus, why does He still let us be tempted?
5. Why did some people who shouted "Hosanna" in praise to Jesus at His entry into Jerusalem five days later shout "Crucify Him"?
6. Jesus' experience shows how jealousy and insecurity can lead to hatred and eventually even murder. Have you ever witnessed an evil act that might have been sparked by jealousy and insecurity? What can you do to help people not feel threatened by the success of others?

# HARVEST
When men listen, God speaks. When men obey, God works (Unknown).

# Blessings and Curses

**Lesson Scripture: Deuteronomy 28:1-68**

 little boy, hearing the story of Noah and the Flood, startled his mother by asking, "When God destroyed the world with a flood, why didn't He drown Satan?" That's not only an interesting question, it's an important one. Sometimes it takes a child to come up with questions we ourselves hesitate to ask.

We blame the devil for all that's wrong in our world— from minor aches and pains to global wars and terrifying calamities. But if we could just get rid of Satan, would everything straighten out and get back to normal?

Granted, Satan brought sin into existence. In heaven, he first came to distrust God's wisdom and decided to break away from His dominion. By his own choice, Lucifer transformed himself from a magnificent angel into a self-serving demon. He chose to rebel against God. He introduced to the universe a cleverly devised alternative—a self-centered existence. This evil of focusing on self, which Adam and Eve chose in the Garden of Eden, triggered a continuous whirlwind of wickedness that extends to this very day.

Sin can be defined simply as selfishness. It turns our thoughts and desires inward, making us live for self rather than for God and the good of others. Sin enthrones self as the ruler, who dictates the course and calls the shots. With self at the controls, it is only natural for us to live primarily for our own glory.

The essence of sin is a state of separation and rebellion against God, and the effects are destructive and far-reaching. Like a fire, sin has a way of getting out of control. Sin will always take you farther than you want to go. We have no idea the many ways our sin will affect ourselves and others. Certainly Adam and Eve never imagined the incredible consequences their one act of disobedience would bring.

God established the basic laws by which all life is governed, based on physical as well as spiritual reality. They are not arbitrary rules or restrictions. They are designed to protect the stability and order of the universe, to promote the well-being of God's creation, and to safeguard loving relationships and spiritual harmony.

If people are going to live, work, or play together, they must have laws that govern their activity and agree to stick by them. That's why we have referees, umpires, police officers, supervisors, governors, presidents, kings, and, ultimately, God. Can you imagine what kind of universe would exist if there were no laws to define what is right and no authority to put them into effect?

God's laws are an expression of His love. They are designed to ensure our happiness and safety. He originally planned that created beings would remain faithful to His laws of love and thus experience the blessings of obedience. In the garden, Satan tempted Eve to distrust God. He deceived her into believing that disobeying would be to her advantage and that the consequences God had warned her about would never happen. The first recorded lie in the Bible was the deceiver saying to Eve, "You will not surely die" (Genesis 3:4, NKJV).

Still, we continue to disbelieve God's distinct warnings regarding the sure results of transgression. Forgiveness brings a change of heart and peace of mind, but it doesn't prevent sin's consequences. Each sin carries with it its own curse, not as a punishment from God, but as the consequence of our own wrongdoing.

God spells out very plainly

this important principle in Galatians: "Do not be deceived, God is not mocked; for whatever a man sows, that he will also reap" (Galatians 6:7, NKJV). One of the earliest lessons we must learn in life is that thoughts and actions have consequences. Through Ellen White, God counsels parents, "Teach your children to reason from cause to effect. Show them that if they violate the laws of their being they must pay the penalty in suffering" (*Counsels to Parents, Teachers, and Students,* 126).

Sin can appear attractive and advantageous, no matter what God says about the pain it will bring to the guilty and to the innocent. Countless numbers of people have experienced lifelong, crippling injuries, untold anguish and fear, or the loss of everything that is dear to them because of someone else's foolhardy decision.

But you may object, "That's not fair! Why doesn't God do something about all the suffering that goes on? Can't He do anything, or is He just unwilling to help us out?" But most of the suffering that takes place results from our choices. We make the

weapons, sell and take drugs, pull the trigger, steal, cheat, and lie, as well as carry out all the other evil desires of our hearts. It was Satan's choice to bring sin into the world, but we choose whether it remains the ruling force in our lives.

God gives us the freedom to choose. If He ruled as a dictator, He could guarantee His own desired results. But God

views freedom of thought and expression as absolutely essential for created beings. He granted the power of choice, knowing full well that abuse of this decisive privilege was a very real possibility. Freedom is risky. It demands responsibility on our part. God, in His love and infinite wisdom, gave us freedom, even knowing the cost our misuse would bring.

But God determined not to let humanity's disobedience negate His plans for this world. When sin did burst upon the scene, God allowed the consequences to run their course for our own good. Suffering confronts us with the reality of sin. Then, if we are willing, God steps in and turns mistakes into opportunities for change and growth. God whispers to us in our joys but shouts to us in our pain. Suffering often turns our eyes heavenward for comfort, strength, and guidance. The psalmist testifies to this when he writes, "The punishment you gave me was the best thing that could have happened to me, for it taught me to pay attention to your laws" (Psalm 119:71, TLB).

The Bible clearly presents the negative effects of sin. Yet its primary focus is on the positive. God wants us to understand that as surely as curses follow disobedience, blessings come to those who obey Him. Scripture presents an all-powerful God committed to providing for the spiritual needs of a now-lost creation. If we will acknowledge our sin and repent, He freely offers us not only forgiveness, but the Spirit's power to heal, comfort, and to give victory over sin.

Having the freedom of choice, our basic options remain the same: the curses of a selfish life or the blessings of Christ as our Lord and Saviour. "Behold, I set before you today a blessing and a curse: the blessing, if you obey the commandments of the Lord your God . . . and the curse, if you do not obey the commandments of the Lord your God" (Deuteronomy 11:26-28, NKJV).

When freedom was abused and sin entered, the Creator determined to step in and become our Redeemer. He determined to win back for us everything sin marred and destroyed. Christ took upon Himself the ultimate curse of sin, the death penalty for our wrongdoing, and willingly died on the cross in our behalf.

This process of restoration will be completed in the new earth. The Creator will again personally dwell with the human family. "God himself will be with them, and he will be their God. He will wipe away all tears from their eyes. There will be no more death, no more grief or crying or pain. The old things have disappeared"

(Revelation 21:3, 4, TEV). The "best of all possible worlds" will now be an eternal reality.

Jesus gave us free will and choice. He provided saving grace and eternal life. Wouldn't you say He is our greatest Blessing?

 # Memory Focus

"See, I am setting before you today a blessing and a curse—the blessing if you obey the commands of the Lord your God that I am giving you today; the curse if you disobey the commands of the Lord your God and turn from the way that I command you today by following other gods, which you have not known" (Deuteronomy 11:26-28, NIV).

OR

"Do not be deceived: God cannot be mocked. A man reaps what he sows" (Galatians 6:7, NIV).

 # Into the Bible

1. The second commandment (Exodus 20:4-6) describes how far-reaching the consequences of obedience and disobedience really are. Read and analyze this commandment by writing in your own words the effects of obeying and disobeying God's commandments.

2. Curses and blessings are spiritual concepts that run all through the Scriptures. The most vivid and detailed description of the consequences of serving the Lord or rejecting Him is found in Deuteronomy 28. Read this chapter; then answer the following questions:

   A. Deuteronomy 28:1-14 focuses on the blessings. What great promises does God hold out to His people in verses 1 and

13 if they remain faithful to Him?

    B. According to Deuteronomy 28:2-12, what specific aspects of the lives of God's people would be blessed by their obedience to God?

3. According to Deuteronomy 28:15-68, no facet of Israel's existence would be left untouched by their disobedience to God. Sickness, pestilence, famine, and natural disasters of every kind would plague them. Use the worksheet provided by your teacher to write a brief summary of the predicted calamity or disaster that is given in each of the listed texts.

 # Projects

1. Write a brief explanation of how some of the predictions in Deuteronomy 28 came to pass.
   A. 2 Kings 6:24-29
   B. 2 Kings 17:5-18
   C. 2 Chronicles 36:11-21

2. Jesus acknowledged the reality of the law of cause and effect by illustrating in His teaching the different ways this principle works in people's lives. You will be asked to read selected texts, summarize the thought of each one, and explain what it means to you. Your teacher will provide you with a worksheet on which to record your responses.

3. The book of Proverbs presents some remarkably keen insights regarding the way the law of cause and effect works in the lives of people. You will be asked to read selected texts, summarize the thought of each one, and explain what it means to you. Your teacher will provide you with a worksheet on which to record your responses.

4. Draw a picture or create a poster to illustrate any of the cause/effect relationships that are listed in Projects 2 and 3.

 **Focus Questions**

1. When things go wrong, why are people so quick to blame either God or the devil, rather than themselves?
2. Instead of removing Adam and Eve from the Garden of Eden, why didn't God simply forgive them for their wrongdoing and give them another chance to prove themselves?
3. Since God has chosen to allow us to experience physical consequences of our sins, doesn't that mean that pain is really a punishment from God?
4. God knew that the freedom of choice would ultimately make this the best of all possible worlds, even if humankind chose to disobey. Do you agree or disagree? Why?
5. Although Israel as a nation never reached the standard God had designed for them, there were some individuals who came much closer to God's ideal. Name some of these people, and explain how.
6. How can parents teach their children "to reason from cause to effect"?
7. What determines whether a personal experience is a curse or a blessing? Can some experiences start out as a curse and end up as a blessing? Or vice versa?
8. In our society today, what evidences are there that the consequences of sin can affect even the third and fourth generations?

# DESTINY

God never leads His childen otherwise than they would choose to be led, if they could see the end from the beginning (*The Desire of Ages*, 224).

# The Final Warning

## Lesson Scripture: Matthew 23:1-39

If you were arrested for being a Christian, would there be enough evidence to convict you? Taking it one step farther, what kind of evidence do you think the judge would be looking for?

These somewhat unusual questions should draw our attention to a very important issue. What makes a person a Christian? What one believes? Or whom one worships? Some might suggest that a Christian is someone who's been born again or one who truly loves and cares about others. At this point, you're probably saying to yourself that all of these are important aspects of the Christian life. And you're right. Perhaps you may have thought of some other factors that could be added to the list. But in the most simple terms, Christianity is generally viewed as a religion whose primary focus is on Jesus Christ as Saviour and Lord and whose fundamental beliefs and practices are based on the Holy Scriptures.

Many of the world's religions share some common features or even uphold similar teachings, but in one crucial way, Christianity stands apart from all the rest. Other religions tend to emphasize human's quest for God. Humanity is viewed as reaching outward or sometimes inward to discover divinity and to develop some form of religious worship based on that discovery. From such a perspective, it is our pursuit and performance that take center stage in religion.

In contrast, the focus of Christianity is God's search for humans. God is seen as reaching down to a lost and dying humanity and personally revealing Himself to us as our Creator and Redeemer. A religion that saves and restores from sin is not derived from the sinner himself, but rather, it's revealed by God, through His Word and through His Son. From a Biblical viewpoint, saving humankind is the Creator's work. It is His life, His plan, His dying, His love and grace that stand at the very heart of Christianity. Keep in mind that whomever we acknowledge as the source of salvation gets our worship and praise. Therefore, in Christianity, it is only fitting that believers exult and rejoice in God's work of atonement, rather than in their attainment.

However, because we're so prone to glory in our own wisdom, bask in our goodness, and rely upon our own efforts for salvation, the Bible boldly reminds us that "whoever wants to boast must boast of what the Lord has done" (1 Corinthians 1:31, TEV). This theme is so beautifully expressed by the redeemed who stand on heaven's "sea of glass" and fervently praise their Redeemer with these words:

"Lord God Almighty, how great and wonderful are your deeds!

King of the nations, how right and true are your ways!

Who will not stand in awe of you, Lord?

Who will refuse to declare your greatness?

You alone are holy. All the nations will come and worship you,

because your just actions are seen by all" —(Revelation 15:3-5, TEV).

We must understand that within the human heart there is a natural inclination to worship self in the place of God. For this reason, the issues at stake in religious controversies are basically the same in every age. As far back as the deadly dispute between Cain and Abel, the real struggle has been between the religion that comes from God and that which is devised by humankind. The real significance of this is very clearly explained by Ellen White when she writes, "The religion that comes from God is the only religion that can lead to God" (*Testimonies for the Church*, 9:156).

Throughout the history of the Jewish people, the most decisive issue was whether their worship and religious practices were God-centered or human-centered. This was made very evident by Israel's request that an earthly king rule over them, rather than God. Their objective was to be governed by a human ruler "like all the nations" around them (1 Samuel 8:5, TEV).

The recurring rebellion of God's chosen people during the entire span of the Old Testament was simply a replay of this vital point. Who was to rule? Whose authority was to be obeyed, and whose commands were to be followed? The natural outworking of sin is to replace the rulership, authority, and teachings of God with our own. And the more humans take over a religion, the more their rules and regulations supplant God's ways, the more oppressive that religion becomes, and the less saving value it will have.

These same principles were involved in the conflict between Jesus and the Jewish leaders. All during His ministry, Jesus had to deal with religious authorities who had severely perverted the worship of God by "teach-ing as doctrines the commandment of men" (Matthew 15:9, NKJV). At one point Jesus rebuked the Pharisees by declaring, "All too well you reject the commandments of God, that you may keep your tradition" (Mark 7:9, NKJV). To understand the reason for Christ's open criticism of the Jewish leadership, we need to take a look at what happened within Judaism in the years preceding the coming of Christ.

In their efforts to safeguard their beliefs from heathen influence, the Jews gradually developed a very formal and regimented religion. They formulated an assortment of rules to deal with every aspect of Jewish life. Slowly, but surely, the simple and deeply spiritual lifestyle of Judaism turned into a very complex and awkward system of religion, controlled by a vast array of man-made regulations.

As these oral teachings were handed down from one generation to another, they became established "traditions," growing in importance until they were considered equal to, or at times even of greater importance than, Scripture itself. These highly revered traditions

**225**

were collected and compiled between 200 B.C. and A.D. 135 and became known as the Mishnah. It was these man-made teachings that became the primary textbook in the

Jewish schools and the basis for most of the conflicts between Jesus and the Pharisees.

This entire process, so destructive to Christ-centered spirituality, was magnified with the writing of the Gemara, a lengthy commentary on the Mishnah. These two were eventually combined into what is known as the Talmud. The Talmud is a very detailed explanation and interpretation of

the laws of Moses and the oral traditions of the Mishnah. This massive accumulation of Jewish wisdom, philosophy, laws and regulations, as well as folklore and legends, was compiled by approximately two thousand scribes and rabbis over a period of 250 years, from A.D. 250-500. An English edition of this work would fill thirty-six volumes of one thousand pages per volume![1]

In the time of Christ, man-made observances were carried out to achieve maximum attention and display. Every ritual was an opportunity for the Jewish hierarchy (ruling clergy) to show off their esteemed piety and devotion, boast of their exalted rank and title, and, of course, flaunt their pretense of moral excellence. Such spiritual pride and pompous exhibition could only lead to formalism—a focus on outward show rather than inward sincerity—and bring about legalism—conformity to law to gain God's approval. Such religious practices were very widespread in Christ's day.

Whenever human opinions are elevated to the realm of

[1] *Nelson's Illustrated Bible Dictionary* (Nashville, Tenn.: Thomas Nelson Publishers, 1986).

"the commandments of men," those who do not measure up will not only be oppressed but carry a heavy load of guilt and despair. As Jesus ministered to these people, He shared with them the gospel, "the good news," that whoever believed on Him for salvation was free from any obligation to earn it by their own works. "Come to me, all of you who are tired from carrying heavy loads, and I will give you rest. . . . For the yoke I will give you is easy, and the load I will put on you is light" (Matthew 11:28, 30, TEV).

In His first public discourse, Jesus affirmed the joyful blessings (Beatitudes) that would come to those who would relate to God in the spirit of humility and meekness. Eight times Jesus held out a promised blessing to those who, by believing in Him, would become spiritual citizens of "the kingdom of heaven" (see Matthew 5:3-12).

How very much like Moses, who had declared to the people 1,500 years earlier, "All these blessings will come upon you and accompany you if you obey the Lord your God" (Deuteronomy 28:2, NIV).

But just as surely as Moses had spoken of both the blessings and the curses, so Jesus, in His final public sermon, boldly pronounced the curses on a people who had rejected God's way of salvation and refused to accept Him as the true Messiah. In His final appeal to the people He so deeply loved, Jesus uttered His "woes," not to merely condemn their hypocrisy and spiritual blindness, but to awaken them to their lost condition and arouse them to repent.

It has been said that the sun that melts the butter is the same sun that hardens the cement. No doubt there were people in the temple that day who responded in a positive way to what Jesus said. They were convicted that their hearts needed to be cleansed just as the temple had been the day before. On the other hand, the Pharisees saw Christ's clear-cut rebuke as a threat to their self-serving ways, and rather than crucify self, they chose to crucify Him. How are we to relate to all of this? Do Christ's censure and His appeal apply as much to us as they did to them? What was it Jesus said that awakened a new life in some and embittered others? Let's open our Bibles and find out!

# Memory Focus

"The greatest among you will be your servant" (Matthew 23:11, NIV).

OR

"This is what the Lord says: 'Let not the wise man boast of his wisdom or the strong man boast of his strength or the rich man boast of his riches, but let him who boasts boast about this: that he understands and knows me, that I am the Lord, who exercises kindness, justice and righteousness on earth, for in these I delight,' declares the Lord" (Jeremiah 9:23, 24, NIV).

# Into the Bible

Christ's final public sermon was spoken in the temple at Jerusalem on Tuesday, three days before His crucifixion. This ultimate appeal to the Jewish people, but especially the leaders, is recorded in Matthew 23 and can be divided into three sections. Read each section listed below, and answer the questions about it.

1. Verses 1 to 12: Jesus exposes the true character of the Jewish leaders.
   A. What two accusations did Jesus make in verses 1 through 4?
   B. List at least five ways that the Jewish leaders tried to exalt themselves (verses 5 through 10).
   C. What did Jesus say was the true indication or mark of greatness (verses 11, 12)?
2. Verses 13 to 32: Jesus rebukes their spiritual conduct and blatant hypocrisy.

In the verses of this passage, Jesus pronounces seven "woes" against the Jewish leaders. Complete the worksheet your teacher will give you that summarizes the seven "woes" against the Jewish leaders.

3. Verses 33 to 39: Jesus reveals the tragic consequences of their sin.
   A. In concluding His final appeal, what predictions did Jesus make regarding those who had steadfastly refused to believe Him?
   B. What attitude does Jesus manifest toward His listeners?

 # Projects

1. This assignment examines Matthew 23. You will need volume 5 of the *SDA Bible Commentary* and several translations of the Bible in order to answer the following questions.
   A. Explain what Jesus meant when He said that "the Pharisees sit in Moses' seat." Why was He critical of them for doing this (verse 2)?
   B. Identify the "heavy burdens" that the Pharisees laid on the people (verse 4). Explain what Mark 7:9 has to say about this.
   C. Define a "phylactery," which the Pharisees used to draw attention to themselves (verse 5). Some modern versions do not use this term. Read this verse in several translations, and write out different ways this term is translated.
   D. Why was Jesus so critical of the Pharisees for seeking after various titles (verses 7-10)?
   E. Explain what Jesus meant when He said, "The greatest one among you must be your servant" (verse 11, TEV).

F. According to verses 23, 24, what was Christ's attitude toward tithing? What point was He trying to make when referring to "mint, dill, and cumin"?

G. Explain what Jesus was talking about when He referred to the "more important matters of the law" (verse 23). Why are they more important? Read several different versions of this text, and write out the various ways these "more important matters" are translated.

H. Explain what the Pharisees had done so that they had "shut the kingdom of heaven" to other people (verses 13-15).

I. What did Jesus mean when He told the Pharisees to "clean what is inside the cup first, and then the outside will be clean too" (verses 25, 26)? See also Mark 7:18-23.

J. Analyze Christ's statement regarding the Pharisees' claim that had they lived during the time of their forefathers, they would not have done what they did (verses 29-32). What does this tell us about comparing ourselves to former generations of people?

 Focus Questions

1. What is your definition of a Christian? Can you find some biblical texts that support your definition?

2. Why are there so many different Christian churches and yet they all claim their teachings are based on the Bible?

3. Jesus referred to the Pharisees as hypocrites. What is your definition of a hypocrite? Is it ever right or appropriate to call someone a hypocrite?

4. What would you say was the main evil of the Pharisees? Why do you feel that way?
5. When we see evil being done in our church or school, should we ever denounce it as Jesus did in His day? How should we respond to the wrongs that others do?
6. What can you do to avoid making the same mistakes the Pharisees made?
7. Jesus accused the Jewish leaders of straining at a gnat and swallowing a camel. What are "the gnats" that are getting too much attention in our day?
8. Are motives more important in spiritual matters than in secular or everyday life?
9. How do the church and the world encourage us to focus on the outward and glorify self?
10. There are many popular religious traditions today, such as worshiping on Sunday. What other examples can you give? Are all "traditions" harmful or wrong? What determines whether a tradition is good or bad?

# ONE DAY AT A TIME
Don't let the future frighten you—you only face it one day at a time
(*Quips & Quotes*).

# lesson 25

## Focus on the Future

**Lesson Scripture: Matthew 24**

**END-TIME SIGNALS**

"Can you believe the way Jesus was talking about the Pharisees?" Michael whispered to his friend Philip, as they crouched behind the wall. "Imagine calling them snakes!"

"And saying that they might be going to hell," Philip added. "I always thought the Pharisees were so good, so righteous. Now, I wonder if they really are."

"Here they come. Let's hide!" The two best friends were glad they didn't have to work in the market today. It gave them a chance to find out in person about this Jesus everyone was talking about.

Michael and Philip dropped down out of sight as Jesus and some of His disciples walked by. When they looked up, Jesus had disappeared through the gate. "Quick, let's follow them," Michael said.

They jumped up and ran through the gate. "Excuse me," Michael gasped as he bumped into one of the disciples. "Sorry."

With a puzzled smile, the disciple turned back to Jesus. Michael and Philip stood behind them all and listened.

"Jesus," one of the disciples was saying, "look at these buildings. Surely this temple will stand forever as a symbol of the one true God."

What Jesus said next was so astounding that Michael and Philip just stood there with their mouths hanging open while the group of men walked away.

"Did you hear that?" Philip finally said. "The whole temple destroyed. Not one stone on top of another. That's unbelievable."

"He must be talking about the end of the world," Michael gasped. "And it must be coming soon." The two young men paused, each one caught up in his own reflective thoughts.

"I sure wouldn't want to be in the temple when it happens," Philip said. "I wonder how we can tell if it's going to happen today or tomorrow or whenever."

"I don't know, but I intend to find out. Come on. We've got to hear more." With that, Michael ran down the street, hot on the trail of Jesus' small group. Philip was right behind him.

Although the Bible doesn't say so, the disciples must have felt a lot like Michael and Philip in our story. The temple was so strong and so secure they were sure that it would last forever. If the temple was going to be destroyed, then the end of the world must be coming too.

Later, after they left the temple, several of the disciples joined Jesus on the Mount of Olives and asked, "When are these things going to happen? And what will be the signs of Your return and the end of the world?"

Jesus mixed the answers to those questions together. He knew that they weren't ready to hear the bald truth about the future. To protect their weak faith, He blended the descriptions of the two events together. He knew that later they could study out the meaning for themselves.

So, many of the signs Jesus gives in Matthew 24 apply to both the destruction of Jerusalem and the time of the end. As you read through the chapter, you can see that the signs fall into three categories: events in nature, the actions of people, and the work of Satan.

You can see examples of each in verses 5 through 7, where Jesus mentions false Christs, wars, and earthquakes. These events were to take place before the destruction of the temple and before the return of Jesus at the end of time.

Jesus does give some warning for those who would be facing the destruction of Jerusalem. Verses 15 through 20 tell the people in Judea to leave without delay when they see the sign. In Luke's record of this talk, Jesus is even more specific.

"When you see Jerusalem being surrounded by armies, you will know that its desolation is near" (Luke 21:20, NIV). Forty years later, Jerusalem was surrounded by Roman armies. The Jewish people were certain their great city would not fall. Then, for reasons unknown by the local people, the armies withdrew. The city broke out into a major celebration, happy to have outlasted the enemy. But the Christians in Jerusalem, remembering Jesus' words of warning, got out of the city as fast as they could. When the Roman armies returned, Jerusalem was again surrounded. This time, the siege worked. The citizens were starved into madness. Many killed and ate their weaker neighbors and children. Finally, the armies broke in and destroyed the city. The temple was burned and demolished. But no Christians died. Remembering Jesus' warning, they were safely hidden in the mountains and wilderness.

In the same way, those Christians who are alive at the end of time will be able to rely on Jesus' words to guide them.

**BEING READY**

If you've ever been on a commercial air flight, you've heard and seen the flight attendants present their preflight safety lecture and demonstration. It's pretty easy to ignore them. After all, most of us can fasten our seat belts without instructions.

But if your flight was ever in danger, if there was a fire or you had to make an emergency landing, you would quickly be wanting to remember their important instructions. Suddenly, their words would be critical to remember.

There is an emergency situation developing in our future, and Matthew 24 gives us important instructions on how to survive it. The most important things to remember from Matthew 24 are these:

1. **The end of the world is coming. Soon!**
2. **Don't be deceived.** Many have claimed and will claim that they are Christ. The checkout stand tabloids are full of news about people

who claim to be prophets. Today, many people in the New Age movement claim to be led by "spirit guides" who will teach them to become a god like Jesus. Don't let them lead you away from the true God.

3. **If you watch, you'll see signs that the end is near.** Read today's paper, or watch the news tonight. Some of the things Jesus predicted are happening now.

4. **We have a work to do.** One of the signs of the end is that the gospel is being preached to all the world. Today, more of the world than ever is open to Christianity. What is needed are people to go and tell what they know about Jesus.

5. **God is in control.** Matthew 24 describes a lot of awful things happening to the earth and to God's followers. But the chapter reminds us that God is in control. He will bring about the time of the end when the time is right. He will bring pain and suffering to an end as soon as possible.

6. **Be ready!** The whole purpose of this chapter is to warn Christians not to get ready, but to be ready. The end will sneak up on those who are too busy to be prepared. Being ready is being a true Christian. It's something you do every day, all day long.

**FLIGHT DELAY**

Many biblical scholars interpreted the tribulation mentioned in verses 21 and 22 as pointing to the great persecutions of the Middle Ages when millions of Christians were killed. Following this time period, the early advent believers saw the "dark day," which occurred in New England on May 19, 1780, and the meteorite shower of November 13, 1833, as a fulfillment of verse 29.

More people have been martyred for their political or religious beliefs in the twentieth century than in all preceding centuries taken together. Communism, the primary persecuting power behind most of these deaths, collapsed dramatically between 1989 and 1991. Yet oppressive governments, religious conflicts, and ethnic turmoil continue to take the lives of thousands of Christians throughout the

world each year. Natural disasters and human carnage on an awesome scale propel people into a search for global solutions and personal peace.

According to verses 30 and 31, the next event should be the return of Jesus. When will it happen?

Obviously, there's been a delay. What could cause God to put off His return? Read Matthew 24:14 for the one specific sign Jesus gives that must be fulfilled prior to His return. Couple this with 2 Peter 3:9, which says He didn't want any to be lost. In 1888, Ellen White was shown that Jesus could have already returned. Now, more than a hundred years later, He still hasn't come. Look around. Look at yourself. How many of us are ready for Jesus to split the sky and step through?

Not many. So, what can we do to be ready?

The problem is that few of us really want the end to come. We lack the security in Christ—and without this security, we aren't anxious for Him to return.

First and foremost, we can personally accept the gospel, which is the "power of God for salvation to everyone who

believes." The Bible says: God . . . "has saved us and called us to a holy life—not because of anything we have done but because of his own purpose and grace" (2 Timothy 1:9, NIV). Then we can share the "good news" with others.

We can shorten the delay by doing the work Jesus left for us. He said that the gospel would go to all the world before He returned. Although the Seventh-day Adventist Church

is proportionately growing at a faster rate than the world's population, more people are being born than are hearing the gospel. Every year, there are more people who haven't heard of Jesus than ever before.

The church desperately needs people to dedicate their lives, no matter what their profession or job, to sharing the gospel with a world running out of time.

There are limits to the delay. God will only allow sin to continue so long, and then He will put an end to it, whether we choose to be ready or not. And all around us, we can see that the earth itself is reaching its limits. Humankind is over-populating, overusing, and over-polluting the earth. Before we can kill ourselves off with wars or choke ourselves to death on garbage and pollution, God will come and wipe the earth clean.

Matthew 24 is a red-flag warning. There is an emergency situation just ahead, but people need to know God has already provided a way of escape in Christ. The end is coming. Keep your eyes open. Be ready! "How shall we escape if we ignore such a great salvation?" (Hebrews 2:3, NIV).

 Memory Focus

"And this gospel of the kingdom will be preached in the whole world as a testimony to all nations, and then the end will come" (Matthew 24:14, NIV).

OR

"I tell you the truth, this generation will certainly not pass away until all these things have happened. Heaven and earth will pass away, but my words will never pass away" (Matthew 24:34, 35, NIV).

 # Into the Bible

1. From Matthew 24:32-51, list the four different stories or illustrations that warn us to be ready for the end.
2. In John 17, Jesus prayed for His disciples and for us who live in anticipation of the second coming. Read each of the following verses, and write out in your own words what Jesus asks God the Father to do for the disciples and for you.
   A. John 17:11
   B. John 17:15
   C. John 17:17
   D. John 17:23
   E. John 17:24
3. Read Matthew 24:4-14. Then complete the chart your teacher will provide, listing each sign given in this chapter under the appropriate heading. Be sure to indicate the scriptural reference for each sign.
4. Matthew 25 is part of Jesus' discourse about the second coming. (Matthew 24 tells us about many signs of Jesus' return.) Matthew 25 shows us how to live and prepare for the second coming. Read Matthew 25 carefully; then answer the following questions:
   A. Why did the virgins fall asleep?
   B. What did they lack when the bridegroom came? Since this represents the Holy Spirit, how do you think this applies to being ready for the second coming?
   C. In the parable of the talents, why didn't the wicked servant invest the one talent?
   D. Talents may represent our abilities or gifts. What do you think this parable teaches about preparing for the second coming?
   E. In the parable of the sheep and the goats, what characteristics or qualities of the righteous (sheep) are commended by Jesus?
5. The question-and-answer session Jesus held on the Mount of

Olives was filled with intense information. But what took place just before this session that sparked the curiosity of the disciples about last-day events? Find out by looking up the following texts and answering the questions.

A. Matthew 23:1—Who was Jesus talking to just before His Sermon on the Mount of Olives?

B. Matthew 23:13—To whom did Jesus specifically address His remarks?

C. Matthew 24:1—After condemning the Pharisees, what did Jesus do, and what did His disciples do?

D. Matthew 24:2—What dramatic prophecy did Jesus make at this time that ignited the disciples' questions on the Mount of Olives?

 # Projects

1. What can you and your classmates do (in a practical way) to help the people about you look forward with joy to Jesus' return? Form groups, and list five practical ideas and ways you might carry them out.

2. Research what two other denominations or religions teach about the end of the world, and present your conclusions to the class. You may gather material from the following: pastors of other denominations, commentaries or other books in the library, someone who is a non-Adventist.

3. The second coming of Jesus and the events that accompany it bring a lot of fear into the hearts of most people, even among Christians. List ten things about this event that portray it as positive and joyous.

4. Make a list of the signs that Jesus gave in Matthew 24:4-14 that lead up to His second coming. Use newspaper and magazine articles and pictures to make a collage on posterboard of current events that fulfill each one of the signs.

#  Focus Questions

1. How did the Jewish people feel about the temple?
2. What events might lead the disciples into thinking that the end had come?
3. What event might lead you into thinking the end was near?
4. Why are false Christs and false prophets such a serious deception? Why would someone believe in a false prophet?
5. According to 2 Peter 3:9 and Matthew 24:14, why is there a delay in Christ's return?
6. What questions about the end of time would you ask Jesus if you could?
7. If Jesus never would return, what difference would it make in your life?
8. Why do you think Jesus did not tell us exactly when He will return?
9. Do you think the second coming is a blessing or an inconvenience? Why?
10. What do you want to do before Jesus comes?

# 241

CROSSROADS SERIES

# unit 4

# Jesus and the Cross

# Jesus' Last Days—Passion Week

Unit four moves through the ministry of Jesus' final days to His betrayal, trial, crucifixion, and resurrection. It seeks to lead to an understanding of the eternal value of these events and to draw each individual into a personal experience of salvation.

Note: Top line represents our method of calculating days—midnight to midnight. Bottom line represents Jewish method of calculating days—sundown to sundown.

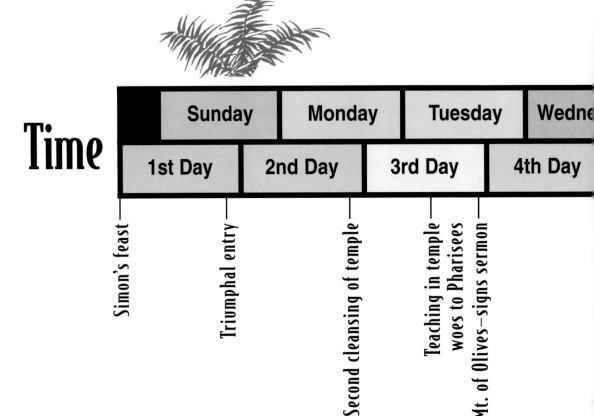

| | Sunday | Monday | Tuesday | Wedne |
|---|---|---|---|---|

**Time**

| 1st Day | 2nd Day | 3rd Day | 4th Day |
|---|---|---|---|

- Simon's feast
- Triumphal entry
- Second cleansing of temple
- Teaching in temple woes to Pharisees
- Mt. of Olives—signs sermon

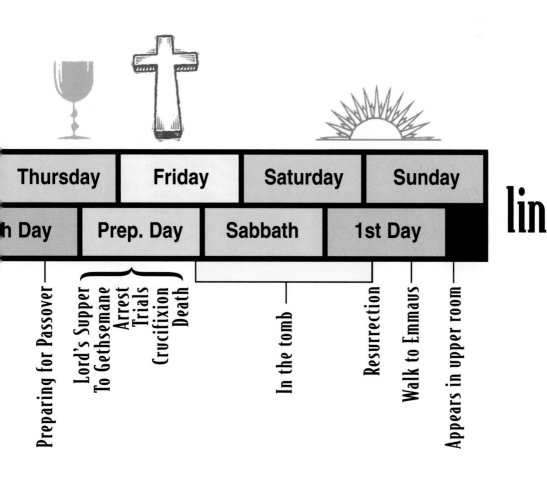

Thursday | Friday | Saturday | Sunday

...h Day | Prep. Day | Sabbath | 1st Day

line

Preparing for Passover

Lord's Supper
To Gethsemane
Arrest
Trials
Crucifixion
Death

In the tomb

Resurrection

Walk to Emmaus

Appears in upper room

# SHOW ME

In Christianity, love is much more easily demonstrated than defined
*(Quips and Quotes).*

# The Last Supper

**Lesson Scriptures: Matthew 26:20-35; John 13:1-17**

ur choir was to sing for vespers. That meant two hours of trying to keep from splitting the seams of my too-tight tuxedo. It was a Communion vespers, and that meant foot washing! I should have followed through with my dream of arranging a home leave for the weekend.

And it was raining.

I made eyes at JoAnne, joked with David, and tried not to think about Communion. After all, I was already a Christian, baptized and all! Why should I have to go through this archaic ritual, anyway?

The organ struck up our song, and Mrs. Price raised her arms, closed her eyes, and pointed to the basses. We sang our hearts and lungs out for her. Up and down the scales on music much too difficult for our little choir. We sang as if we were at Kennedy Center for an inaugural ball. We wowed 'em!

And they liked us. They applauded and applauded. Then it was over, and Communion was beginning.

Mrs. Price had to leave for another choral appointment, but she thanked us for our performance before she bolted through the back door into the rain. David and I watched her raincoat flying toward her old Buick, closed the door, gritted our teeth, prayed for deliverance from Communion, and began a hesitant march toward the sanctuary.

But the door exploded

open behind us, spraying rain-water down the hallway. Mrs. Price, raincoat covered with mud, stockings torn and hair plastered to her forehead, called to us. "Bradley, David, Bud, Terry! My car is stuck in the mud! Please come help me!"

Gladly, we dashed through the door into the deliverance of mercy. The rusty old Buick was truly mired, and it took all of us pushing like a band of steroid-powered penguins before the beast finally began to move. Then its angry tires effectively ended our evening. Mud flew, covering every thread of our soggy tuxedos. Mrs. Price rolled down the window and shouted a genuine "thanks" as she sped toward her appointment.

Everyone ran back toward the dorm except David and me. Somehow, we ended up at the curb in front of the church. The drain was plugged, the water was already nearly a foot deep, and a wading pool was forming. We splashed the mud from our tuxedos, and then something overwhelming sat us down on the curb. We looked at each other in amazement, removed our soggy shoes and squashy socks, and washed each other's feet with the rainwater.

To this day, I'm not at all sure what made us do it. But I know I've never felt the same about Communion. It was an unlikely setting—a curb, mud, rain-soaked clothing, but it was here that God spoke to us. We heard God ask if we really wanted to be His servants. He offered a deep pool of clean rainwater, and we had dirty feet and hearts that needed to be washed.

Neither David nor I worried whether someone was watching or if we could sit with JoAnne and Donna for the bread and wine. This time we just washed, sat there in the rain, and then prayed for each other.

David had to return to the dorm with trousers beyond repair. But something drew me up the stairs to the church sanctuary. The deacon was hor-rified by my hair, tux, and bare feet but reluctantly allowed me to enter and sit in the very back pew. The other kids were all up front, so I participated alone, like an included outcast, blan-keted with forgiveness and grace.

The bread was small, yet large enough to remind me of the Saviour who gave His all that I might freely eat. The "wine" was sparkling and sweet, and in it I saw the crimson shadow of a cross.

The choir sang for vespers. I can't remember what we sang. But the Communion service God held for me behind the Buick, at the curb, and on the back row still reverberates through my life.

My successes are worthless, nothing.

Only in His service is there true success.

Only in the pure blood of His death can my life be purified.

Only at the cross can my hunger for self-confidence be relieved.

Only at the cross can my thirst for peace be quenched.

His success for me is invaluable, eternal!

The unusual story you have just read captures some of the same mixed emotions the disciples experienced at the first Lord's Supper. They were preoccupied with their struggles for personal power and identity, and they avoided anything that would require humility or unselfishness. They could only think of the place they would

have in the kingdom that Jesus would soon establish. They wondered how and when Jesus would assert Himself as the King of the Jews.

The week had been full of tumultuous events. It began with that glorious entry into Jerusalem as hundreds of people praised Jesus as the promised Messiah. Then on Monday, in an act of radical holiness, Jesus cleansed the temple—again. There was a new and passionate urgency that the disciples sensed in Jesus now. Just two days ago, they had heard Him boldly rebuke the Pharisees as He spoke to the crowds in the temple courtyard. And then, the door to the future had been nudged ajar as their Master revealed His predictions and plans.

Now, this evening, their heads swirled with conflicting ideas. Each was so involved with his own thoughts that there was no room to be concerned about others and their needs. It was in this setting that Jesus reached out to each disciple—with a towel, a basin, some bread, and some wine.

And it is with these same symbols that He still reaches out today.

# Memory Focus

"And he took bread, gave thanks and broke it, and gave it to them, saying, 'This is my body given for you; do this in remembrance of me.' In the same way, after the supper he took the cup, saying, 'This cup is the new covenant in my blood, which is poured out for you' " (Luke 22:19, 20, NIV).

# Into the Bible

Luke 22:20—Here is Christ's assurance that by His shed blood, He would institute the new covenant promised in the Old Testament book of Jeremiah.

This new covenant brings to an end the old covenant God gave Israel through Moses, consisting of special ceremonies and

rituals and laws. They were designed to instruct the people about the coming Messiah and how God would accomplish the forgiveness of their sins and give them salvation through Christ. Jesus was the fulfillment of all the Old Testament "shadows" that pointed forward to His suffering and sacrificial death. Thus He put an end to the ceremonial animal sacrifices of the Old Testament (see Hebrews 9:26 and 10:1-4).

1. Bread is used in the Old Testament as a symbol of God's providing for His people. Summarize the story of Exodus 16:1-7 of how God provided food for His people in the wilderness.
2. Examine John 6:50, 51, 53. What do you learn about Jesus from each verse?
3. Read Hebrews 9:22 and Leviticus 17:11 to discover why there is so much emphasis on the blood of Jesus. Summarize the reasons.
4. Read 1 Corinthians 11:23-26, and answer the following questions:
   A. What does it mean "to proclaim"? (You may wish to use a dictionary.)
   B. What is to be proclaimed?
   C. Explain the connection between the shed blood of Christ and the covenant. You may wish to use a dictionary to define covenant. Consult Matthew 26:28; Hebrews 8:10-12; 9:15; 13:20 for further information.
5. Passover, for the Jews, was considered a great spiritual festival. As Jesus had the Last Supper with the disciples, they were actually participating in the last Passover that would ever be needed and at the same time observing the first Communion service. Using Exodus 12; Luke 22:7-20; *Patriarchs and Prophets*, pages 273-280; and *The Desire of Ages*, pages 652-661, compare these two services. Use the chart your teacher will provide in making the comparisons.

 **Projects**

1. Christians hold three primary views on the relationship of Christ and the substance of the bread and wine. While Seventh-day Adventists believe that the bread and wine are only symbols of the body and blood of Christ in what is known as the "reformed" tradition, Lutherans hold a position sometimes called "consubstantiation," and Roman Catholics hold the view known as "transubstantiation." Use a dictionary to define these terms. You may wish to call a Lutheran minister or a Roman Catholic priest and ask them to explain their position. Report your findings to the class.

2. Use one or more Bible commentaries to obtain information about the preparation for the Passover. Matthew 26:17-19; Mark 14:12-16; Luke 22:7-13. List five facts that you found about the activities involving the Passover Feast.

3. Contact two or three members of the Jewish community, or do library research to find out how the Passover is celebrated today. Summarize your findings, and identify changes in the celebration from that in Jesus' time.

4. Contact two or three persons who are members of other Christian churches, and ask for information about how they celebrate the Communion service. Summarize your findings, and identify differences and similarities in the service.

 **Focus Questions**

1. Should every worship service include Communion? Why or why not?
2. What is the relationship of the spoken word (the preaching of the gospel) and the Communion service?
3. Must a person have a true personal relationship with Christ in order for the Communion service to bring God's blessing?
4. Is foot washing a necessary element in the Communion service?
5. Why do you think Jesus chose bread to represent His body?
6. If the Lord's Supper is so important, why do so many Christians avoid it?
7. Jesus used foot washing as a symbol of humility and service. If He were to choose a new symbol today, what do you think He would choose?
8. If Jesus came here to wash your feet today, what would you say to Him?

# LISTENING

If you would have God hear you when you pray,
you must hear Him when He speaks *(Quips and Quotes)*.

# The Divine Comforter

**Lesson Scriptures: John 14:15-25; 16:5-15**

The flames of the campfire flickered lower as John sacrificed the last marshmallow on the glowing coals. "Good night, guys. Watch out for those mosquitoes," Pastor Bob called as another group of campers disappeared into the tents.

John thought while he ate his marshmallow. Then he said, "Pastor Bob, to me, the whole idea of the Holy Spirit is really confusing. Especially this 'unpardonable sin' stuff. Can I really do something so bad that God won't forgive me?"

"Well, you know the stories in the Bible. People are forgiven for murder, adultery, lying, . . ."

"See what I mean! What worse sin can there be? Or is the Holy Spirit more picky than Jesus, more easily offended?"

"No, John, I don't think I'd say that."

"So, what is it? For all I know, I've already done it, and I'm wasting my time going to church and everything."

"All right. Let me explain this way." Pastor Bob stirred the fire with a long stick. "Suppose you were the only one out here, lost in the middle of this forest, in the middle of the night, many miles from civilization."

"OK."

"And suppose your only hope was to sit here by a big burning fire that would attract the rescuers. Your greatest danger would be wandering away from the fire."

"It would be stupid to do that," John said.

"True," Pastor Bob agreed with a smile. "Because if you

did, you might get lost in the darkness. No matter how big the fire was, no matter how brightly it burned, you could get so far away that you could not see it."

"I'm sure I could," John agreed.

"Now, imagine, in spite of how dumb it was, you did go off into the darkness, farther and farther from the fire. Slowly, it would seem like only a small fire, then just a flicker between the trees. Soon it would only be a glow in the distance, until finally it was completely out of sight. There you would be, totally lost, with no idea which way to go."

"That wouldn't be too bright. But what does this tell me about the unpardonable sin?"

Pastor Bob waved the burning stick toward John. "Let's say the Holy Spirit is like that fire. Only He can lead us to salvation, because He is our connection to Jesus."

"And the light of the fire would be like His influence, His efforts to reach out to us and draw us to God?" John asked.

"That's right. And while He tries to attract us and lead us to God, He never stands in the way of our freedom to choose.

If we want to walk away from Him and not listen, we are free to go."

"So when does He not forgive us anymore?"

"Well, think back on the story. When were you lost, with no chance to find your way out?"

"When I couldn't see the fire anymore."

"Right. Not because the fire went out, but because you left. It's the same with the Holy Spirit. He doesn't stop caring for you or calling to you. You just can't hear Him anymore, and when you can no longer sense His attraction, then you are lost. Forever."

"And that's the unpardonable sin? When you can't hear His voice anymore?"

"There is no sin that God won't forgive if we sincerely repent. But the only thing that draws us to Him to ask for forgiveness is the influence of the Holy Spirit. If we can't sense that, we are unpardonable because we're unreachable."

"So, the Holy Spirit doesn't cut us off because we make a big mistake. We cut Him off," responded John. Then he tossed some more wood on the fire. "Maybe the Holy Spirit isn't as confusing as I thought."

Sometimes, understanding God is difficult. God the Father, God the Son, and God the Holy Spirit, three Persons who are like One, but what are They like?

Especially God the Holy Spirit. We think of the Father as, well, a father. But the term *Spirit* or *Ghost* conjures up thoughts of some wispy character with no real body or form, not someone like Jesus.

And what does the Holy Spirit do? If we pray to the Father in Jesus' name, does the Holy Spirit take the message to heaven? Or do the angels do that? Or do they take it to the Holy Spirit so He can relay it to heaven? When we ask for Jesus to be with us through the day, is He? Or is the Holy Spirit with us in His place? Is there a difference?

Confusing, isn't it? Let's try to sort this out by starting at the beginning. Let's realize that we are trying to understand in human terms things that are not human. In communicating with humanity, God has expressed Himself in terms that humans can understand. "Father," "Son," and "Holy Spirit" are titles used for our benefit.

This world and its people are definitely a group project.

In the beginning, it was Jesus who created the heavens and the earth. But the second verse of the Bible, Genesis 1:2, says that the Spirit of God was present when the world was created. And again at Jesus' baptism, the group was present. The Father spoke from heaven, and the Holy Spirit came down like a dove. The Holy Spirit continued to be involved during Jesus' life here on earth, apparently directing Jesus' daily plans.

Most of what we know about the Holy Spirit is found in John 14 and 16. In those chapters, Jesus tells His disciples that He is leaving. But He promises that Someone else is coming to help them.

In this kind of tag-team approach, Jesus hands off the responsibility of working directly with humans to the Holy Spirit. Jesus doesn't describe the Holy Spirit's appearance or say that the disciples will see Him, but He introduces the Holy Spirit as a Person.

Jesus says that the Holy Spirit is coming down to continue the work that He started, the work of the Father in heaven. What does Jesus say this other God-Person will do?

In John 14:16, Jesus says, "I

will ask the Father, and he will give you another Helper" (NCV). The Greek word translated "helper" can also mean "intercessor," "mediator," or "advocate." All of those words refer to someone who works to bring two sides together. The King James Version translates the word as "comforter."

Some people have wondered why Jesus says that the Father will send "another Comforter." Who was the first Comforter? When we realize that the Holy Spirit's work as Comforter and Helper is to draw humans to God's love, it's easy to see who the first Comforter must have been. It was Jesus Himself, who came to earth to show us what God was really like.

So Jesus sent the Holy Spirit to continue His work of bringing God and humans back together. Jesus said that the Holy Spirit would also teach the disciples truth and help them remember the things Jesus had taught them (see John 14:26).

The Holy Spirit would also have a mission to the rest of the world. He would "prove to the people of the world the truth about sin, about being right with God, and about judgment" (John 16:8, NCV). So in addition to teaching and guiding the church, the Holy Spirit is also out in the world working on people's minds, preparing them to hear and accept the message of God's love.

So what is the Holy Spirit's role in the plan of salvation?

1. He draws people to Jesus and to the truth (John 16:8-13). He influences the minds of believers and those who don't know God.
2. He brings the presence of Jesus (John 14:17, 18). He fulfills Jesus' promise to be with us always.
3. He guides the operation of the church (Acts 16:6, 7). He helped the early believers select missionaries (Acts 13:1, 2). Paul reminded the early church leaders that the Holy Spirit had placed them in that position (Acts 20:28).

Today, the church prays for guidance from the Holy Spirit and looks for evidence that the Holy Spirit has "called" a person to be a minister.

4. He gives the church special gifts. Whether gifts of ministry (1 Corinthians 12:7-11), artistic gifts (Exodus 31:3), or the power to preach the gospel (Acts 1:8), the Holy Spirit gives believers what they need to do the work God asks them to do.

5. He illuminates the hearts of believers. When a person is baptized, the Holy Spirit fills the heart with God's love and peace (John 3:6, 7). And He changes us, making us more and more like Jesus (Titus 3:5).

One of the most confusing things about the Holy Spirit is the "unpardonable sin." The idea of a sin that cannot be forgiven comes from something Jesus said:

"So I tell you, people can be forgiven for every sin and everything they say against God. But whoever speaks against the Holy Spirit will not be forgiven" (Matthew 12:31, NCV).

That sounds pretty final. But when you look at the ear-lier verses in that chapter, you see what is really going on. The Pharisees, the church leaders of Israel, saw that more and more people were following Jesus. That meant fewer and fewer were listening to them. When Jesus refused to follow their guidelines, they spoke out against Him.

"Do not listen to this man," they told the people. "He is not from God."

"Then how," the people asked, "do you explain the miracles He does?"

The Pharisees were stuck. Obviously, the miracles were real. Blind people who can suddenly see are hard to argue with. But if Jesus didn't agree with the Pharisees, then He couldn't be from God. So, they said, He must heal people with the power of the devil.

This was when Jesus said that anyone who speaks against the Holy Spirit cannot be forgiven. Believing that the work of the Holy Spirit was really the work of the devil showed that the Pharisees' minds were completely closed to the Holy Spirit. They had cut themselves off from Jesus and from the Holy Spirit, who was trying to bring them to Jesus.

Since the Holy Spirit could

not reach them, they would never change and never want forgiveness. So that sin could never be forgiven.

How do you know if you've committed the unpardonable sin? Remember that every good thing in this world comes from God. Every time a person says or does something truly good or unselfish, it is because the Holy Spirit is working on his or her heart. So when you do or say anything that is unselfish or good, the Holy Spirit is still working on you, trying to draw you closer to God.

The Holy Spirit is the escape route, the bridge, the connection between us and Jesus. To someone who is fighting against the pressures and the unfairness of a world full of sin, He's the best ally you could have.

 ## Memory Focus

"I have told you all these things while I am with you. But the Helper will teach you everything and He will cause you to remember all that I told you" (John 14:25, 26, NCV).

 ## Into the Bible

1. The Holy Spirit is not just a Person, He's a busy Person! Read the following verses, and write a summary that describes what the Holy Spirit is doing in each of the verses.
   A. Genesis 6:3
   B. Luke 12:12
   C. Acts 13:2
   D. John 16:8
   E. Romans 8:26
   F. 1 Peter 1:2
   G. John 14:25
2. John 13 and 14 describe the events at the time Jesus promised that the Holy Spirit would be sent.
   A. List the events described in these chapters.
   B. In your own words, describe what Jesus told His disciples about the Holy Spirit.
3. In John 16, Jesus talked about the work of the Holy Spirit.

A. Read verses 8 through 11, and indicate the three things the Holy Spirit convicted the world of, and why.

B. Use a Bible commentary, and write a summary that describes why the "world" would be convicted of each.

4. According to John 16:12, 13, what three things would the Holy Spirit do that Jesus could not do?

 # Projects

1. Interview a pastor or teacher to find out what he/she thinks it means to be called by the Holy Spirit to be a minister or teacher.
2. Look up John 16:7 in several versions.
   A. Write down how the word *comforter* is translated in each one.
   B. Then use a dictionary to write down a definition of each word. Include *intercessor, mediator,* and *advocate* in your list.
3. Read the part of the lesson that compares the Holy Spirit to a fire. Write a short description that will compare the Holy Spirit to one of the following:

   A. a telephone     D. an elevator

   B. a referee       E. a bridge

   C. an army general

 # Focus Questions

1. In the story, does it make sense to compare the Holy Spirit to a campfire? What does the comparison say about the Holy Spirit?
2. What thoughts come to your mind when you hear the words, *Holy Spirit?*
3. What is the Holy Spirit's place in the Godhead? What does He do?
4. In what way are this world and its people a "group project"?
5. What is the Holy Spirit's role in your salvation?
6. What is the unpardonable sin? How can a person know if he/she has committed the unpardonable sin?

Mark Wellman, a paraplegic, is being helped to the top of Half Dome.

# CRISIS MANAGEMENT
The daily tests of life determine our decisions in the great crises of life
(Unknown).

# lesson 28

# Jesus and Gethsemane

## Lesson Scripture: Mark 14:32-42

Ordinarily, the gatekeeper would have been just a bit suspicious of twelve men leaving the city all together in the middle of the night. At some other time of year, he might have delayed them, questioned them, thrown his weight around a bit. But it was Thursday night of Passover week, and he expected the unusual at this time of year. Thousands of pilgrims had descended on Jerusalem for the yearly celebration of this ancient festival. Even now, the moon glowed softly on their tents, pitched as far as the eye could see around the city walls. This group of men asking him to open the gate were no doubt just another bunch of pilgrims making their way back to their tents in the dead of night.

Jesus and eleven of His disciples descended the rocky path out of the city in somber silence. There was much to talk about, but no one felt like making conversation, especially since Jesus was so strangely silent. As they crossed the Brook Kidron, each of them was lost in his own thoughts, remembering the unusual supper they'd just finished in their rented upstairs room.

Jesus had been in a solemn mood, saying baffling things about death and betrayal. He'd been talking like this for weeks, but they still weren't sure what He meant. Who would want to kill Him? Who would be desperate enough to betray Him? If that wasn't enough of a mys-

tery, there was Judas's bizarre behavior. Where was he, anyway? What possessed him to leave the room in the middle of supper?

The disciples followed silently behind Jesus, watching Him in the dim moonlight. He didn't seem merely preoccupied; He seemed anxious and troubled. Suddenly, He stopped and looked around. "My soul is full of a deathly sorrow," He said mournfully. Two of the disciples rushed forward to support Him as He stumbled along the path. They all became alarmed. What was this strange sadness overwhelming their Teacher and Friend?

Could it really kill Him? Was that why He'd seemed so preoccupied with death?

The disciples knew where Jesus was going and were anxious to get there soon. The Garden of Gethsemane was Jesus' favorite place. He'd often gone there for privacy and prayer. Perhaps some rest in the garden would cheer Him up. *He must be sick or exhausted,* they thought, *and just needs a good night's rest.*

Jesus asked eight of His followers to wait near the garden gate. They didn't need to be persuaded. They were worn-out, too, and anxious to shut out the eerie gloom of this night. They huddled in groups on the ground and fell quickly to sleep.

Jesus asked Peter, James, and John to follow Him deeper into the olive grove. They hiked for some distance. Finally, Jesus told them to wait while He went off by Himself to pray. He asked them to pray for Him while He was gone. He didn't say it in so many words, but He was trying to tell them He needed their support. He needed to know that He could count on their love and loyalty during His terrible crisis. As long as He'd known them, He had prayed for them. Now He needed their prayers.

They may have had the best intentions, but Peter, James, and John were as tired as the others out by the gate. Besides, none of them really grasped the significance of what was happening. They'd heard Jesus talk about His impending death at supper that night. They'd seen Judas go out of the room at the mention of betrayal. But they just hadn't put it all together in their minds. If they had realized that the world's salvation, including their own, was at stake that night, they would have made more of an effort to stay awake. As it was, Jesus came back to them twice for some company and encouragement, and both times He found them fast asleep.

Why was Jesus in such a terrible state of mind that night in the Garden of Gethsemane? Why was He in such agony that some accounts say He sweated great drops of blood? The simplest answer is the terror He felt facing a torturous death. But that can't be the whole explanation. Not when you consider that for centuries after this, Christian martyrs—men, women, and even children—went to their deaths by stoning, burning, and wild animals, singing hymns and praising God. We've all heard stories of heroic men and women in times of war or disaster who faced death without so much as a whine or whimper.

So Jesus wasn't simply afraid of dying. His anguish was the result of sin, separation, and surrender—all interrelated and all contributing to His conflict in the garden that night.

**Sin.** Some people who have survived near-death experiences report later that their "whole lives passed before them." They see, like a video on fast forward, all the bad things they've ever done. They're filled with remorse and long for the chance to make things right.

We've all felt the pressure of guilt, whether we have lied, stolen, cheated on an exam, or betrayed a friend. Guilt is a healthy emotion if it leads to repentance, confession, forgiveness, and restoration. But without these remedies, guilt can be crushing, causing physical pain, mental illness, and even suicide.

The mystery of Jesus in the garden is that it wasn't His own guilt He was feeling but the crushing burden of the guilt of the whole human race. He who "knew no sin" became "sin for us" (2 Corinthians 5:21). Under such a weight of guilt, Jesus became the embodiment of sin, that most hated thing in God's universe. His suffering was partly the result of wondering if His relationship with God could survive this experience.

**Separation.** Have you ever seen a two-year-old left with a baby sitter? At this age, most toddlers go through a long phase of something called separation anxiety. They've bonded

with their parents and rely on them completely. The thought of being separated from them is more than they can bear. They don't understand time, so they aren't comforted when they're told Mom and Dad will be back soon. They only know that Mom and Dad are gone, and any time at all is forever.

Luckily, we grow out of this phase. But all through life we face different degrees of separation—summer camp, boarding school, business trips, death. But in each case, there is the hope of being reunited—at the end of summer, when school is out, next week, or in eternity.

Jesus' agony in the garden, and later on the cross, was grounded in the fear that so much sin would separate Him from God forever. That even if He succeeded in carrying all of humanity's sins to His grave, the price of crossing such a chasm would be that He could never return to His Father.

*Surrender.* It's easy to talk tough before the other guy shows up for the fight. It's easy to be blasé before the lights go down and the curtain goes up. Before He took the form of a human being, Jesus had volunteered to rescue the world

from sin. He had even spoken matter-of-factly about His death. But now He faced it for real. Now it was either drink from the cup handed Him or pass it on to the whole world. Faced with what He knew would surely happen in the next few hours, Jesus asked God three times, "If you are willing, take this cup from me" (Luke 22:42, NIV).

Satan, of course, couldn't let such a vulnerable moment pass. He'd been waiting for an opening ever since his defeat in the wilderness. Now He came to add to Jesus' suffering by suggesting an easy, even reasonable, option. "Why put Yourself through this?" he whispered. "Who really believes in You, anyway? Your companions are all asleep. Judas has betrayed You. Peter will say he doesn't know You. All of them will run away. And these are Your friends I'm talking about! The church leaders are out to kill You. If the whole human race wants to hurtle into oblivion without You, why not let them!"

It would have been easy to do. There seemed to be so little reward for such a sacrifice. In the end, only one thing persuaded Jesus. He looked back

and forward into the future of human history and saw thousands and millions who had believed and would believe in Him and receive the gift of eternal life that only He could give. Allowing His people to be lost would be more agonizing than what He faced tonight. Though He asked three times if there was any other way, Jesus firmly said, "Not my will, but yours be done" (Luke 22:42, NIV). The struggle over, Jesus fell exhausted to the ground.

### EPILOGUE

They awoke to the sound of a mob approaching the garden gate, their torches casting eerie shadows among the trees. The leaders asked for Jesus of Nazareth, and Jesus replied, "I am He." For an instant, a flash of divine light paralyzed the mob, and they staggered back. But when the brilliance faded, the soldiers got a grip on their courage and stepped forward to arrest Jesus.

Judas did what had been predicted and what he would forever be known by—he identified Jesus with a kiss. Peter suddenly remembered his own promise to stick by Jesus and,

not finding anything more useful to do, he grabbed a sword and started swinging, succeeding only in cutting off the ear of the high priest's servant. Far from being impressed by this macho display, Jesus told Peter to put the sword away, "for all who draw the sword will die by the sword" (Matthew 26:52, NIV). Then He touched the servant and healed his ear.

When it became clear to Peter that Jesus was not going to resist arrest, he suggested to his friends that they do what they could to save themselves. Acting swiftly on this suggestion, "all the disciples deserted him" (Matthew 26:56, NIV).

## OUR GETHSEMANE

All of us can expect to face a lot of suffering in this life—sickness, death, bigotry, the misery of broken families. But no matter how painful, these crises are not equivalent to Jesus' agony in the Garden of Gethsemane. Our Gethsemane comes, just as it did for Jesus, in the battle between our will and God's will.

In Philippians 3:10, Paul speaks about knowing Jesus and "the fellowship of his suffering." All who receive eternal life will have fought against their own selfish desires and let God win.

There's a big difference, though, between Jesus' struggle and ours. Jesus wrestled with the decision to take our sin and guilt; we struggle to give it up. Jesus' greatest pain was separation from God; ours is separating ourselves from sin. He had everything to lose; we have everything to gain.

 # Memory Focus

"In that He Himself has suffered, being tempted, He is able to aid those who are tempted" (Hebrews 2:18, NKJV).

 # Into the Bible

1. Peter, who was so quick to take up the sword, later wrote on the subject of self-defense. Read 1 Peter 2:13-15, 18-23; 3:14, 17. What do you think made the difference?
2. Identify how Christ's crucifixion on the cross is a continuation of the agony that began in the Garden of Gethsemane as recorded in the following Scriptures: Matthew 26:38, 39; 27:46.
3. What was the "cup" from which Jesus drank? Matthew 26:39, 27, 28; 20:22, 28; Jeremiah 25:15; Isaiah 51:17; Romans 5:9; Revelation 14:9,10. (Notice the use of the word *too* in verse 10, NIV.)
4. Jesus tried to warn His disciples of the tragic events associated with His arrest, trial, and crucifixion. He even quoted an Old

Testament prophecy predicting their response to these events. Read the prophecy found in Zechariah 13:7, Jesus' warning in Mark 14:27, and the fulfillment of these predictions found in Mark 14:49-51. Why do you think the disciples responded in the manner they did even after being warned of their weaknesses?

 Projects

1. You are a reporter for the *Jerusalem Times*. You worked late. It is night, and you are on the way home when you see a mob of men led by the high priest leaving the city. Your curiosity is aroused, so you follow them. They go to the Garden of Gethsemane, where they arrest and take a man away. Write a brief report of your eyewitness account of the events that took place. From what you saw, indicate why you think the man was arrested.

2. Choose one of the following individuals, and write a report as to what you think was going through his mind during the events that took place that night in the Garden of Gethsemane.
   A. Peter
   B. Servant
   C. High priest
   D. Judas Iscariot

 Focus Questions

1. Was it possible for Jesus to fail His mission to redeem the world?
2. Why was it so difficult for the disciples to stay awake and pray for Jesus and themselves?
3. Jesus took on the full weight of all the sins of humanity. Does that mean that we have nothing to do?
4. How is Christ's struggle different from ours?

# THE WITNESS

Jesus Christ does not grant us the privilege of being secret believers (Unknown).

# lesson 29

# That Incredible Mistrial

**Lesson Scriptures: Matt. 26:57-75; 27:3-26; Luke 22:66-71; 23:6-12; John 18:12-38**

Eyes filled with bitter tears, minds reeled in shock and dismay as people woke up on that fateful Friday to the news that Jesus had been arrested, tried, found guilty, and sentenced to die. And since all of this had taken place while Jerusalem slept, there were many who wondered, "Why the hurry and coverup? Why such underhanded flurry by the highest court in the land?"

But there were others in Jerusalem that morning who breathed a sigh of relief when they learned that the one they considered to be a blasphemer and self-proclaimed Messiah was about to be silenced. How grateful they were for a judicial system that could move so decisively when dealing with those who were such an annoying threat to the nation's spiritual well-being.

Earlier in Christ's ministry, one of His disciples observed that "there was a division among the people because of Him" (John 7:43, NKJV). No doubt this was a fitting description of the people's response to Jesus, whether to His teachings, His miracles, or His condemnation and death.

## THE MISTRIAL

In any civilized nation, where justice and equality are eagerly pursued and valued, the judicial system—the courtroom, the judge, the jury—plays an extremely important role. It is assumed that in a society where obedience to law is highly esteemed, as it was in Israel, truth and justice will prevail whenever a person or an issue is given a hearing. Naturally, the more crucial the case, and the more serious the crime, the more deliberate the judicial process will be to assure a fair and lawful verdict. If this essential procedure breaks down, if a nation's highest court is corrupted by self-interest and political gain, then that nation is dangerously close to national chaos and ruin.

*Webster's Dictionary* defines a mistrial as "a trial that has no legal effect by reason of some error or serious prejudicial misconduct in the proceedings." What were some of these illegal, behind-the-scene maneuvers that made the trial of Jesus one of the most tragic events in all of human history? If that sounds like an exaggeration, bear in mind that this deplorable affair involved the Creator Himself, the Supreme Ruler of all the universe, being mocked, spit upon, tortured, and condemned to die the most painful and humiliating death ever devised. How the Almighty God, garbed in human flesh, could take such insult and abuse by men under the control of Satan, without complaint or reproach, is certainly beyond our comprehension.

## THE BACKGROUND

In Christ's time, there was a great deal of turmoil and unrest among the Jews. As a nation fiercely loyal to the God of their ancestors, it was extremely painful to be under the rule and dominion of a heathen government. Repeated rebellion against the oppression of Rome was commonplace.

The rulers that Caesar had appointed to govern the Jews, Herod the Great in Galilee and Pilate in Judea, greatly angered the people with their heavy-handed policies and cruelty. Herod had taxed the people unmercifully to sustain a life of luxury for himself, as well as to rebuild the temple in Jerusalem. It was he who had ordered the slaying of the babies in Bethlehem at Christ's birth. When this Herod died, his son, Herod Antipas, took the throne and is best remembered for having beheaded John the Baptist and taken part in Christ's trial. Pilate was appointed governor of Judea in A.D. 26 and was intensely despised by the Jews for his brutal and savage treatment of those who interfered with his rule. Bloodshed, riots, and violent confrontations between the Jews and Roman authorities were everyday occurrences.

This outbreak of revolution and civil defiance of Rome must have been discussed daily in Nazareth as Jesus worked at the carpenter's bench. Yet, when Jesus emerged as the Messiah proclaiming the good news of the kingdom of heaven, His primary attack was not against the tyranny of Roman rule, but rather, the abuses of the religious leaders.

Naturally, such fearless rebuke from an unschooled Galilean inflamed the wrath of the Jewish clergy. For men like these, Jesus was a "thorn in the flesh," not only for exposing their self-serving practices, but for meddling with their lucrative business in the temple. Seeing Jesus as a rival to their position of authority rather than as a hoped-for liberator from Rome, the Pharisees and Sadducees united with one common objective in mind—to bring to an end the life and ministry of Jesus at any cost.

## THE TACTICS

With their primary goal being to eliminate Jesus, not to test the truth of His teachings, any strategy that would accom-

plish this purpose was considered appropriate to them. Nothing would stand in their way! Matthew confirms this when he says, "The chief priests, the scribes, and the elders of the people assembled at the palace of the high priest, who was called Caiaphas, and plotted to take Jesus by trickery and kill Him" (Matthew 26:3, 4, NKJV).

Such coldblooded treachery was already taking place several months earlier, when following Christ's raising of Lazarus, Caiaphas "gave counsel to the Jews that it was expedient that one man [Jesus] should die for the people" (John 18:14, NKJV). *Webster's* defines *expedient* as being "governed by self-interest." When the Jewish leadership disregarded principles of justice simply to safeguard their established positions and to promote their selfish interests, what else could such an immoral behavior bring about but a mistrial of the very worst kind.

## THE VIOLATIONS

In order to step up the pace of the trial, provide as much secrecy as possible, and assure a guilty verdict, the Sanhedrin committed violations of Jewish law from the beginning to the very end of the trial. In all crim-

inal cases, Jewish law provided strict control of court proceedings, especially in capital cases where the death penalty might be involved. Although there were scores of legal infractions,

we will examine only some of the more serious violations that occurred during the Jewish or religious phase of the trial.

1. Jewish law did not permit the trial of a potential capital case to be held at night, on the Sabbath, or during a religious festival. Christ's trial began after midnight on Thursday, and Friday was the first day of the Feast of Unleavened Bread.

2. The prescribed place for such a trial before the Sanhedrin was an inner courtroom of the temple. Only there could a death sentence be handed down. Since the temple doors were locked at sundown, the trial took place in the palace of the high priest.

3. Jesus was never formally indicted. Instead, accusations were drummed up against Him.

4. Any witnesses and their testimony had to be carefully screened and validated. No one could be found guilty of any charge except by the undisputed testimony of at least two witnesses. During the trial, two witnesses were bribed to conjure up false testimony.

5. Contrary to law, the high priest and the members of the Sanhedrin served as prosecutor, judge, and jury.

6. Jewish law forbade convicting or sentencing a criminal based on his own testimony, as was done in this case.

7. For a conviction involving a capital offense, sentence could not be passed on the same day as the trial. Christ was pronounced guilty, sentenced, and executed all on the same day.

8. Throughout the trial, Jesus was repeatedly abused and

beaten, even by officers of the court. Such unruly conduct was strictly forbidden.

9. The balloting was done by group acclamation rather than by individual polling of each member, starting with the youngest and moving up to the oldest, as the law required.

10. After the Jewish (religious) phase of the trial was over, the charges against Jesus were changed from a religious to a civil crime.

### THE CHARGE

Obviously, the key issue in the whole trial was the specific crime for which Jesus was charged. When He was brought before Pilate during the Roman or civil phase of the trial, Pilate began with a logical question, "What charges are you bringing against this man?" (John 18:29, NIV). At first, the Jewish leaders endeavored to sidestep this inquiry with an evasive answer, but finally they stated their contention: "This fellow has been leading our people to ruin by telling them not to pay their taxes to the Roman government and by claiming he is our Messiah—a King" (Luke 23:2, TLB).

When this indictment is compared to the one that had been pronounced earlier that morning, there is a strange twist. Having condemned Jesus for religious misconduct, the charge is now altered to focus on treason and civil disobedience, hoping of course, to alarm Pilate and gain his approval for Christ's death.

But the REAL reason for demanding Christ's death was not based on anything that Jesus had done, which is generally the primary issue in a criminal case. Jesus, however, was declared worthy of death for whom He claimed to be—"the Son of the Blessed One" (Mark 14:61, 62, NIV). Granted, Jesus had said and done a great deal that had exposed and angered the Jewish leaders, but if Jesus was merely a deluded, self-proclaimed Messiah, then He could simply be ignored and put away. If, on the other hand, He truly was "the Son of God" as He claimed, then all that He had spoken and carried out was indeed true, and it was they who stood condemned. In their spiritual pride and arrogance, they refused to acknowledge the error of their ways, choosing instead to crucify Him who is "the way, the truth, and the life" (John 14:6, KJV).

This tragic episode of nearly two thousand years ago has a very definite connection with the present. Pilate's question to the people, "What shall I do, then, with Jesus?" (Matthew 27:22, NIV), is a question none of us can escape or ignore. Each of us must answer it for ourselves. It's been said that within the heart of every person there is a throne and a cross. If Jesus is invited to rule on the throne, then self will be placed on the cross to die. But if self is allowed to reign supreme in our lives, by that choice we are in effect "crucifying the Son of God all over again" (Hebrews 6:6, NIV). The choice is ours.

### THE TRIAL OF JESUS

The following is a summary of Jesus' trial. It includes the sequence of events, the approximate time and place, and those presiding over the hearings.

### THE RELIGIOUS (JEWISH) TRIAL

1. A preliminary hearing before Annas, who had served as the high priest from A.D. 7 to A.D. 15. This hearing took place shortly after midnight, in the early hours of Friday morning.

2. A hearing before Caiaphas, the high priest who was in office from A.D. 18 to A.D. 36. This hearing took place in the palace of the high priest from about 2:00 a.m. to 3:00 a.m. During this time, the call went out for the members of the Sanhedrin to assemble.

3. The night trial of the Sanhedrin, the Jewish Council, convened in the palace of the high priest from around 3:00 a.m. to 4:00 a.m. It was during this hearing that Peter denied Jesus.

4. The day trial took place before the reassembled Sanhedrin, shortly after sunrise, in the council chamber in the temple. At this time, Judas confessed to the leaders and went out and hanged himself.

### THE CIVIL (ROMAN) TRIAL

5. The hearing before Pilate, governor of Judea from A.D. 26 to A.D. 36, took place in the governor's palace in the early morning hours.

6. The hearing before Herod Antipas, who ruled Galilee from 4 B.C. to A.D. 39, probably took place at his

palace around 7:00 a.m.

7. The final phase of the trial was a second hearing before Pilate, probably taking place at his palace around 8:00 a.m.

# Memory Focus

" 'He committed no sin, and no deceit was found in his mouth.' When they hurled their insults at him, he did not retaliate; when he suffered, he made no threats. Instead, he entrusted himself to him who judges justly" (1 Peter 2:22, 23, NIV).

# Into the Bible

The trial of Jesus is recorded in all four Gospels. Its importance is revealed by the fact that it receives more attention in these four books than any other event in Christ's life. Your teacher will give you a worksheet that will help you examine the various phases of the trial and related events in the order in which they took place. Complete the worksheet by answering each question.

# Projects

1. **AN IN-DEPTH STUDY:** The book *The Desire of Ages* by Ellen G. White provides a commentary on the various phases of the trial of Jesus and related events. On the worksheet provided by your teacher, answer the questions, using the references listed with each question.

2. **LETTER WRITING:** You have been a personal witness to the trial of Jesus. You are going to respond to what you have just experienced by writing a letter based on one of the following situations:

   A. You are writing a letter to Caiaphas as a Jew, who, prior to

the trial, was convinced that Jesus was nothing more than a deluded pretender.

B. As a close friend of Judas, you are writing a letter to him that will be read at his memorial service.

C. As a concerned resident of Jerusalem, you are writing a letter to the editor of the *Jerusalem Daily News* expressing your opinion regarding the trial.

D. As a believer in Jesus, you are writing a letter to Him (to be delivered on Monday) sharing with Him your feelings as to what this trial meant to you and its effect upon your life.

3. **POSITION PAPER:** Imagine what might have happened if the disciples had demonstrated spiritual courage and spunk and had defended Jesus before the Sanhedrin and Pilate. Let's say the disciples decided that Peter would be their official spokesman.

A. Based on the disciples' beliefs about Christ's role as the Messiah, write what you think Peter might have said to the Sanhedrin and to Pilate in Jesus' defense.

B. If the disciples would have listened to Jesus and fully accepted what He told them about Himself and His work as the Messiah, write what kind of defense Peter would now have presented to the Sanhedrin and/or Pilate.

4. **RESEARCH PROJECT:** Respond to the following topics. Use a Bible dictionary, encyclopedia, and *Index to Writings of E. G. White* for references.

A. The SANHEDRIN:
  (1) What was the primary work and function of this Jewish council?
  (2) How did one become a member? Were there any qualifications for membership?
  (3) What was the scope, as well as the limitations, of its religious and civil authority?

B. PILATE, HEROD and CAIAPHAS:
  (1) Describe the kind of person/ruler he was.
  (2) What happened to him after the trial?
  (3) Identify any special accomplishment or misdeed for which he is remembered. Resources: Bible dictionaries and Bible encyclopedias.

#  Focus Questions

1. What is the difference between denial and betrayal? Describe ways that you and I can be guilty of these acts of disloyalty to God.
2. Have you ever been in a situation in which you were abused or felt that your rights were violated? How should a Christian deal with these kinds of injustices?
3. The Bible says that after his denial, Peter wept bitterly. Is such remorse always a good experience? Do you think Peter would have become the fearless apostle he became without going through the experience of denying Jesus?
4. What aspects of the trial do you feel were the most difficult and painful for Jesus? Why? *The Desire of Ages*, 710:2.
5. Which of the violations of Jewish legal procedure do you find the most deplorable? Why?
6. What do you think was the real reason Judas betrayed Jesus?
7. Why do you think Jesus predicted Peter's denial and the betrayal of Judas?
8. What would you say is the main reason the Jewish leaders hated Jesus?
9. What do you think the people who believed in Jesus as the promised Messiah expected to happen during the trial? *The Desire of Ages*, 700:4.
10. How do you feel about the religious leaders who were involved in the trial? What makes a religious person so hardhearted?
11. Do you think Judas committed the unpardonable sin? How does one commit such a sin?
12. Why does Jesus come across as a winner even though He was the abused victim? Who would you say ended up the biggest loser in this tragic affair? What important lesson does this teach us?
13. If you had been at the trial, what comments or questions would you have liked to direct to Judas, Pilate, Caiaphas, Peter, Herod, or Jesus?
14. What do you see as the main lesson to be learned from the trial of Jesus?

# C O N N E C T I O N

The hand that sustains the worlds in space . . . is the hand that was nailed to the cross (*Acts of the Apostles*, 472).

# lesson 30

# All Eyes on Calvary

**Lesson Scriptures: Matthew 27:26-66; Mark 15:15-47; Luke 23:25-56; John 19:16-42**

The anguished cries of the dying could be heard everywhere. History records that literally thousands of villages were nearly wiped out by the bubonic plague that raged across Europe during the years of 1632 and 1633. One small Bavarian town of about 1,600 people watched in horror as hundreds of its inhabitants fell victim to this devastating illness. At the height of the crisis, the town leaders got together and eventually came to a unanimous decision. They would ask God to intervene in behalf of their dying village, and in turn, they vowed that from that day forward, every ten years, their town would perform a reenact-ment of the crucifixion of Jesus.

According to the official Oberammergau guidebook, from the hour the vow was made, no other villager died from the plague.

Oberammergau's first passion play was performed in 1634 as a genuine act of homage and unspeakable gratitude to God for His mercy in sparing their lives.

Ever since that time, the people of Oberammergau have lived up to the vow of their ancestors. Even with the passing of centuries, the performances that are presented every ten years from May through September not only survive, they thrive. At first, the passion play was performed in a meadow with only one performance. In 1710 it grew to two perform-

**281**

ances and in 1810 to four. From 1820 on, the number steadily increased until it reached one hundred performances in 1980. And at a special day-long jubilee presentation in 1984, the play attracted 470,000 spectators.

From the town's population of only 4,500 people come 1,000 actors, 125 of them with major speaking parts. All the participants must have been born in Oberammergau or have lived there for at least twenty years. In addition, they must have an unblemished reputation. The actor who portrays Jesus has to memorize his speaking part of over seven thousand words. Since he must undergo a torturous physical ordeal when he hangs on the cross, he must prepare himself by spending several months engaged in special exercises to build up body strength and stamina.

The entire play takes place on an immense outdoor stage that is vulnerable to rain and cold weather. The audience is seated in a covered pavilion. The action is played out in true-to-life stage settings of narrow Jerusalem streets, palace and temple façades, courtyards,

as well as a main center stage.

The depth of commitment of the residents is impressive. To them, they do not perform merely a play or a drama; it is reality. As one witnesses the reenactment of the sufferings and death of Jesus, one is readily caught up in the soul-stirring fervor of the drama. In fact, it is virtually impossible to be merely a spectator. Those who believe in Jesus literally become participants in the most heart-wrenching event ever observed by mortal eyes—the crucifixion of Jesus.

## THE HISTORY OF CRUCIFIXION

Crucifixion was considered the most painful and degrading form of death in the ancient world, though its origin is still uncertain. It was used by many nations, including Assyria, Medo-Persia, and Greece. By the time of Christ, crucifixion had been adopted by the Romans and used throughout the empire. Rome perfected it as an instrument of torture and execution, designing it to bring about a slow death with maximum pain and suffering.

Because it was the most severe and shameful way of

dying, Roman citizens were exempt from crucifixion. It was reserved for the vilest of criminals, such as runaway slaves and pirates, as well as political criminals such as deserters and traitors.

During the Old Testament time, there is no evidence that the Jews used the cross as a means of capital punishment. The law of Moses directed that the death penalty be carried out by stoning, though it did allow for public display or "hanging" of a lawbreaker's body "on a tree." This was done primarily to discourage civil disobedience or to mock and ridicule defeated military foes. The law also commanded that the body was not to remain on the tree overnight. In heathen countries, however, the body was allowed to be devoured by scavengers or simply rot away.

Jews believed that persons who were hanged from a tree were accursed of God. They viewed crucifixion as the most humiliating and degrading form of death. For that reason, it is truly astounding that the nation's spiritual leaders sought and obtained Roman approval to have Jesus crucified.

How could it happen that God's chosen people could, with malice and disgust, put to death the very One they were to accept and proclaim as the Saviour of the world? Clearly, the crucifixion of Jesus exposes the depths of cruelty to which the human heart sinks when hardened and blinded by pride and selfishness.

## THE PROCESS OF THE CRUCIFIXION

A person condemned to be crucified was first publicly flogged. In this legal but brutal preliminary to a Roman execution, the prisoner was stripped of his clothing, and his hands were stretched above his head and tied to a post. The usual flogging instrument was a short whip known as a *flagellum*. It consisted of a handle equipped with braided leather thongs, tipped with sharp pieces of sheep bone or jagged pieces of iron. With each stroke alternately delivered by two able-bodied soldiers, the jagged slugs would bury themselves into the flesh of the victim. These lacerations left behind shreds of torn, bleeding tissue right down to the bone. The excruciating pain was accompanied by massive hemorrhaging.

283

The lash of the whip was applied to different parts of the body, sometimes including the face. So inhuman and brutal was a Roman flogging that many a person died from the scourging alone. It isn't certain that the Romans followed the Jewish practice of prohibiting more than forty lashes. What is certain is that twice the centurion commanded Jesus to be flogged.

The soldiers had heard the Jewish leaders' accusation that Jesus claimed to be a king. To these Romans, this was viewed as a most serious charge, and so after flogging Him, Jesus was mocked and scorned. As far as the soldiers were concerned, Jesus deserved such treatment. A robe was thrown over Christ's shoulders, and a crown made up of flexible thorn branches was forced upon his brow until the blood flowed freely down His face. After He was shamefully abused by being spat upon, struck in the face, and verbally insulted, the robe was wrenched from His back. This would have caused indescribable agony as the partially dried wounds were reopened.

It was customary for the condemned person, stripped of his clothing, to carry the cross from the flogging post to the place of crucifixion outside the city walls. Since the weight of the entire cross could exceed three hundred pounds, only the upper crossbar was generally carried by the victim. The arms of the person were usually tied to the crossbar as he clumsily conveyed it through the crowded streets.

Somewhere along the three-hundred-yard route of two or three city blocks, Jesus' brave attempt to carry the heavy beam failed, and Simon of Cyrene was ordered to carry it for Him. This painful trek to the death site was led by a garrison of Roman soldiers, headed by a centurion who was in command. A tablet stating the criminal's name and his crime was placed around his neck, and at the time of crucifixion it was nailed to the cross.

## THE ORDEAL OF CRUCIFIXION

The word *crucify* is defined by Webster as "to torture" or "to put to death by nailing or binding the hands and feet to a cross." The act of crucifixion was generally carried out in a very open and public manner so the greatest possible number of people could witness the execution. Jewish leaders had hoped that Christ's execution would be carried out as quickly and unceremoniously as possible. But it wasn't.

Jesus was crucified in a place called "Golgotha" in Hebrew and "Calvary" in Latin. These names mean "place of the skull" or just "skull," probably referring to the skull-like shape of the hill itself. According to the Bible, the crucifixion took place around nine o'clock in the morning. When the procession arrived at Golgotha, the soldiers proceeded to nail Jesus' wrists to the crossbar. Usually, both ropes and nails were used to hold the body to the cross. When Jesus was lifted up, the cross beam was attached to the upright beam, and His feet were nailed to that beam as well. The victim was generally nailed about fifteen to eighteen inches above the ground, making him more vulnerable to the taunts and abuse of those watching.

Jesus hung from the cross that had been prepared for Barabbas. By this transaction, a guilty man was set free, and the innocent One died in his place. In this exchange, the whole purpose of Christ's sacrifice is clearly demonstrated—Jesus, the sinless One, dies for me, the guilty one!

To help support the body and thus prolong the dying process, a wooden block was placed at the base of the feet or attached midway down the upright beam, thus serving as a crude seat for the victim. The weight of the body pulling down on the outstretched arms would cause the muscles that control the breathing apparatus to convulse and cease to function in a normal manner. By utilizing the attached block or seat, the victim could prolong his life by painfully pushing himself up and thus reactivating the paralyzed muscles. Regarding this ordeal, Ellen White penned these words, "Never was a criminal treated in so inhuman a manner as was the Son of God" (*The Desire of Ages*, 710).

The length of survival on the cross generally ranged from several hours to up to a week or longer. During that time, the victim was exposed to insects, birds of prey, predatory animals, as well as heat prostration, extreme dehydration, and tetanus (blood poisoning) from the wounds.

Death could be hastened by breaking the legs, leading to shock and asphyxiation. With the legs broken, the victim was prevented from pushing himself upward. Unable to relieve the severe tension placed on the respiratory muscles, suffocation would quickly occur. The Roman guards could not leave until they were sure that death had occurred. Thus it was their custom to pierce the body (in the region of the heart) with a sword or spear to ensure the victim's death.

## CHRIST AND HIS CRUCIFIXION

As one reads the biblical account of the crucifixion, it becomes obvious that the Gospel writers chose not to dwell on the physical suffering of Jesus. Perhaps one reason was that Jesus Himself never uttered any complaints regarding the physical anguish He willingly endured. His admission "I thirst," spoken through parched lips and faltering breath, is as close as He comes to acknowledging His extremely agonizing condition. Though the physical torture of the crucifixion was unbelievably intense, yet it was the mental anguish of bearing the sins of the world that caused the most extreme suffering for Jesus. "So great was this agony that the physical pain was hardly felt" (*The Desire of Ages*, 753).

Yet even during those hours of suffering, the primary concern of Christ was not the evil that others were doing to Him, but rather, the good He might do for others. Jesus had always taught: "Love your enemies, bless those who curse you, do good to those who hate you, and pray for those who spitefully use you and persecute

**286**

you" (Matthew 5:44, NKJV). From this text we can know that during all the confusion and turmoil of the trial, Jesus was praying for Judas and Peter, for Pilate, Herod, and even Caiaphas and the members of the Sanhedrin. He did not pray for His life to be spared. He knew He had to die. For this hour He had come. His main concern was their spiritual struggle. The burden of His heart was that their eternal welfare hung in the balance.

As Jesus struggled to Calvary, He stopped to express His sorrow for the women who stood weeping. On the cross, He again prayed for His persecutors and promised a dying thief a place in His kingdom. He acknowledged the presence of His mother and thoughtfully committed her to the care of His disciple, John. Only after the needs of the people around Him were taken care of did Jesus express any personal anguish.

As Jesus died, a supernatural darkness abruptly blotted out the sun. It was midnight at midday. Darkness reigned, symbolizing the light of God's presence being withdrawn from His Son. The "outer darkness" affirmed the inner darkness of soul that Jesus experienced as He suffered and died for the sins of the whole world. Yet by this darkness over the land, the Father also mercifully veiled the unbelievable suffering of His Son from the leering gaze of the unruly crowd.

At the moment of Christ's death, there was a violent earthquake. It was even more frightening than the darkness. People were thrown about. There was mass panic and confusion. Nature and the earth itself seemed to writhe and convulse in protest at the death of their Creator. In the Old Testament, the earthquake always symbolizes the coming of God in judgment. This shows Calvary to be God's judgment on "the sins of the whole world" (1 John 2:2, NIV). Even as the earthquake split open graves and spewed forth the dead, so Christ's sacrifice prepared the way for the dead to come forth in the power of God. The actual resurrection of a select number of people took place when Jesus Himself came forth from the tomb as "the firstfruits of those who have fallen asleep" (1 Corinthians 15:20; Matthew 27:53, NIV).

Finally, at Christ's death, there was a rending noise in the sacred precincts of the temple. The majestic veil that hung between the Holy and the Most Holy Place was torn from top to bottom by an unseen hand. Thus God dramatically revealed an important spiritual truth in a very visible way. Obviously, He didn't want us to miss the point! Why did He tear the temple veil at the very moment the torn body of Jesus died on the cross? He was declaring that through the blood of Christ we now have direct and unobstructed access into His very presence.

He desired the world to know that the Jewish system of animal sacrifices, earthly priests, and temple services was finished. Down through the centuries, these sacrifices had pointed forward to the saving work of Christ. With that work accomplished, the sacrificial sys-tem was replaced by a new and living way. Jesus Himself is now our all-sufficient sacrifice for sin. He is now our High Priest who lives forever to make intercession for us in heaven itself. "Not with the blood of goats and calves, but with His own blood He entered the Most Holy Place once for all, having obtained eternal redemption" (Hebrews 9:12, NKJV). The torn veil exposed the Most Holy Place to the eyes of all, signifying that the earth temple was no longer sacred, and the presence of God was no longer there.

"Seeing then that we have a great High Priest who has passed through the heavens, Jesus the Son of God. . . . Let us therefore come boldly to the throne of grace, that we may obtain mercy and find grace to help in time of need" (Hebrews 4:14, 16, NKJV).

# Memory Focus

"For the message of the cross is foolishness to those who are perishing, but to us who are being saved it is the power of God" (1 Corinthians 1:18, NIV).

# Into the Bible

1. There is no story in the Bible that receives as much attention as the last events of Christ's life. In order to get a complete picture of what took place at the crucifixion, all four Gospels need to be studied. Your teacher will give you a worksheet that contains texts from the four Gospels. You will be asked to read the texts and write a summary of each of the events that happened on that fateful Friday.

2. Isaiah 53 is one of the great Messianic chapters in the Old Testament. It prophetically declares Christ's first coming as the Messiah and details the purpose and glory of the suffering He endured. Read Isaiah 53:3-12, and complete the following writing assignment.
   A. List the phrases that describe the reason for Christ's suffering.
   B. List the phrases that describe the reaction of Jesus to His suffering.

3. Psalm 22 is another Messianic chapter. In this chapter, David seems to be describing his own personal experience. But the New Testament writers have interpreted this chapter to have a deeper meaning—pointing to the sufferings of Jesus while on the cross. On the worksheet your teacher will give you, summarize the verses that describe Christ's sufferings or condition while on the cross.

4. There were many characters in the drama of Jesus'

crucifixion. Read the following texts, and identify three of
these people and the reaction of each to the events.
A. Matthew 26:57-68
B. Matthew 27:11-26
C. Matthew 27:45-54

 **Projects**

1. *The Desire of Ages* contains three chapters on the crucifixion.
   They are: "Calvary," "It Is Finished," and a portion of "In
   Joseph's Tomb." In these chapters, various individuals and
   groups who witnessed Christ's death are discussed. Use the
   worksheet provided by your teacher to summarize the impact
   this event had on the lives of the people listed.
2. Study pictures provided by your teacher or from other sources
   depicting Christ on the cross. Write a report describing the
   similarities and differences of the pictures. What aspects make
   some of them more historically accurate than others? Where
   possible, include photocopies of the pictures or drawings.
3. On a worksheet your teacher will provide, you will be asked to
   write a brief monologue of how you think some of the people
   involved in the story of the crucifixion might have thought
   and felt as Jesus was crucified. You then may be asked to read
   one of your descriptions as part of a dramatic reading.
   Capture the emotions of the people in your monologues.

 Focus Questions

1. If Jesus lived in our day, who do you think would crucify Him? What would be the charge against Him?
2. Do you think Satan wanted Jesus to be put to death, or would he have preferred to have Jesus save Himself?
3. What relationship do you see between thorns mentioned in the Garden of Eden as the result of sin and Jesus wearing a crown of thorns?
4. What do you believe is the main reason for the disciples being absent (except for John) at the crucifixion?
5. Which of Jesus' followers do you think best understood what was happening on the day Jesus died? Why?

# L O V E
Greater love has no one than this, that he lay down his life
for his friends (John 15:13, NIV).

# The Final Words

## Lesson Scripture: Luke 23:32-49

**S**IXES AND SEVENS

What a deal! A Christian faces life's battles knowing the war has already been won. We work from victory—not toward it. God declares us to be more than conquerors, all because of a life we never lived—and a death we never died. All because of six hours one Friday.

Six hours one Friday. Those six hours are either the hinge of human history or the greatest hoax of history. The Bible says our salvation was accomplished on that day. But how can six hours equal salvation?

On that Friday, for six hours, Jesus took the guilt of sin, yours and mine, and took it away: "We all, like sheep, have gone astray, each of us has turned to his own way; and the Lord has laid on him the iniquity of us all" (Isaiah 53:6, NIV).

Jesus' sixth statement on the cross, during those six hours on the sixth day, just before He died, was: "It is finished!" Done! Accomplished! Completed! For us.

As author Max Lucado says so well, three basic realities flow from understanding what Christ accomplished on the cross.[1]

1. Our lives are not futile.
2. Our failures are not fatal.
3. Our death is not final.

In other words, what Christ accomplished by dying and rising gives our lives meaning, courage, and hope. His cross accomplished our salvation.

How? What happened during those six hours?

---

[1] Max Lucado, *Six Hours One Friday*, 25 (Multnomah Press, 1985).

Another number, seven, helps explain the Lord's crucifixion. Seven has a specific symbolic meaning in the Bible. It stands for fullness, completion, and perfection—which leads to salvation and rest. Seven always points us to God's work, never to ours. The first mention of seven in the Bible illustrates this.

In six days God finished everything that needed to be done for the new man and woman to have a joy-filled life, secure in His love. At the end of the first six days, God drew close to the first couple and said: "Let's celebrate on the seventh day, the first full day of your new life. We will call it the Sabbath, and it will be a perpetual symbol of your rest in My provisions and love."

Then the long night of sin entered into the world. It shrouded God's presence, perverted man's purity, and caused people to reject His rest and hide from His love. But God didn't give up. He came close. He clothed Himself in the fragile armor of flesh and blood and came to do battle for His lost creation. He came to win us back. He came to restore our relationship with Him.

The decisive battle of that rescue mission was accomplished during six awesome hours on that terrible—and wonderful—Friday. Now we need to go back to Calvary and discover the sevens that help explain how Immanuel (God with us) stooped low to save our lost race.

He was the perfect Sacrifice for sin, and everything about His suffering points to His perfection. There were seven statements made by others that testified to His innocence (Pilate's wife, Pilate [twice], Judas, the scribes and priests at the cross, the dying thief, the Roman centurion). And to explain the meaning of His suffering, Jesus, while still on the cross, was the perfect teacher. He spoke seven times. Seven witnesses—and then seven words.

Just seven short statements. But they contained infinite love. To understand them is to know the way of salvation and the heart of true discipleship. Let's explore them.

**STATEMENT 1**
**THE POWER OF FORGIVENESS**
*"Father, forgive them, for they do not know what they are doing"*
*(Luke 23:34, NIV).*
In a New England village,

there is a little country church with a high white steeple and a graveyard out back. A low black iron fence encircles the old tombstones, which lean at various angles. In the middle of the graveyard, a marble column rises above the rest of the tombstones. At its top is a cross. And on its base one word is carved four times, once on every side, so that it faces the resting place of each Christian buried there. The one word is: *FORGIVEN*.

*Forgiveness*. What a wonderful word. It is our entrance into Christianity and the path along which we walk. Sometimes we forget how precious it is, and how needed. In Lisbon, Portugal, a letter appeared in the newspaper from a father to his estranged son. It read:

Dear Pancho,

I am sorry for all the struggles we've had. All is forgiven. I love you and want you to come home. Please meet me at the cathedral at noon on Sunday.

Your Father

That Sunday morning, a reporter went early to the cathedral. He wanted to see this reunion. When he arrived, there were over a hundred Panchos waiting, each one hoping the letter was meant for him.

*Forgiveness*. Sometimes we forget how costly it was for Jesus to make it available. Picture the scene. Crucifixion was a horrible way to die, reserved only for the vilest of criminals. Men like that didn't give in without a struggle when they were nailed to a cross. They kicked and cursed and screamed.

But Jesus, who could have called a legion of warrior angels to His side or annihilated the Roman soldiers and arrogant priests with a word, submitted quietly to the nails. No cursing. No fighting. No screams. As the nails were pounded into His flesh and the blood began to flow, His very first words were: "Father, forgive them . . ." He responded to their hate with love, their cruelty with compassion, and their injustice with mercy.

Later, the apostle Paul applied that moment to all of us, saying we have already received redemption through His blood for the forgiveness of our sins. His blood—our forgiveness. He came to be our salvation, and He allowed the nails to drive His point home.

The cost of our forgiveness was nothing less than the death of Jesus. He purchased us with His own blood.

This first statement of Jesus from the cross removes the guilt of our past.

Long before we were born, Christ provided forgiveness to all of us who, by our sins, crucified Him. He gave His seamless robe away to all the crucifiers who knelt at the foot of His cross. He still does. That forgiveness is ours the minute we turn to Him in faith and remains ours as long as we walk with Him in faith—as His second statement proves.

### STATEMENT 2
### SECURITY OF ASSURANCE
*"I tell you the truth, today you will be with me in paradise"*
*(Luke 23:43, NIV).*

Remember, Jesus was crucified between two criminals. Two other men. Both equally guilty, both equally sinners. One cursed Christ and turned from Him. He died without hope, forever lost. The other acknowledged his guilt and Jesus' innocence, then simply said: "Lord, remember me." That was it. Nothing more.

But it was enough. Jesus turned to him and said: "You're in! I guarantee it." A lost, crucified criminal received the assurance of salvation. The promise of eternity. The one difference between these two thieves was how each responded to the cross in their midst.

Those two men still symbolize all men and women everywhere. God still places the cross in our midst, and how we respond to it still determines our destiny. Jesus' second statement from the cross offers the assurance of salvation for all who, knowing their great need, turn to Him with nothing to offer but faith and submission. His blood removes the guilt of our past. Then He offers assurance for the future. A sure hope. The knowledge that eternity is the last turn in the road and that this one pathetic little inch we call life is only the preface to a million miles of unending adventure in an earth made new.

### STATEMENT 3
### PROVISION FOR OUR NEEDS

In the first three statements from the cross, Jesus concentrated on the needs of others before focusing on His own suffering. His third statement

reveals the heart of a concerned son, as well as the heart of a Saviour.

*"Dear woman, here is your son"* *(John 19:26, NIV).* At Calvary, Christ ruled from the cross, providing for the needs of His people. He would not leave Mary, His mother, alone, but committed her to the apostle John to be cared for.

Protestant Christians do not accept the exaltation and adoration of Mary as the Queen of Heaven as taught by Roman Catholics. But we must not react so much that we miss the beautiful symbolism in these verses. As the mother of Jesus and as one of His disciples, Mary symbolizes the church. Jesus is leaving her. She will see Him no more. But He will not leave her destitute and uncared for. And He provides for her through the care of His apostle.

So with the church. Jesus promised us He would not leave us alone. He gave us the apostles' teaching (the New Testament) to guide us and His Spirit to care for us. The third statement from the cross illustrates the ongoing provisions of Christ for our daily needs. Writing to the Christians in Rome, Paul joyfully proclaimed:

"If God is for us, who can be against us? He who did not spare his own Son, but gave him up [to die] for us all—how will he not also, along with him, graciously give us all things?" (Romans 8:31, 32, NIV).

Think about the fears we all have in life. We have fear about our past and the things we shouldn't have done. We have fears about the future and what might happen to us. We have fears in the present as we face the struggles of each day.

In the first three statements

from the cross, Jesus shatters all those fears. He removes the guilt of our past, the insecurity of our future, and the loneliness of our present struggles. He is the One who is, and was, and is to come, and He promises: "I am with you always, to the very end" (Matthew 28:20, NIV). And His first three statements from the cross give our lives unshakable security:

1. "Father, forgive them"—forgiveness for the past.
2. "You will be with Me"—assurance for the future.
3. "Dear woman, behold"—provisions for the present.

Now we enter into the deepest mystery of the cross.

### STATEMENT 4
### THE BROKEN HEART OF THE CROSS

*"My God, my God, why have you forsaken me?"*
*(Matthew 27:46, NIV).*

Why, indeed?

Why would God forsake His Son? Why would God turn away from the Righteous One? Why would God lay the curse on the one Person in all of human history who deserved the fullness of His presence? Had not God twice said: "This is my Son, whom I love; with him I am well pleased" (Matthew 3:17; 17:5, NIV)?

What is going on here? Jesus knew what He was saying. He really was forsaken. He didn't just feel it; it was fact. At noon it became night; the brightness of midday became the darkness of midnight as the Father withdrew His presence for the first time in all eternity from His Son.

For three hours on the cross (12:00 to 3:00 p.m.), Jesus experienced the outer darkness and inner torment of the lost. He descended into the depths and experienced the "second death"—the death of a soul separated from God. The death of those who will have no hope beyond the grave. All die a physical death, but no one else in history, other than Christ, has yet tasted the agony of this cup of final retribution. Indeed, He alone has "tasted [the second] death for everyone."

But why? Why would God forsake His Son? There can be only one answer. Jesus was forsaken in order that we might never be. If Jesus was not truly forsaken, if He did not truly experience the wrath of God against sin, then we are not truly accepted, forgiven, and

acquitted. He experienced the outer darkness and inner anguish of the second death in our place and on our behalf—for our sins. He was receiving what we deserve: "For Christ died for sins, once for all, the righteous for the unrighteous, to bring you to God" (1 Peter 3:18, NIV).

During those dark hours, God reached forward in time and brought the final judgment of the entire human race back to Calvary. On the cross, Jesus accepted the guilt of every single sinner and experienced the wrath of a holy God against their sins. He was giving birth to a redeemed church—and the labor pains were excruciating.

Though He had no sin in Him, Jesus took the guilt of all our sins upon Him, so that we who have no saving righteousness in us could have His perfect righteousness placed upon us. This is the gospel—God's great exchange in Christ. God "made Him who knew no sin to be sin on our behalf, that we might become the righteousness of God in Him" (2 Corinthians 5:21, NASB).

Nowhere else are the Bible writers so bold as they are here, trying to explain this deep mystery of infinite Love offering itself up to save its lost creation. Paul declares Christ literally became the curse for us in order to redeem us from the curse of the broken Law and open to us the blessing of God.

But we must be careful to understand this right. Calvary was not the Father against the Son or the Father forcing the Son to die. Nor was it a merciful Son trying to stop the vengeance of an angry God. No! It was Father and Son together enduring the agony of the cross so we might be saved. God does not love us because Christ died for us. Rather, Christ died for us because God loves us: "For God so loved the world He gave . . ." God, Father and Son, united together in a costly plan to redeem the race. Both suffered; two infinite hearts were broken at Calvary.

Why? So that you and I might live. The old saying is true: God does hate sin and yet loves the sinners. And God could not sacrifice His holiness in order to show His love, nor could He stop loving to preserve His holiness. So in holy love, He sacrificed Himself, in the person of the Son, in order to save every sinner who turns

to Him in faith. Because of the cross, He can be both "just (the penalty was paid) and the One who justifies (declares not guilty) those who have faith in Jesus."

God, Father and Son, could do no more.

## STATEMENT 5
## THE FULFILLMENT OF PROPHECY

"After this, Jesus, knowing that all things had already been accomplished, in order that the Scripture might be fulfilled, said, *'I am thirsty'* "(John 19:28, NASB).

On the cross, Jesus quoted from two psalms, 22 and 69. In both cases, He was demonstrating how all the prophecies spoken of the suffering Messiah were fulfilled in Him. He Himself was the true temple, high priest, and atoning sacrifice—the true Lamb of God who truly takes away the sins of the world so that after this sacrifice for sins there would be no need for any other. At Calvary, reality swallowed up symbol:

"When this priest had offered for all time one sacrifice for sins, he sat down at the right hand of God. Since that time he waits for his enemies to be made his footstool, because by one sacrifice he has made perfect forever those who are being made holy" (Hebrews 10:12-14, NIV).

Psalm 69:21 says that the Messiah would be given "gall," a terrible mixture of wine and vinegar, for His thirst. Only at the conclusion of His suffering, only after He knew "all things were already accomplished" and the battle was His, did Jesus acknowledge His thirst and take a sip of this sour wine from the sponge.

For six hours He had suffered terrible thirst. He endured it so we might drink again from those waters that alone truly quench our thirst: "Whoever is thirsty, let him come; and whoever wishes, let him take the free gift of the water of life" (Revelation 22:17, NIV).

## STATEMENT 6
## THE VICTORY SHOUT

"When Jesus therefore had received the sour wine, He said, *'It is finished!'* And He bowed His head, and gave up His spirit" (John 19:30, NASB).

"And Jesus cried out again with a loud voice, and yielded up His spirit. And behold, the

veil of the temple was torn in two from top to bottom; and the earth quaked, and the rocks were split" (Matthew 27:50, 51, NKJV).

When we put John's and Matthew's accounts of the sixth statement together, we get an accurate feeling of what it was like. In the original Greek, it was just one word. Imagine Jesus' tone as He spoke that word: "It is finished." Was it a sign of defeat, a gasp of despair, the dying whimper of a conquered man?

No! It was a loud cry. A victory shout. The conquering cry of a mighty Warrior. Only when He knew He had finished what He came to do did He submit to death. It is a shout that compels us to ask: "What is finished?" And what does it mean for us?

This shout was aimed primarily at the Father (though Satan heard it and knew his kingdom was crushed and his doom sure). To the Father, Jesus declared that all things anyone needed—redemption—had been achieved. His perfect life and perfect sacrifice, His flawless obedience and infinite suffering on our behalf—for our sins—was finished.

The Bible is clear. No one can see God's face who is not perfect in righteousness, flawless in performance—every minute of every hour of every day. Yet we in ourselves stand before the searching gaze of a holy God as those who are stained by sin, inwardly and outwardly. No one has the sinless life. So Christ undertook the task of keeping the Law of God fully, of becoming the second Adam who would keep the Law in all its heights and depths, who would not sin no matter what the cost.

And He did it! He was obedient even until death. His was a life of perfect trust, perfect kindness, and perfect love. Now it was finished. In all points He had been tempted like us, yet without sin. Every missile in Satan's arsenal had been fired at Him, the last blasphemous insult, the last wicked temptation had been hurled at Him, the last demonic cruelty had spent its full fury on Him. Yet Jesus could still declare that Satan could "find nothing of his spirit in Me."

"I have finished the work which You have given Me to do. And now, O Father, glorify Me together with Yourself" (John 17:4, NKJV).

Grasp what that is saying. Only Jesus could truly say: "Father, I have done all You require. By My outward actions and inward thoughts I have always honored Your name. In public and in private, toward enemy and friend, I have done all—omitting nothing—so that even Your divinely discerning and infinitely pure Law could require nothing more. Now I offer up My life for My church as a saving garment that is without spot or wrinkle or any stain. Father—it is finished."

The word *finished* is translated in other places to mean "made an end of," "paid in full," "completely performed and accomplished." He accomplished a righteousness He didn't need and died a death He didn't deserve—for us.

### STATEMENT 7
### THE FINAL WORD

The sixth statement from the cross belongs to Jesus alone. His was the work of salvation, and He achieved it alone. We had no part. But as we accept His finished and perfect work for our salvation and turn from our own imperfect and inadequate performance as a basis of hope, we are called to say with Him, *"Father, into your hands I commit my spirit"* (Luke 23:46, NIV).

Only Luke records this final statement. That is fitting. Luke's account is the Gospel of hope. To Luke is given the privilege of recording this last expression of rest and trust.

The first and the last statements of Jesus from the cross begin with "Father." During the hours of darkness, when Jesus experienced the curse of sin and separation, He could not call God "Father," but still called Him "My God." Now as darkness lifts and death descends upon His soul, Jesus again says "Father." And He ends His suffering with a statement we can use to begin each day in light of so great a salvation. "Into your hands I commit my spirit" (Luke 23:46, NIV).

When the words of Jesus were finished and the earthquake rumbled through the city, there was one last statement spoken at Calvary. It came from the mouth of a battle-hardened pagan who had seen everything that happened that day. Mark records that "when the centurion, who stood there in front of Jesus, heard his cry and saw how he died, he said, 'Surely this man was the Son of God!' " (Mark 15:39b, NIV).

 # Memory Focus

"For God was pleased to have all his fullness dwell in him, and through him to reconcile to himself all things, whether things on earth or things in heaven, by making peace through his blood, shed on the cross" (Colossians 1:19, 20, NIV).

 # Into the Bible

1. There were six witnesses who made statements during Christ's trial and crucifixion that affirmed His innocence. On the worksheet provided by your teacher, identify the key witness, and record the key word or phrase that reveals Christ's true character in the midst of the false accusations.

2. Some Christians believe it is wrong to have a present personal assurance of salvation. Some go the other way and say once you ask for salvation you can never lose it (once saved, always saved). Read carefully the passages on the worksheet provided by your teacher, and write the phrases that describe what each passage says about present assurance of salvation.

3. The judgment is often viewed as a frightening event at which no one can be sure of the outcome; where the big issue is, "Am I good enough to get in?" The Bible clearly teaches there is a final judgment at the end of history. But if Calvary was God's decisive judgment upon sin, and Christ died "for the sins of the whole world" (1 John 2:2, NIV), then the primary issue is no longer whether we are good enough. We are not good enough; that's why Jesus had to die. Then what is the central issue in judgment? Read the following texts from the Gospel of John. Briefly summarize what the passage says the central issue is in the final judgment:
   A. John 3:18, 36
   B. John 5:24
   C. John 6:28, 29

4. The Bible is clear that we do not gain salvation by our works. Our salvation is based on faith in Christ's finished work alone. The Bible is equally clear that there is still a work for us to do—a holy life we are called to live. From the following texts, identify at least three reasons why Christians continue to strive to do God's will other than to receive salvation:
A. Acts 20:24
B. Galatians 5:13, 14
C. 1 Peter 2:9

5. During the final hours of Jesus on the cross, He spoke words that were significant then and have significance to us today. These are usually referred to as the seven last words (statements) of Christ. Use the worksheet provided by your teacher to identify these statements, and record what meaning they hold for us today.

 # Projects

1. Locate two additional stories, one in the Bible and one from literature outside the Bible, in which the great need of an individual was to be forgiven. Name and briefly describe each story. Be prepared to discuss what makes such stories so meaningful.

2. Read the following statement by Ellen White. Then answer these three questions:
A. Why did Christ have to die?
B. According to the quote, what three things did Christ come to accomplish?
C. How did God react to Christ's sacrifice, and what does God's reaction mean to us?

"Satan declared that human beings could not keep the law. Christ has proved this statement false. He came to this earth, and lived among men the law of God. He died on the cross to bear witness to the unchanging character of the law. This law

had been broken, and only by the offering of Christ's blood could the penalty be paid. . . . He planted the cross between heaven and earth, and when the Father beheld the sacrifice of His Son, He bowed before it in recognition of its perfection. 'It is enough,' He said. 'The atonement is complete.'

"Could the law have been changed, Christ need not have died. But it was impossible for God to change. The penalty of transgression must be borne. Therefore, that the human race might not perish, the Son of God came into this world to live in our behalf a life of perfect obedience, and by the sacrifice of Himself to meet the demands of justice.

"See the Saviour, sinless and undefiled, yet bearing the penalty of sin. Why?—That we might be spared. 'God so loved the world, that He gave His only begotten Son, that whosoever believeth in Him should not perish, but have everlasting life.' God could not do more than He has done for us. He has left us without excuse" (*Review and Herald*, 24 September 1901).

3. Create a dramatic reading based on the seven last sayings of Jesus. Your teacher will give you instructions.

4. Write a diary entry describing what your thoughts might have been if you had been at the crucifixion and had just buried your closest friend, Jesus. Use the writing guide your teacher will provide.

 **Focus Questions**

1. Jesus said: "Forgive them, for they do not know what they do." Who do you think "them" refers to? Is a sin still wrong when we commit it unknowingly?

2. How could Jesus have experienced the second death and not remain in the grave?

3. Which motivates us more quickly to do the right thing: love or fear? Which do you think is the better motivation to achieve long-term results?

4. What do you think motivates God's angels not to sin?

# CENTERED

God desires the same place in your heart that He holds in the universe
*(Daily Walk).*

# lesson 32

# He's Alive!

**Lesson Scriptures: Matthew 28:1-10; Mark 16:1-12; John 20:1-18**

Once in a while, mathematics gives you an answer that is so strange, it's terrifying.

Not to mention gross and disgusting.

Take the simple question of just what relationship George Washington has to a two-liter bottle of soda, for instance.

With a little bit of research and a pocket calculator, you see, it's easy enough to figure out that there are roughly thirty million trillion trillion trillion molecules of water on planet Earth. (That's a three with forty-six zeros after it, for those of you who want to write it out.)

And if you'll push a few more buttons on that calculator, you'll learn that a two-liter bottle of soda contains roughly sixty million trillion molecules of water—or about two-trillionths of a trillionth of the total number of water molecules on this planet.

Now hang on, because this is where it starts to get really strange.

As a young man, George Washington weighed about 175 pounds—which means that one of his body's essential ingredients was about forty liters, or about one trillion trillion molecules of water. (Trust me.)

Now since he is no longer using those trillion trillion molecules (which is a pretty safe assumption to make) and assuming that those molecules are randomly scattered over the surface of the earth (which is a pretty safe assumption, given the two hundred years they've had to wander around), then

what have you got?

You've got a million or so water molecules that used to belong to George Washington floating around in that two-liter bottle of soda.[1]

(No, don't worry—it won't affect the taste. After all, we're talking about less than a trillionth of one drop. Then, too, water is water, no matter where it comes from.)

### HOW DOES GOD DO IT?

All this may seem like a strange way to begin a lesson on the resurrection. But there's one question that always comes up in a Bible class whenever this subject is discussed. It's "What happens to the guy who was eaten by a shark?" Isn't God going to have a hard time putting together the pieces of someone who's been so thoroughly digested?

But as you can learn from a two-liter bottle of soda, there has to be more to the resurrection than just reanimation. I mean, if all God does on judgment day is scrape together the bits that once were you and "zaps" them back to life, then what is He going to do with the bits that have taken up residence someplace else? Like inside that two-liter bottle, for instance. Or as part of a sunflower. Or a flashlight battery.

Or even somebody else. Making up part of your flesh and blood and bone are more than a few million atoms that once did the same for George Washington. As well as other atoms that did the same for Joan of Arc. And Cleopatra. And Moses. And Eve. And there's a good chance that some of the atoms you're currently using have cycled through the bodies of hundreds—even millions—of people.

So, again, when it comes to the resurrection, how does God put together all the pieces that once were you? And how does He do so in such a way that it really is you and not just a copy?

### IT'S IMPOSSIBLE—ISN'T IT?

Start asking those questions, and you'll begin to understand

---

[1.] Actually, it's a great deal worse than what I've let on. You don't "own" a set of water molecules for life, after all. Every single atom in your body is going to be replaced several times over during your lifetime. Then, too, water molecules themselves aren't eternal—they're continually forming or breaking apart in any one of the numberless chemical transformations that take place on this planet. But life is complicated enough as it is, so I've tried to simplify it.

why the people of Athens laughed at Paul. These were not uneducated fools, after all. They were philosophers, professional thinkers, who practiced their trade in the very birthplace of logic and rational thought. Socrates had taught not far from where Paul stood. So had Plato and Aristotle. Paul's audience, in other words, was a group who knew the difference between sense and nonsense.

And they knew that Paul's talk about the resurrection of the body was nonsense. The idea that this Jesus whom Paul kept talking about had risen from the dead! That His body had come back to life! That the same thing would someday happen to our bodies as well. Even the thought of this happening was enough to convince them that the whole idea of a "resurrection" was absurd.

No, it made much more sense to believe that when you were dead, you were dead, and that was all there was to it. Or that "something" survived your death, some sort of "spark" or "spirit," that would find a new home elsewhere. The Epicureans who were listening to Paul believed the first (when you were dead there was nothing more); the Stoics in his audience believed the second (something survived the death of a person that would find a new home elsewhere).

And people today believe much the same. In fact, some go so far as to say that Jesus didn't really rise from the dead. No, they say, we should understand the story of His resurrection as a kind of parable, a story that can teach us spiritual truth, even if it never happened.

## A MATTER OF LIFE AND DEATH

Compare this attitude with that of Saul (Paul). Here was a man who had every reason not to believe. He was smart, after all. Educated. And certainly no friend of Jesus or His disciples.

Yet here was a man whose life was turned around, a man who was willing to risk both the ridicule of his enemies and death because he believed that Jesus was alive. He certainly didn't believe that Christ's resurrection was some sort of "parable." In fact, he went so far as to say that:

"If Christ has not been raised, then our preaching is in vain and your faith is in vain. We are even found to be misrepresenting God, because we testified of God that he raised

Christ, whom he did not raise if it is true that the dead are not raised. For if the dead are not raised, then Christ has not been raised. If Christ has not been raised, your faith is futile and you are still in your sins. Then those also who have fallen

asleep in Christ have perished. If in this life we who are in Christ have only hope, we are of all men most to be pitied" (1 Corinthians 15:14-19, RSV).

What Paul is saying is that if Jesus wasn't resurrected from the dead, then we are lost in sin and doomed to perish. However, he confidently states that Jesus "was delivered over to death for our sins and was raised to life for our justification" (Romans 4:25, NIV). The resurrection

confirmed that Jesus had fulfilled His Messianic claims and that His Father had accepted His all-sufficient sacrifice.

Jesus trusted God to take care of Him—just as we should. God took care of Jesus by resurrecting Him from the dead, and this provides proof that we, too, can trust Him.

But if God had not raised Jesus from the dead, then He would have broken His promise to His Son. He would have failed someone who trusted Him. And if God would let down someone like Jesus, well, the future wouldn't look promising for us.

## EVIDENCE THAT MAKES SENSE

Certainly Paul believed that Christ had appeared to him on the road to Damascus. That personal encounter was what first convinced him that Jesus was alive.

But something else may have played a part as well—the simple fact of believing in Christ's resurrection makes more sense than not believing in it!

If that sounds hard to believe, then take a look at some of the ways people have tried to "explain away" Christ's

empty tomb:

1. "The story of Christ's resurrection was made up by His followers a long time after He died."

Clearly, the resurrection was one of the earliest teachings of Christ's followers. First Thessalonians, for instance, was one of the first New Testament books to have been written. In chapter 4, Paul simply assumes that his readers both already know about and believe in Christ's resurrection (see 1 Thessalonians 4:14).

What's more, in 1 Corinthians 15:5-8, Paul says there were over five hundred eyewitnesses to the fact that Jesus rose from the dead. He wrote these words in A.D. 55—close enough to the event that many of the five hundred were still alive and could still testify as to what they had said.

Far from being some "new" teaching that crept into the church, the good news about Christ's resurrection was something Christians proclaimed right from the start.

2. "Jesus didn't really die on the cross. He fainted, and the coolness of the tomb revived Him."

To believe this, one would have to—

Ignore the spear that pierced His heart.

Ignore the professional judgment of the soldiers who allowed Christ's disciples to remove His body, soldiers who had crucified many people and could be expected to know what a dead body looked like.

Ignore the fact that an overnight stay in a stone-cold tomb would not have "revived" someone who had been through what Jesus endured. Instead, he would more likely have died from shock, hypothermia, and/or loss of blood.

Ignore these objections, any one of which would be enough to kill this argument, and you're still left with a question: "How could a man who had endured both a public beating and a crucifixion roll away the stone that blocked the entrance to his tomb and fight his way past the guards who were posted to make sure that something precisely like this did not happen?"

The answer? Obviously,

he couldn't.

3. "Christ's followers stole His body and then said Jesus had been raised from the dead."

This was the story the council paid the soldiers who'd been guarding Christ's tomb to tell. But no sooner was it told than people must have begun asking two questions: how and who?

First, the how. How do you sneak past a squad of soldiers, every one of whom knows he will die a gruesome death if he's found sleeping while on guard, lever an enormous stone out of its place in front of the entrance to the tomb, steal a body, and do all this without waking any of the soldiers?

Next, the who. Who steals the body? Not the disciples, surely. They'd shown no desire for confrontation with the authorities. They didn't believe Jesus when He told them He'd rise from the dead. And they didn't believe the women who told them He had risen from the dead. So if Christ's followers didn't steal His body, and they didn't give any evidence that they were heroic or fanatical enough for the deed, then who did?

4. "Christ's followers lied or were misled. Perhaps they honestly believed He had risen from the dead; maybe they simply came to the wrong tomb early on that morning."

Later, almost all of Christ's original followers died horrible deaths as a result of their belief in Him. Will people die for something they know to be a lie?

Perhaps.

But if people were spreading the rumor that Jesus had been raised from the dead, all the authorities had to do in order to stop such reports was to produce His body for a public "show and tell." That would have stopped Christianity in its tracks.

The fact that they didn't do so, however, suggests something. It suggests that they didn't produce Christ's body because they couldn't produce it. And they couldn't produce His body because there was no body to be found.

And if there was no body to be found, then where did it go?

## WHAT WE KNOW

Granted, there are a lot of things about the resurrection we don't understand. There are probably even more things about it that we can't understand. How did Jesus come back from the dead? What was it like? What would you or I have seen had we been standing there in the tomb when it happened?

The Bible doesn't answer these questions. It doesn't speculate, and neither should we.

Though some questions remain unanswered, Scripture is clear: Jesus rose from the dead. The Father, the Son, and the Holy Spirit each participated in His resurrection. We can rejoice in God's promise that regardless of what happens to our physical bodies, God will raise us as real and distinct individuals when Jesus returns. And we will have all of eternity to get answers to our questions about Jesus' resurrection and ours.

 Memory Focus

"But the angel said to the women, 'Do not be afraid; for I know that you seek Jesus who was crucified. He is not here; for he has risen, as he said. Come, see the place where he lay' " (Matthew 28:5, 6, RSV).

OR

"For as by a man came death, by a man has come also the resurrection of the dead. For as in Adam all die, so also in Christ shall all be made alive" (1 Corinthians 15:21, 22, RSV).

 Into the Bible

1. Prepare a report of the events that took place on the day of and during the next few days and weeks following the resurrection of Jesus. Use the "Witness Report" worksheet that your teacher will provide.
2. Luke 24:27 states that Jesus explained to two disciples on the

road to Emmaus how His death and resurrection had been foretold in Scripture. In each of the following chapters locate statements that Jesus might have used in explaining these events to the two disciples. Write down the specific verses, and summarize what was foretold. Some chapters will contain more than one verse.

Example: Isaiah 53:3—Jesus was despised by many Jewish leaders who caused the people to demand that He be crucified.

Texts:   Genesis 3          Isaiah 53
         Psalm 22           Zechariah 11
         Psalm 69

3. Study the following three events that took place after Christ's resurrection. Write a news story (one paragraph for each event) that describes the significance of the event and what the person or group of persons did and said under the circumstances given. Be as descriptive as you can—use all five senses.

   A. Mary Magdalene when telling the disciples about Christ's appearance to her in the garden. Matthew 28:1-8; Mark 16:9; Luke 24:1-11; John 20:1, 11-18.
   B. The Jewish leaders' response to the report of the captain of the squad of soldiers that had been guarding Christ's tomb. Matthew 28:11-15.
   C. Christ's ascension on Sunday as told by those who were visiting with Him when the event took place. Acts 1:7-11.

4. Use the worksheet that your teacher will provide to compare what the disciples actually did after the death and burial of Jesus. Imagine how different things might have been had they believed Jesus when He told them that He would rise from the grave.

 Projects

1. Using the *Seventh-day Adventist Bible Dictionary*, the encyclopedia, and other available resources, write a short report on

what one of the following groups believed about life after death: the Essenes, the Pharisees, the Sadducees.

2. If you use a modern translation of the Bible, you may notice that it brings Mark's Gospel to a close at Mark 16:8. If you use an older version, it may end at Mark 16:20. Use the *Seventh-day Adventist Bible Commentary* to find out why this difference exists.

3. First Peter 3:18-20 says that Jesus "was put to death in the flesh but made alive in the spirit; in which he went and preached to the spirits in prison." Some think this means that Jesus spent the three days between His death and resurrection preaching to people in hell. Use the *Seventh-day Adventist Bible Commentary* to help you write a brief explanation of how Seventh-day Adventists interpret these verses.

 # Focus Questions

1. Does the resurrection of Jesus help answer the age-old problem of God and human suffering?

2. What do you think is the most powerful evidence for Christ's resurrection?

3. How are we today who believe in the resurrection of Jesus even more blessed than was the disciple Thomas, who saw the resurrected Lord?

4. Would it be worthwhile to be a Christian, even if there were no life after death?

5. What might have been different during Jesus' final week on earth if the disciples had believed His predictions of death and resurrection?

6. What practical difference does it make whether one goes immediately to heaven at death or waits in "sleep" until the second coming of Jesus?

# WALK WITH ME

Tell me . . . and I'll forget. Show me . . . and I'll remember.
Walk with me . . . and I'll understand (Unknown).

# He's Still Alive!

**Lesson Scriptures: Matthew 28:16-20; John 20:19-30; John 21**

 e tend to keep track of winners.

If you want to know who won the gold medal in the 100-meter run during the 1936 Olympics, for instance, you can easily look it up; any almanac will tell you it was Jesse Owens of the United States, with a time of 10.3 seconds.

Likewise, the same almanac will tell you the name of Miss America for 1952 (Coleen Kay Hutchins, of Salt Lake City, Utah), as well as the winner of the Nobel Prize for Physics in 1903 (Svante A. Arrhenius, of Sweden).

Even the winner of the 1980 Lady Byng Memorial Trophy given for "most gentlemanly player" in the National Hockey League hasn't been forgotten—it was Wayne Gretsky, who played for the Edmonton Oilers at that time.

Granted, you may not have known (or much cared to know) the names that were just listed.

But chances are you've a list of winners you do care about; a list you wouldn't mind being on yourself. Maybe it's on one of those "Most Valuable Player" plaques they keep in your school's trophy case; maybe it's on the "Student Council Officers" page in your school's yearbook.

Or maybe the list that's important to you is more of an informal one—one that's kept by you and your friends, perhaps. A list of who's in and

who's out, who's up and who's down, who's hot and who's not.

Whatever the list, as I said, you probably want to be on it. If you're on the winner's list, after all, you get noticed. You get attention. You get your five minutes of fame. . . .

Which may not be much, but it's a whole lot more than the losers get.

Think of Nelson Harding, for instance. The fact he's the only person ever to win the Pulitzer Prize for Editorial Cartooning two years in a row probably doesn't mean much to you. (Maybe because he won these prizes in 1927 and 1928.)

But just try to find out who the runner-up was those two years. Or who was voted "Miss Congeniality" during the 1952 Miss America pageant. Or who won the silver medal in the 100-meter run during the 1936 Olympics (much less the bronze, much less fourth and fifth place).

Not that you can't find out who these people are; it's just harder. A lot harder. And the farther you get from number one, the easier it is to get lost in the crowd with all the other losers.

Maybe that's why so many

of us think it's important to win—we know what happens if we don't. Maybe that's why so many people work so hard to make it to the top. Maybe that's why so many people try so hard not to make mistakes, try so hard not to do anything that might keep them out of the winner's circle.

And there's the problem—because most of us do make mistakes. On any given measure of excellence, as a matter of fact, precisely half of us will rank below average.

Even the people we think of as winners don't always succeed. Think of George Herman Ruth, for instance. During his career in baseball, "the Babe" hit 714 home runs—more than any player in history except Hank Aaron. In 1924, he led the American League with a batting average of .378; during the four games of the 1928 World Series, he hit an incredible .625.

But Ruth never managed a Major League team (which was something he very much wanted to do). Why? Because people said Ruth was "too irresponsible" to be a manager. (And they were right; he was.) Even someone as successful as

the Babe knew what it meant to lose out at something that was very important to him.

Failure's inevitable, in other words. We might as well learn how to live with it.

But how can we learn to live with it, when people are continually telling us that "winning's not everything; it's the only thing"? How can we keep from feeling as though we're a failure when we fail?

Good question.

Fortunately, there's a good answer—though it's one that requires a little bit of patience if you're going to understand how it applies to your life.

Dealing with failure is a lot easier, you see, if you understand what Christ's resurrection really means. It means that the universe is a place where you don't have to settle for a sad ending. Because it means that God is a God of second chances.

Think back to that first resurrection morning, for instance. The disciples believed Jesus was dead—which is another way of saying they believed He was a failure. Everything He'd done, everything He'd tried to accomplish, had apparently come to nothing.

Worse yet, the disciples

believed they had failed Him. And they had. Peter had denied Him. Peter, James, and John had slept when Jesus had asked them to pray with Him in the Garden of Gethsemane. Peter, James, John, and all the rest of the disciples had fled when Jesus was arrested.

Humanly speaking, there was no way they could make right what they'd done. Humanly speaking, there was no way they could even apologize to the man they'd wronged—Jesus was dead, remember?

Except that now He isn't. Now He is alive.

And one of the first things He does now that He's alive is

go back to His disciples and tell them they're still His disciples.

Granted, it's not easy for the disciples to believe they have this kind of second chance. They doubted the women who came to them with the good news; Thomas doubted even when everybody else believed.

But Jesus was patient, even with Thomas. (Which is good news for those of us who have a hard time believing sometimes.)

And Jesus was patient, even with Peter. (Which is good news for those of us who make mistakes—big mistakes—every now and then.)

What's more, Jesus was more than patient with all His disciples. Given the way they'd treated Him, after all, Jesus would have been within His right to send them all back to Galilee and start off fresh with a new batch of disciples. But it was this very same group of disciples, the very ones who'd betrayed Him, that Jesus sent out to the world with His message.

The most important job in the world, and to whom did Jesus give it?

You guessed it; losers.

And Jesus is still in the resurrection business, by the way.

Yes, there'll be God's great "second chance" at the end of time—that day when everyone who's trusted Him will be raised back to life. On that day, all misunderstandings will be cleared up. All hurt feelings will be healed. All sad endings will be rewritten.

But in some way, what's even more important is the resurrection that can take place in your life today.

Paul wrote about this in Philippians 3:10, when he talked about how he wanted to know "the power of the resurrection." He knew the mistakes he'd made; he knew how prone he was to bumble and fumble and just plain foul up.

But he also knew that God was the kind of God who could make great things happen, even when He was working with losers like Paul. And Paul knew he needed this "second-chance power" in his life, if he was to accomplish anything worthwhile.

And that's the good news that can help us cope with failure in our own lives; it's the good news that no one who trusts God blows it completely. No one who trusts God fails in the end. No one who trusts God bungles it so badly that

God can't cope with the results.

Simply put, the resurrection tells us God can give every loser a second chance to become a winner.

That's not saying mistakes don't matter—it may take God all of this lifetime to work things out to His satisfaction.

But sooner or later, God will work it out—if you let Him. If you give Him a chance, in other words, God will give you a second chance.

Hard to believe?

Then ask yourself why everybody knows the names of losers like Peter, James, and John.

Hardly anybody knows the name of who won the Lady Byng Memorial Trophy for 1981.

 # Memory Focus

"Go therefore and make disciples of all nations, baptizing them in the name of the Father and of the Son and of the Holy Spirit, teaching them to observe all that I have commanded you; and lo, I am with you always, to the close of the age" (Matthew 28:19, 20, RSV).

OR

"For the Lord himself will descend from heaven with a cry of command, with the archangel's call, and with the sound of the trumpet of God. And the dead in Christ will rise first; then we who are alive, who are left, shall be caught up together with them in the clouds to meet the Lord in the air; and so we shall always be with the Lord" (1 Thessalonians 4:16, 17, RSV).

 # Into the Bible

1. Matthew 28:19, 20 is often called "The Great Commission." Read the text, and do the following:

A. List the four things Jesus told His disciples to do.

B. Why do you think each of these four things is important?

C. What promise did Jesus give His disciples?

D. How long did Jesus say this promise would be in effect?

E. Why would this promise be important, in light of the task Jesus had given them?

2. Read 1 Thessalonians 4:13-18, and answer these questions.

A. In verses 13, 14, Paul explains death to be like what condition?

B. According to verse 16, what must happen before the dead in Christ shall rise?

C. According to verse 17, what happens after the dead are raised back to life?

D. How long does verse 17 say we will be with the Lord?

E. How might the message given by Paul in verses 13 to 18 bring comfort to someone who is mourning the death of a loved one?

3. Read 1 Corinthians 15. Identify the verses and the statements that refute the following common misconceptions about life after death.

A. "When you're dead, you're dead—that's all there is to it."

B. "When you die, you go straight to heaven or hell and spend all eternity there."

C. "When you die, you come back to earth in another body" (reincarnation).

................................................................

 # Projects

1. Write a first-person narrative account of the events in John 21, using the viewpoint of one of the disciples who was present.

2. Write a paragraph in which you project yourself into the future and imagine how you will fulfill the "Great Commission" of Matthew 28:19, 20 through your chosen career.

3. Compare/contrast the task given to Peter by Jesus in John 21:5-17 with "The Great Commission" Jesus gave all His disciples in Matthew 28:19, 20. Write your response in two paragraphs, one showing the similarities and the other the differences.
4. Your class will be divided into small groups for this project. Each group is to create a piece of artwork such as a poster, stick art, etc., depicting the theme expressed in the song "In Heaven's Eyes There Are No Losers" or another song selected by your teacher. The completed art is to be shared with the class and the idea portrayed explained.
5. Research and write a one-page paper on some well-known person who at one time in his/her life had been considered a failure.

 Focus Questions

1. Is it easier or more difficult to tell people about the gospel today than it was in the time of Christ?
2. What can you do now—other than pray or donate money—to fulfill Christ's "Great Commission"?
3. Why was Jesus willing to trust Peter again after he had failed Him before?
4. Is it wrong to strive for achievement or recognition?
5. Why are winners given so much adulation?
6. Compare/contrast "making mistakes" and "failure." Are they the same? If not, how are they different?
7. How can "making mistakes" be a good thing?

# ACKNOWLEDGMENTS

Grateful acknowledgment and recognition is given to those who made a valuable contribution to the development of books 1 and 2 of the **CROSSROADS SERIES** for grades 9 and 10—*IN THE BEGINNING GOD . . .* and *GOD'S GIFT ♦ OUR CHOICE.*

## • SECONDARY BIBLE TEXTBOOK STEERING COMMITTEE •

The following served on the Secondary Bible Textbook Steering Committee and were responsible for supervising development of Student Textbooks, Teacher's Edition, and Teacher Resource Manual for *IN THE BEGINNING GOD . . .* and *GOD'S GIFT ♦ OUR CHOICE.*

Gerry E. Thompson, chair
Ed Boyatt
Richard Fredericks
Gordon Kainer
Edward M. Norton
Glenn E. Russell
Don L. Weatherall

## • CONSULTANTS AND STAFF •

The following provided valuable support services to the Steering Committee during the development of one or more components.

Bonnie Casey, editorial assistance.
Victor H. Fullerton, coordinator.
Shirley Goodridge, editorial assistant and copyright authorizations.
Marion Hartlein, North American Division Office of Education consultant.
Alyce Pudewell, art consultant.
Lorene Beaulieu, word processing and formatting of manuscripts for Student Textbook and Teacher's Edition.
Beverly Benson, word processing of manuscripts for Student

Textbook and Teacher's Edition.

Ardyce Weatherall, word processing of manuscripts for Teacher's Edition and Teacher Resource Manual.

### • WRITERS •

The following functioned as writers of one or more lessons. Each writer brought to his or her work a rich background of experiences and a writing style that adds interest and variety in approaches to the topics covered.

DeWayne Boyer, Greg Brothers, Steve Case, Renee Coffee, Des Cummings, Jr., Richard Duerksen, Richard Fredericks, L. R. Holmes, Gordon Kainer, Gayle Norton, Jerry Thomas, Alden Thompson, Stuart Tyner, Martin Weber.

### • TEACHERS AND STUDENTS •

The sixty-seven teachers and approximately 1,500 students in junior and senior academies of the North American Division who field-tested lessons during the 1993–1994 school year. Their responses on the survey questionnaires provided valuable input and insights.

### • TEACHER RESOURCE MANUAL WORKSHOP COMMITTEE •

The following Bible teachers and other education personnel served on the 1994 summer workshop committee that developed the Teacher Resource Manual.

Don L. Weatherall, Chair
Ron Aguilera
Lyle Bennett
Brett Hadley
Gordon Kainer
Victor H. Fullerton
Gerry E. Thompson

**• PACIFIC PRESS PUBLISHING ASSOCIATION •**

Paul A. Hey, liaison with the Secondary Bible Textbook Steering Committee
Robert Mason and Michelle C. Petz, designers
Glen Robinson, editor

**• PUBLISHERS, AUTHORS, AND AGENTS •**

Grateful acknowledgment is made to the following publishers, authors, and agents for permission to use and adapt copyrighted materials.

For *God's Gift* ◆ *Our Choice*

Baker Book House Company quotations from *14,000 Quips & Quotes*, by E.C. McKenzie. Copyright © 1980. Used by permission.

The Review and Herald Publishing Association for "Dear Lord and Father" verse two from the *Seventh-day Adventist Hymnal.*

Walk Thru the Bible, Inc., for quotations from *Daily Walk* magazines. Used by permission.

Warner Bros. Publications Inc. for the lyrics to "Show Me the Way," by Dennis De Young. Copyright (c) 1990 Grand Illusion Music (ASCAP), c/o Almo Music Corp.(ASCAP). Used by permission of WARNER BROS. PUBLICATIONS INC., Miami, FL. 33014.

Word, Incorporated for *In the Eye of the Storm*, by Max Lucado. Copyright (c) 1991 Word Publishing. Used by permission.

Opening quotations for lessons are from the following sources: The Bible - NIV (31); Phillips (14); TEV (6); TLB (13), Paraphrase (1); *Daily Walk* (4, 9, 32); *14,000 Quips & Quotes* (3, 7, 8, 11, 16, 17, 18, 20, 25, 26, 27); Unknown (10, 12, 19, 21, 22, 23, 28, 29, 33); Ellen G. White, *The Acts of the Apostles*, p. 472 (30), *The Desire of Ages*, pp. 48, 480, 224 (5, 15, 24), *The Ministry of Healing*, p. 470 (2).

Illustrations for opening pages of units and lessons were provided by the following: pp. 8-9, Nathan Bilow/Allsport; p. 12,

Wayne Aldridge/International Stock; p. 18, C. Purcell/Photo
Researchers; p. 30, Flip Chalfaut/Image Bank; p. 38, Jeff
Foott/Alaska Stock; p. 46, Tony Stone Image; Visions of Nature; p.
52, Loubat**Vandystadt/Photo Researchers; p. 60, Chris
Falkenstein/ Falk Photo; p. 70, Robert Winslow/Tom Stack and
Associates; pp. 84-85, Nathan Bilow/Allsport; p. 88, Roger Allyn
Lee/Superstock; p. 94, Gary Crandall; p. 104, Darrell Gulin/Tony
Stone Images; Visions of Nature; p. 116, Ernest Braun/Natural
Selection Stock Photo, Inc.; p. 124, Harvey Lloyd/The Stock
Market; p. 132, Mark Muench; p. 140, Bill Tucker Studio,
Inc./International Stock; p. 148, Renee Lynn, Tony Stone Images;
Visions of Nature; p. 158, Michael Philip Manheim/International
Stock; p. 168, B. Seitz/Photo Researchers; pp. 174-175, Christophe
Profit/Allsport/Vandystadt; p. 178, The Dickmans/Westlight; p.
186, R. Lynn, Photo Researchers; p. 194, Jim Erickson/Stock
Market; p. 204, W. & D. McIntyre/Photo Researchers; p. 214,
Harald Sund/Image Bank; p. 222, Clark Mishler/Alaska Stock; p.
232, Miwako Ikeda/International Stock; pp. 242-243, Pascal
Tournaire/Vandystadt/Allsport; p. 246, Scott Barrow, Inc.; p. 254,
D. Boyer/Photo Researchers; p. 262, Chris Falkenstein/Falk
Photo; p. 270, Art Wolfe/Tony Stone Images; Visions of Nature; p.
280, Ken & Carl Fischer; p. 292, John Terence Turner/FPG
International; p. 306, C. Butler/Photo Researchers; p. 316, Dave
Reede/Westlight.

Cover illustration by Harvey Lloyd/The Stock Market.

All Scripture references not otherwise credited are from the
Holy Bible: New International Version.

Every effort has been made to trace the ownership of all copyrighted material in this book and to obtain permission for its use.

Sincere appreciation is given to the many others who have
contributed to the manuscript whose names may not be included.